WILL ROGERS

Will Rogers and his verbal lariat.

WILL ROGERS
A Bio-Bibliography

Peter C. Rollins

Popular Culture Bio-Bibliographies

Greenwood Press
Westport, Connecticut • London, England

Library of Congress Cataloging in Publication Data

Rollins, Peter C.
    Will Rogers: a bio-bibliography.

    (Popular culture bio-bibliographies, ISSN 0193-6891)
    Includes index.
    1. Rogers, Will, 1879-1935 — Bibliography. I. Title.
II. Series.
Z8754.5.R64   1984   016.7927′028′0924 [B]   83-10696
[PN2287.R74]
ISBN 0-313-22633-4 (lib. bdg.)

Library of Congress Catalog Card Number: 83-10696
ISBN: 0-313-22633-4
ISSN: 0193-6891

First published in 1984

Greenwood Press
A division of Congressional Information Service, Inc.
88 Post Road West
Westport, Connecticut 06881

Printed in the United States of America

10 9 8 7 6 5 4 3 2 1

TO THE MEMORY OF ROBERT W. LOVE

a true Oklahoman who always had
room in his house for stray dogs
and visiting scholars

CONTENTS

ILLUSTRATIONS

PREFACE

A decade has passed since I first came into contact with the Will Rogers activities at Oklahoma State University, and *Will Rogers: A Bio-Bibliography* represents the ripe fruit of that decade of immersion in Will Rogers materials of all kinds — from memorabilia and bric-a-brac to book-length works and feature films. My training in American Studies and constant involvement in the popular culture studies movement have kept me attuned to multiple ways in which Will Rogers related to the ideas and events of his time. Chapters 1 and 2 spell out in detail the major facts and significant interpretations of the man and his biography. Many who have not been exposed to the Will Rogers tradition will be surprised by the intelligence and warmth of the man, qualities that account for his impact on contemporaries. Chapter 3 takes an exegetical approach to the humor of Will Rogers: short quotations are analyzed in close detail to highlight the specific humor strategies employed by the Oklahoman. Whenever possible, lesser known passages have been selected for this "intellectual montage." Chapter 4 is a long bibliographical essay which has been written in the style of Dr. Johnson; my hope was that an opinionated approach — even when wrong — would make the reading more interesting. I am sure that other Will Rogers scholars would have different evaluations to offer were they to treat the same materials.

From Chapter 5 through the remainder of the volume, the materials become more factual and clerical. Chapter 5 alone provides the reader with accurate information concerning the authors, dates, films and filmmakers, audiovisual presentations, and recordings available by or about Will Rogers. Reference librarians should find this section of great value as will scholars of popular culture. Great efforts have been made to tabulate every article, book, film, and record important to the Rogers legacy.

In Chapter 6, a selective chronology attempts to link up developments in the life of Will Rogers with ongoing events in the world around him. Special emphasis has been put on technological and political events in these parallel time strands because these were issues that caught Rogers' eye. All of Rogers' silent and sound films are briefly summarized, and the credits in each case have been checked against three different sources. The major radio programs which Rogers made are summarized to give a flavor of what he did before the national microphone. Finally, some original research has been conducted to give a taste of the kind of presentations which Rogers delivered to civic and charity groups in the New York area where he was a willing speaker at luncheons, conventions, and gala events — for a price. These extemporaneous utterances have been unearthed to round out the picture of Will Rogers the orator.

One of the major goals of the Greenwood bio-bibliography series is to provide scholars with information about archival sources for the study of major figures in popular culture, and the Will Rogers bio-bibliography is no exception. Chapter 7 provides the *first* public listing of the papers of Will Rogers held in the Claremore Memorial. It is hoped that this detailed list will allow scholars at great geographical distances to decide whether a trip to Tulsa–Claremore is worth the effort. I suspect that many dissertation writers will find the list very attractive indeed. In any case, I thank Will Rogers, Jr. for allowing me to publish the Memorial manuscript list in this book for the first time. Other lists from the Margaret Herrick Library at the Motion Picture Academy of Arts and Sciences; the Archives of the Performing Arts, University of Southern California; and the National Archives will stimulate research ideas among scholars of American popular culture. The net has been thrown out far; very little in the realm of original sources has been missed. As a result, scholars should find *Will Rogers: A Bio-Bibliography* an extremely useful source; early chapters interpret, while later sections of the book provide guides to materials which will allow scholars to form their own interpretations.

During the past decade, I have accrued many debts to supervisors, co-workers, and students. Clinton Keeler, my first department head, urged my involvement in the Will Rogers Publication Project. Later, Gordon Weaver, the current department head, took a personal interest in my connection with the project and in all other creative ventures. Both men helped me to function effectively as a scholar in the area of popular culture. At a greater geographical distance, Ray B. Browne fostered national help by publicizing Oklahoma State University's Will Rogers efforts. Joseph A. Stout, Jr., the second director of the Will Rogers Project, taught me to write directly, clearly, and effectively; his influence has permeated all that I have done using words since our few years of common labor on *The Writings of Will Rogers.* Will Rogers led me to filmmaking. While working on *Will Rogers' 1920s,* Richard Raack taught me how to weave music with film, while Patrick Griffin and William Malloch added perceptions about the relationships between image and sound. Finally, the late Robert W. Love deserves the dedication at the head of this volume. He helped me to understand the rootedness of Will Rogers' perceptions.

A great number of people assisted in the collection, transcription, and verification efforts of this bio-bibliography. Ken Pilcher proved to be an indefatigable research assistant, blending his energy with a Rogers-like sense of humor. Tom Slater and Michael Moore were extremely helpful with the film and radio synopses, a difficult and tedious job because of the great number of details involved. The checklist of books was enhanced by the work of Charles Mangus, Michael McDonough, and Salwa Khoddam. Ms. Khoddam also helped prepare the hundreds of interlibrary loan requests which brought books and articles about Will Rogers to the door of my carrel in the Oklahoma State University library. Humanities Librarian Terry Bassford facilitated these library connections. His cheerful and intelligent approach to scholars makes research in the Edmon Low Library a pleasure.

Film archives and interested corporations helped in this project. Robert Knutson (University of Southern California's Archives of the Performing Arts) responded promptly to research questions, as did Samuel A. Gill and Val Almendarez (Margaret Herrick Library, Academy of Motion Picture Arts and Sciences), Mrs. Eileen Bowser (Film Department, Museum of Modern Art), Ted Ewing (Blackhawk Films, Inc.), and numerous other institutional representatives. Special thanks go to Steven K. Gragert of the Will Rogers Project at Oklahoma State University, a person of goodwill whose attention to detail has been an asset to *The Writings* and to my efforts in this volume.

Two local influences deserve note. My colleague Leonard Leff has been a constructive daily influence on my work in film studies. Janet B. Rollins has maintained a lively interest in the letter and spirit of the Will Rogers tradition. Her eye for style has affected everything I have written for the page or screen in the last three years. Grace Wynd has been more than a typist.

A special note of thanks is due to Will Rogers, Jr. for his interest in all efforts to collect and interpret the legacy of Will Rogers. His support of scholarship has been completely selfless, and without his help, many of the articles, books, and films listed in this bio-bibliography would not have come to fruition. All researchers owe him a great debt.

The photographs come from the author's private collection.

WILL ROGERS

1. Will Rogers (1879-1935).

1

THE LIFE OF WILL ROGERS (1879-1935) – A BRIEF SKETCH

It seems only appropriate that a commentator on American politics should be born on election day – November 4, 1879. In an autobiographical fragment, Will Rogers claims that his mother, during labor, asked to be moved from the large white house in Oologah to an adjacent log structure: "She had just read the life of Lincoln. So I got the log house end of it OK. All I need now is the other qualifications" (Donald Day, *Autobiography,* p. 3). Both Clement Vann Rogers and Mary America Rogers had high hopes for their eighth – and last – child. Little "Willie" was often told that he must amount to something – his mother hoped that he would become a preacher; his father saw in him a future politician. In ways the parents could not have anticipated, both their dreams for William Penn Adair Rogers came true.

The Clement ("Clem") Vann Rogers family had been part of Indian Territory for fifty years prior to Willie's arrival. Clem's participation in tribal and territorial politics, however, had not been without its ups and downs: he was very successful as a Cherokee tribal senator, but he suffered psychological and economic setbacks as a defeated member of the Confederacy's officer corps. As Indian Territory became the state of Oklahoma, Clem Vann Rogers prospered. Cooweescoowee District, where Oologah and Claremore were located, would be renamed Rogers County in his honor. In his twilight years, "Uncle Clem" would remain a dominant force in local and state politics. Throughout the varying fortunes of his career, Clem Vann Rogers remained one of Oklahoma's power elite.

Will Rogers usually approached his audience in the guise of a simple cowboy fresh from the plains of Oklahoma. Contrary to this image, the real Will Rogers grew up in a wealthy, politically dominant family which took a subscription to the *New York Times* (delivered to Oologah by train). Not only were Willie's parents anxious that he amount to something; they were also ready to smooth the way with money and not-so-gentle persuasion. This background in part explains how a young man, who claimed only to be a cowboy, eventually became the friendly, perceptive, public critic of the world's most important father figures.

Rogers explained on many occasions that his mother, who had more Indian blood (one-fourth) than his father (one-eighth), had been responsible for his sense of humor. None of Rogers' biographers has explored the meaning of this notion. It is too often forgotten that the Cherokees—like other Amerindian peoples—valued laughter. From the Indian perspective, life on the American continent certainly had many painful ironies requiring the balm of laughter. Rogers plays with some of these ironies in describing the source of his name. At the time of Willie's birth, Indian Chief William Penn Adair was staying at the Rogers home. Clem and Mary conveyed the chief's name and the hopes of the American Indian to their son: "I just looked at him when he named me and thought: 'By the time I get to be big enough to be Chief, we won't have any more country than a Jay Bird' " (Donald Day, *Autobiography,* p. 9). Such a reaction mixed the realism and laughter of the Indian culture.

Personal tragedy and loss can often provide conditions for humor to flourish. At the age of ten, Willie lost his mother. For the remainder of his life, he could not mention her name without tears coming to his eyes. She had been an important buffer between the boy and a distant father. The deep strain of negative feelings between the adolescent and his only living parent were not improved by the pangs of growth. The youngster became a loner, an increasingly disruptive pupil who enjoyed the role of class clown. When his roping foolishness got him into big trouble at Kemper Military School in Missouri in 1898, Willie, a devoted reader of pulp Westerns, ran away from his last school to pursue the cowboy dream.

Life as a cowboy was less romantic than the pulps had promised. After working at two Texas ranches, Rogers returned to Oologah in 1902 to oversee his father's cattle interests. As his cousin Spi Trent reports, the work was dull and time consuming. The only audience consisted of four-footed creatures who were unimpressed by singing and held strong negative attitudes toward trick roping. When Rogers fled to South America and Africa, he discovered that cowboy realities in exotic lands were little different from Oologah boredom.

The cowboy myth was something else again. City dwellers in the United States and Europe were fascinated with the dime novels, Wild West shows, films, and news—if it focused on train robberies—of the vanishing West. Oklahomans like Colonel Zack Mulhall and his family were plying the Western myth in Wild West shows for audiences in St. Louis, Chicago, and New York. After a disappointing global search for the myth, Rogers joined the Mulhall troupe in 1904: trick riding and roping before an audience of appreciative city dwellers had all the romance which the dime novels had promised.

During a Mulhall show in Madison Square Garden in 1905, a large steer decided to break down the barriers between fantasy and reality. It broke into the stands, initiating a stampede of terrified New Yorkers. Rogers grabbed his rope, ran directly to the exit he knew the cow would charge for, and saved the day by bringing the steer down. No one was harmed. When New York papers featured stories about the pluck and skill of the cowboy roper from Oklahoma, Rogers was in show business to stay.

WILL ROGERS MAKES HIS STAGE DEBUT

Bringing trick roping from the expanses of Madison Square Garden to the proscenium stage of vaudeville was no easy task. The space was cramped, the horse had to be outfitted with rubber shoes, and there was always a danger that the orchestra might be crushed if the stage was slippery. Rogers either performed his tricks from horseback or demonstrated special throws at the horse as a friend, Buck McKee, rode in circles around him. It was a mini-Wild West show.

At some point in the vaudeville days, Rogers decided that audiences would not pay attention to a strictly silent presentation: whoops and hollers kept the atmosphere alive; descriptions of throws about to be made fostered anticipation; when errors occurred, a joke could smooth over the embarrassment.

In his search for laughter, Rogers was not operating in a vacuum. A staple of vaudeville humor was a character called "the yokel," a country bumpkin thrown down in the middle of the city who was usually the victim of his rustic ignorance of city ways. Rogers adopted the yokel persona, adding to it the cowboy's accent, diction, and metaphors. In the first experiments, the cowboy yokel lines were merely bridges between tricks; as Rogers' career progressed, what the persona said became more important than what he could do physically. In an era of mass migrations to America's cities, the comic device had a special appeal.

Sometime during 1915, an agent for Florenz Ziegfeld "discovered" Will Rogers. Ziegfeld's *Follies* specialized in sophisticated entertainment for wealthy New Yorkers and visitors to the city. The notion of having a frontier cowboy among urban comics and "glorified" American girls struck everyone as an exquisite touch of anachronism. Concurrently, Rogers stumbled over the device of using his cowboy persona to discuss current events, things from the newspapers. Since the *Follies* had a repeat audience, Rogers was forced to find new material daily: he would read three or four newspapers each morning in search of absurdities needing the cowboy treatment. From 1915 onward, Rogers' career flourished in proportion to his ability to bring the comic cowboy persona in contact with newsworthy issues and personalities.

The real Will Rogers was no provincial yokel. Even though he had been an erratic student, he had the equivalent of a high school education; in addition, he had seen much of the world during early ramblings. Letters sent home from South America and Africa reflect an alert mind and a grammatical pen. While on the vaudeville circuit from 1903 to 1908, he wrote a series of some fifty love letters to his fiancée, Betty Blake. These important revelations of his personal feelings — available to researchers at the Will Rogers Memorial — show a sophisticated mind at work and bear no relation to the semiliterate diction which Rogers exploited for rhetorical purposes when speaking in his cowboy persona. Inspection of the library at the Will Rogers Ranch in Santa Monica, California, reveals such resources as the *Congressional Record* and *Foreign Relations of the United States.* Among family and friends, Rogers could be serious, sincere, even eloquent. Still, the cowboy posture brought big rewards: in the *Follies* period, the lasso fit around the island of Manhattan, but as Rogers explored print and electronic media, the loop would eventually surround every American who attended a movie, listened to a radio, or read a morning paper.

FROM HEMP TO VERBAL LARIAT

As early as 1914, the Chicago and New York press started quoting the best of Will Rogers' quips. When Woodrow Wilson picked up one of these quotes about preparedness in a 1916 speech, the lariat began to branch out beyond New York City. During the same year that the president quoted him, Rogers performed in Baltimore before an audience which included Wilson. While a "roasting" technique was a regular part of his *Follies* act, there was some question in Rogers' mind about the propriety of making jokes about a president who was actually in the audience. When Rogers launched into remarks about Wilson's embarrassing policies toward Mexico, both the performer and the audience were relieved that the president joined in the laughter. The president even seemed to welcome the roasting. As a commentator, Rogers saw the evening as a breakthrough: from 1916 onward, he felt free to address world leaders in a familiar, jocular way, treating them like patrons at Ziegfeld's *Follies.* Public figures were pleased to be mentioned in a Will Rogers column or radio program. The publicity always outweighed any criticism.

Prior to 1922, Rogers was known to convert his stage material into newspaper articles, but only occasionally. His two books of 1919, *The Cowboy Philosopher on Prohibition* and *The Cowboy Philosopher on the Peace Conference,* were no more than tossed salads of one liners and personality roasts. In 1922, the McNaught Syndicate approached Rogers with a writing offer. When Rogers accepted, he further increased the size of the audience within his loop. The relationship with McNaught would continue until Rogers' death. Weekly articles would be distributed to Sunday papers; after 1926, a daily article of 150 words would reach millions of American readers.

The *Saturday Evening Post*'s editor, George Horace Lorimer, was an ardent Will Rogers fan; during the 1920s, he dispatched Rogers on a number

2. Public men knew that publicity always outweighed criticism. (Congress-man Rogers, House Speaker Rainey, and Journalist Rogers.)

of special journalistic assignments for America's favorite weekly magazine. The McNaught Syndicate and the *Saturday Evening Post* would be the channels through which Rogers could reach millions of Americans. His books were little more than hard-bound collections of insights first encoun-tered by his audience in local papers or in the large, colorful pages of the *Post*. For many Americans, Will Rogers was a daily, weekly, and monthly companion.

THROWING A LOOP AROUND HOLLYWOOD

As early as 1919, Will Rogers brought his "cowboy yokel" character to the silent screen in a host of short films for Samuel Goldwyn and Hal Roach. While New York City reviewers — who knew Rogers' work from the *Follies* — applauded his efforts, box-office receipts showed a net loss. A brief experiment as an independent producer led Rogers to economic disaster: the mortgage of his home was refinanced to pay debts; his not-so-friendly bank confiscated prints of his films for collateral. Except for retrospective screenings in Oklahoma, the resulting films — *The Roping Fool, The Fruits of Faith,* and the uncompleted *One Day in 365* — would never reach theatres. Silent motion pictures were simply not Rogers' *métier,* nor was business.

When sound came to the movies, Rogers was more than ready, for his stage act — not to mention his journalism — was based entirely on the rhythms of oral speech. Will and Betty started searching for the right properties. Not surprisingly, he chose a series of roles in which he played a Midwestern innocent whose wife believed that *They Had to See Paris* (1929). As Depression conditions grew more extreme, Rogers was cast in nostalgic tales of simpler times: *David Harum* (1934), *In Old Kentucky* (1935), and *Steamboat 'Round the Bend* (1935). A nation uneasy about alternating eras of boom and bust found solace in rural dramas about simpler days. The Fox Film Corporation (later 20th Century-Fox) rewarded its leading box-office attraction handsomely. By 1935, the loop was totally extended.

THE POWER OF RADIO

A photograph at the Will Rogers Memorial shows Rogers making his first radio broadcast in 1922 at station KDKA in Pittsburgh, Pennsylvania. After an initial period of experimentation, Rogers became comfortable with the new medium: whenever possible, he tried to broadcast in front of a live audience. If the studio audience laughed, Rogers knew his act was working. Like a *Follies* performance, a radio broadcast could build toppers, delay stories by digressions, and reach a punchline properly. Like today's viewers of "The Johnny Carson Show," radio audiences delighted in the many digressions and pauses by which Rogers burned up valuable air time. On the air, Rogers sounded like a garrulous neighbor paying a visit.

Rogers was involved in a number of national radio hookups during the 1920s. During a national show broadcast from his ranch in Santa Monica, he humorously impersonated Calvin Coolidge in a foolish, pun-filled report to the nation. It was the sort of spoof that still pleases audiences — witness the popularity of Rich Little. Unfortunately, the president was not delighted to learn that many listeners thought that the speaker was Coolidge himself! In spite of this brouhaha, executives continued to permit Rogers to ad lib on the air.

3. Will and Betty Rogers return from abroad in early 1932.

Will Rogers was on the air regularly during the Depression. In 1931, E. R. Squibb and Company employed him to bring out a series of twelve programs on leading political and show business personalities. Rogers obliged with thoughtful monologues on Charles Lindbergh, Calvin Coolidge, Al Smith, Dwight Morrow, and Henry Ford, as well as other personalities and topics. (Unfortunately, only written transcriptions of these presentations exist today.) In 1933, the Gulf Oil Company paid Rogers handsomely to make a series of broadcasts for "The Good Gulf Show." (Many of these delightful programs were recorded and are still available on records.)

4. Rogers plays a "yokel" role in *The Headless Horseman* (1922).

What made the radio presentations so memorable was the virtuosity with which Rogers modulated his voice. In speaking about the Depression and its victims, he could provide an intonation that aroused sympathy and concern; on the other hand, when ridiculing the panaceas of Father Charles Coughlin or Senator Huey Long, his voice could mix irony with indignation in such a way as to be devastating. In fact, many of the Rogers programs of the 1930s go beyond entertainment. They are gems of American oratory. When Americans tuned in to "The Good Gulf Show," they welcomed a friend into their homes. The friend talked with them about their problems; his humor somehow made more bearable the impact of impersonal economic forces.

WILL ROGERS AS HUMANITARIAN

Many of the reminiscences of show business people testify to Rogers' numerous acts of personal charity. In 1927, and again in 1931, Rogers toured areas of the United States that had been victimized by floods and drought. He played benefits in cities within these regions to raise money for stricken farmers. While people in the Midwest were obviously grateful for the help, press coverage made the entire nation aware of Will Rogers' concern for those in trouble. A nation's sense of gratitude accounts for the special rapport between Rogers and his national audience after 1931. He was a public man who came to the rescue with relief — some of it financial, but much of it the kind of comic relief which his fellow citizens needed even more than money. The cowboy philosopher on these trips of mercy cast his rope around a nation's heart.

BEYOND THE FRONTIER

At the end of July 1935, Will Rogers boarded a plane in Los Angeles and flew to Seattle where he was joined by Wiley Post, fellow Oklahoman and experimental pilot. *Winnie Mae,* Post's plane, was equipped with pontoons and was ready for an extended Arctic trip: Post was scouting for potential routes for airmail flights between North America and Asia, and Rogers was looking forward to seeing Alaska for the first time. When the pair reached Juneau, Rogers recalled that his very first motion picture, *Laughing Bill Hyde* (1918), had been about the wild country he was visiting. The land was covered with game and the people were neighborly. Thinking back to the domestic confusion and international strife plaguing Americans, Rogers meditated that President Franklin D. Roosevelt might draw strength from airborne views of the sublime scenery.

Post and Rogers planned to fly to Point Barrow and then on to Russia. Not far from their intermediate objective, the plane crashed. The deaths were untimely and tragic; on the other hand, the place for the passing seemed poetically correct — Point Barrow is at the most northern tip of the American continent, the ultimate land frontier. The millions of Americans

5. Will Rogers on the road—in this case, the Republican National Convention in Chicago, 1932.

who mourned the loss of Will Rogers knew that more than an individual had died; the cluster of values which he represented had flown out of their lives. Little wonder that people old enough to read a newspaper or listen to a radio in 1935 remember exactly what they were doing and where they were when the news of Rogers' death arrived.

6. Will Rogers and Wiley Post prepare for their last trip, August 1935.

2

THE PROFOUND
APPEAL OF
WILL ROGERS,
1920-1935

The biographical facts of Will Rogers' career, discussed in chapter 1, reveal that he used a variety of forums to broadcast his observations concerning the American scene. Through the Ziegfeld *Follies,* Rogers' droll comments on people in the news reached the upper-class decision-makers of New York, Baltimore, and Washington. Presidents either attended or kept track of these live shows where their recent policies were often gently "roasted" by the cowboy humorist. The Rogers slant on contemporary events reached a new listening audience across the nation beginning in 1922. When radio became more sophisticated in the 1930s, denying most performers the right to extemporize at the microphone, Rogers continued to talk spontaneously about whatever newsworthy events came to mind. Politicians knew that millions listened, and—after 1932—the New Deal administration worked hard to maintain good relations with such an important molder of opinion. Rogers' gifts as a storyteller held stage and radio audiences rapt.

The republication efforts of the Will Rogers Research Project at Oklahoma State University have forced a recognition of how many of Will Rogers' trenchant insights found their way into American newspapers and magazines. There was a host of print journalism ventures: a weekly column began in 1922; a short daily column began circulation in 1926; and finally, Rogers conducted a number of special trips for the *Saturday Evening Post,* trips that brought the cowboy correspondent face-to-face with international personalities and events. When the Oklahoma State University republication project is completed, Rogers' journalistic record will amount to twenty-one volumes. The timeliness of the humor in these writings made them especially influential, although many of the insights are still pertinent. While it is true that Rogers often mirrored current public attitudes, just as often his insights into the human heart clarified complex issues, making Will Rogers the average American's unofficial ambassador to the world.

7. Will Rogers helps lay the cornerstone of the Florenz ("Flo") Ziegfeld Theatre. Earlier, Ziegfeld (in fur coat at right) helped to lay the cornerstone of Rogers' successful career.

8. The late films of Will Rogers radiate humor and humanity. This is a playful scene from *Life Begins at Forty* (1935).

Especially for those who did not grow up in the Will Rogers era, the motion pictures of the man convey insight into his appeal. The silent films deserve much more attention than film historians have given them. The sound films constitute a national treasure for they radiate the humor and humanity which account for the reverence with which Rogers' contemporaries remember him.

Most of the scripts for Rogers' films were based on works of regional literature, thus allowing the Oklahoman to embody the rural values which many Americans feared were being too blithely rejected in an era of pervasive change. People left a Will Rogers film reassured about the goodness of their heritage. As Joseph Schenck (chairman of the board, 20th Century-Fox) correctly observed, Rogers was totally different from other film personalities. He was "loved as a man, as a national character, as the greatest of all home philosophers."[1] When Wiley Post and Will Rogers were killed in an airplane crash in 1935, American movie-goers lost an important avuncular companion.

This chapter examines the unique place of Will Rogers in the hearts of Americans. Although he never held political office, his use of the *Follies,* radio, newspapers, and films made him a constant presence in the popular culture of the United States from 1920 to 1935. The social and intellectual context for his humor is described, with special emphasis on the underlying anxiety felt by even the most enthusiastic celebrants of the novelties of the period. How much of the new developments were "bunk" and how many of the new opportunities afforded by industrialism and industrial values were truly progressive? Will Rogers, his feet planted firmly in a rural tradition, seemed to be in a privileged position to discern what would last and what was ephemeral. In his personal life, Rogers seemed to embody the ideal life-style — progressive, yet concerned about family values. In his writings, radio programs, and films, he provided his fellow Americans with insights into how to balance the good things of tradition with the opportunities of a boom era.

When the Depression set in, Rogers used his forums to reduce the impact of bad times. A man who had never entirely endorsed the excesses of the Jazz Age could remind Americans that getting back to the real things in life was not entirely harmful. Through boom and bust, Rogers evoked strong feelings from all strata of American life. No subsequent humorist has been able to do so — a fact that says much about the unique quality of the Oklahoman as a spokesman of and for his times.

1920s: AN AMBIVALENCE ABOUT PROGRESS

Americans in the 1920s were excited by the rapid changes going on around them. Yet, at the same time they were uneasy, for assuming the new identity as twentieth-century urban Americans entailed a rejection of older modes of life and values. The tension induced by these changes led some Americans to strike out at the new. The infamous Red Scare inspired by A. Mitchell Palmer sought to stamp out the threat of bolshevism. Gathering new members among native-stock, rural Americans, the Ku Klux Klan expanded its crusade against change. Its new enemies included "the city, sexual freedom, modern life . . . [and] . . . liquor."[2] While militant fundamentalists brought John Scopes to trial, the Daughters of the American Revolution and others who feared the rising political power of the immigrant launched their campaign for 100 percent Americanism. The majority of Americans attempted to find a place for themselves in this new world, but unquestionably all Americans in the period were curious about the much celebrated juggernaut of progress—was it steaming toward the good society or away from it?

Industrialism had posed increasing challenges since the end of the Civil War. Those native Americans who went to the city to profit from the new wealth and social mobility available there were rewarded handsomely. A ready supply of docile immigrant labor assured that quick-witted native Americans could rise to the top of the industrial heap. Yet for all their successes, these same newcomers to the good life of industrial America had their anxieties: "For millions of people torn from accustomed rural patterns of culture and thrust into a strange, urban environment, the meaning of industrialism lay in a feeling of uprootedness, in the disintegrations of old ways of life."[3] Many of those who remained behind believed they were left out, creating the paradoxical situation in which the liberated were anxious while the innocent were resentful.

The technique of mass production started what has been called a "second industrial revolution."[4] The United States was transformed as this manufacturing technique was pressed into service to turn out large quantities of automobiles, radios, and other new inventions of the era. The advertising industry expanded its efforts to convince Americans that they required the massive number of goods which could now be produced. Americans were urged to consume, to buy on credit, to become part of this new economy of abundance. If they had money left when they finished shopping, Americans were advised to invest in the stock market. If they had no money left, they were assured that they could buy on the margin.

Parallel with these major changes in economic life, a "revolution in morals" was significantly altering the outlook of Americans.[5] As the authority of religion declined, the gospel according to Saint Freud gained true believers. The family had already lost its economic role; its power as an institution was further lessened by a host of pleas for individual liberation. As a result, many were bothered because new guides of conduct were not being offered to clothe the individual as he stripped off the corset of Puritanism. Perhaps the greatest consternation arose when the new woman appeared. Rather than a socially constructive idealist, like Jane Addams, she turned out to be the flapper and the flirt!

The liberation of writers in elite culture yielded the creative literary work of Hemingway, Faulkner, and Fitzgerald. But in popular culture liberation appeared to have unstopped the bottle of cheap-and-nasty: popular songs on the radio were titled "Hot Lips," "I Need Lovin'," "Burning Kisses," while popular magazines such as *Paris Nights* and *Flapper Experiences* covered the newsstands. Hollywood concentrated all of these pyrotechnic changes into one half-baked city, Los Angeles, California. Advertisements for the "smart" and "sophisticated" films produced there promised "brilliant men, beautiful jazz babies, champagne baths, midnight revels, petting parties in the purple dawn, all ending in one terrific smashing climax that makes you gasp."[6]

According to contemporary social scientist Edward Sapir, industrialism, urbanism, advertising, and the unreflective celebration of the individual all had worked to fragment the traditional culture of the West. Much like Will Rogers, Sapir was careful to explain that so-called progress in the early twentieth century was more a matter of material improvement than an advance in the quality of "genuine culture." Even the most well-adjusted twentieth-century American sensed a certain incompleteness in his life:

> Even if he succeeds in making a fairly satisfactory compromise with his new environment, he is apt to retain an uneasy sense of the loss of some vague and great good, some state of mind that he would be hard put to it to define but which gave him courage and joy that latter-day prosperity never quite seems to have regained for him. What has happened is that he has slipped out of the warm embrace of a culture into a cold air of fragmentary experience.[7]

The price of material conquest of the environment had been paid for by an emotional tax on true happiness:

> Here lies the grimmest joke of our present American civilization. The vast majority of us, deprived of any but an insignificant and cruelly abortive share in the satisfaction of the immediate wants of mankind, are further deprived of both opportunity and stimulation to share in the production of non-utilitarian values. Part of the time we are dray horses; the rest of the time we are listless consumers of goods which have produced no lasting impression on our personalities. In other words, our spiritual selves go hungry, for the most part, pretty much all the time.[8]

From his elevated position as professor of anthropology at Yale, Edward Sapir could see the fragmentation of culture in a historical sweep that went back to the seventeenth century. On the level of popular culture, most Americans sensed the same inadequacies in their lives, but their frame of reference was smaller. Many sought solace in thinking of the 1890s as a lost Eden from which the America of their own postwar era had departed. At least as nostalgically recalled by these unsettled people, that earlier America had been a face-to-face society, a comprehensible world painted in primary colors:

> By 1932, the prewar years had taken on a luminescence that they did not wholly have at the time. In retrospect, the years before World War I seemed like a lost Arcadia. Men remembered country fairs and church socials, spelling bees and sleigh rides, the excitement of the circus train or the wild dash of firehorses from the station house, the cool smell of an ice cream parlor and the warm fragrance of roasted chestnuts. . . . They remembered people: the paper boy with his off-key whistle, the brawny iceman sauntering up the walk with his five-cent cake of ice, the Negro stable boys, the printers and devils in the newspaper offices. They recollected general stores: the bolts of calico and muslin, the jars of cinnamon and gunpowder tea, bins of dried peaches and cornmeal, kegs of mackerel, canisters of striped candy. From the vantage point of 1932, it seemed as though they had danced endlessly at tango teas and strummed mandolins every evening.[9]

Not the realities of the 1890s, but the anxieties of the 1930s tempted Americans to reflect nostalgically on that earlier era, proving that people who burn their candles at both ends will frequently be burned by the hot wax.

WILL ROGERS: A MAN WITH ROOTS, A MAN AT PEACE

Will Rogers was important to Americans in the 1920s and 1930s because he addressed his humor to their basic sense of rootlessness and loss. As a cowboy version of Rip Van Winkle, Rogers passed through this era of change, judging new developments by the standards of the 1890s. And despite the criticism he delivered, he somehow bridged the gap between the old and the new. Because he made the transition without losing his identity, his audience was intensely concerned with his highly publicized "private" life: in a world where divorces were increasing, Rogers remained happily monogamous and committed to a traditional American family life-style; while his audience felt itself to be under constant pressure to perform, he seemed somehow to be unruffled by an active life with its host of commitments. Many Americans worried about the influx of machines. As a friend of Lindbergh and Ford, Will Rogers demonstrated that the machine age could be welcomed without America's losing touch with frontier values. In an era of big government and big business, Will Rogers stood out as a symbol of ready sympathy and practical help, for, unlike his uprooted audience, he seemed to be in contact with "The Real Things of Life."

Love and Marriage

Rogers was admired from the beginning as a man who was somehow able to remain simple and pure, even in an age of puff and artificiality. He seemed miraculously unaffected by the erosion of values. His good qualities were highlighted further by his presence in Hollywood: "He became nonetheless dear to us because of the falsity of much that surrounded him: the spurious nature and illegitimacy of much of the screen threw him into relief as someone really genuine."[10]

Rogers' sexual purity was universally respected. Reviewers of the early Rogers films were surprised that he could succeed on the screen without pandering to the usual demands of romance and sex appeal. He was unique as a male film star in "outwitting the sexy fellows."[11] Many admired Will and Betty Rogers for holding their family together. One reporter, realizing how important this happily monogamous couple was to her audience, breathlessly told her readers the results of a telephone "interview over four thousand miles with a model married man."[12] The readers necessarily understood that Hollywood was the leading edge of sexual liberation, and thus a city where the family was most endangered. In this context of dizzy freedom, "Will Rogers and his wife have been married longer than some stars, several times divorced, have been alive."[13] Rogers himself encouraged the press to report this eccentricity. Proudly (and often) he proclaimed that he was "the only motion picture star who has the same wife he originally started with."[14] The result of all this interest and self-promotion was that the Rogers household was celebrated as "an ideal home" where (in contrast with much of the rest of American homes) parents spent every free moment teaching the children or playing with them.[15]

A review of Rogers' first talkie, *They Had to See Paris* (1929), clearly shows how intensely concerned his film audience was with this reputation for cleanliness and fidelity. When Pike Peters (Will Rogers) and his wife (Irene Rich) reach Paris, Mrs. Peters immediately begins to dress in the styles of the *beau monde*. In a bedroom scene, Pike, pleased by the way his wife looks in her new fashions, gives her a very innocent kiss. Rogers' audience was so involved with their public man off the screen that there was a very intense response to this act on camera: when he "blushingly kissed her," the audience broke into happy applause. They knew it was Will's first screen kiss, and they realized that he never would have done it had it not

9. Two 20th Century-Fox symbols of purity, 1935.

been for the years of devoted friendship that had grown up between them in their pilgrimage to the top of the screen ladder. Also in view of Will's domestic happiness, the roof went off when he admitted that his kiss was almost like infidelity.[16] The film audience admired Will and Betty Rogers for maintaining "a real house, even in Hollywood" because so many families in their own neighborhoods were disintegrating under the acid of change.

Transcending the Pressures of Middle-Class Life

Americans were fascinated by Will Rogers' ability to surmount the pressures of his busy life as entertainer, journalist, and film star. As an admiring newspaperman reported: "Will Rogers probably is the only person alive who can face the Associated Press totally unembarrassed. Big news is but the happenings of a small town to him. To him important personages are but fellers of his acquaintance."[17] Rogers himself delivers a line in *Life Begins at Forty* (1935) which summarizes the lesson his viewers drew: "He solved the problem which all the world has been looking for — how to relax. Just to look at him makes me feel better."

Rogers' freedom from pressure was communicated in numerous ways. When radio was a new invention which stymied a number of professional performers, Rogers made his broadcasts extemporaneously. He conveyed the impression that he was too secure in himself to be worried. As one commentator noted, Rogers was "the only guy in radio who dares to hem and haw away air time."[18] Rogers' movie fans were aware that he was equally blasé on the movie set. Part of the delight in viewing a Rogers movie was watching Rogers deviate from the script and seeing the problems which his improvisation caused for his fellow actors. While this horseplay might have been a pleasure for an audience accustomed to being programmed during working hours, it caused some consternation and confusion on the movie set at 20th Century-Fox. Rochelle Hudson (who played the young female in *Dr. Bull, Mr. Skitch, Judge Priest,* and *Life Begins at Forty*) admitted that Rogers' liberties with the script caused her great distress, for she never recognized her cues. As she recalled, Rogers' proclivity for improvisation left her "listening for cues that never came . . . had me adlibbing to myself in my sleep long before my first picture with Bill was finished."[19] A young and ambitious John Ford (already knowledgeable about the insouciance of Will Rogers and Irvin Cobb on the set) began the filming of *Steamboat 'Round the Bend* (1935) with the simple but knowing question: "Does either of you two gentlemen have the faintest idea of what this story is about?"[20]

Will Rogers' screen audiences were delighted by his improvisations, for his liberty even from the verbal restrictions of a script conveyed the impression that he was a man at ease with himself who (unlike his middle-class audience) was capable of transcending the petty demands of a busy life. One reviewer accurately spoke for millions when he said that "You feel, somehow that he has captured the secret of being happy, and that if you watch the screen carefully, this secret may be yours."[21] As with the other virtues described in this section, the audience believed that this secret applied to Rogers the man as well as the Rogers persona on the screen.

The Sympathetic Spirit

Rogers' humanitarian activities were widely followed and admired. When an earthquake destroyed Managua, Nicaragua, in 1931, he flew south to

10. Rogers pretends to get the inside scoop from Walter Winchell.

lend his name to fund-raising efforts; after floods ripped through the lower Mississippi Valley in 1927, he was on the spot to entertain and to ease the pain of the dispossessed; when Oklahoma and surrounding states became a "Dust Bowl" during the famous drought of the 1930s, he stumped Oklahoma and Arkansas for the Red Cross. The itineraries of what were called Rogers' "tours of mercy" boggle the mind of the ordinary mortal. His contemporaries found it difficult to believe that a man could do so much for so many without some kind of mission of love inspiring him. One contemporary went so far as to say these tours were representative of Will Rogers' "Christ-like spirit of giving." When they reported these tours, newsmen did not hesitate to contrast the personal concern demonstrated by Rogers with the foot-dragging and bureaucratic bungling of a big and indifferent government. There is little doubt that by circumventing the red tape and empty debates, Rogers gave many forgotten men in the age of Calvin Coolidge and Herbert Hoover the sense that someone of national stature was personally concerned about their suffering.

A newspaper cartoon entitled "Relief Map of Oklahoma" conveys this message.[22] Rogers managed to visit almost every major city and county seat of Oklahoma during the disastrous drought of the 1930s. The people of his home state were obviously pleased with the $225,000 in financial relief which these tours yielded, but this cartoon-map has nothing to say about physical or fiscal relief. In fact, it is really not a map at all, but a close-up of Will Rogers: in the foreground, blocking out all but the eastern and western extremities of the outline of the state, is the smiling face of Will Rogers, his hat on the back of his head and his boyish grin warming our hearts. The cartoon really celebrates the spiritual and psychological relief which Rogers' humor brought to suffering people. Other stories and cartoons of this kind make it certain that victims of flood and other natural disasters were relieved when they heard the announcement (this from a New Orleans newspaper) "Will Rogers Is Coming!"

As a representative person, Will Rogers embodied a ready sympathy, a freedom from the selfishness which seemed to be the guiding spirit of the materialistic American 1920s. In a society where dwellers in the same apartment building did not know each other, Rogers seemed to convey the idea that cities and nations (through his example) could be linked by neighborly bonds of affection: "He comes nearer being a *Jongleur de Dieu* than any modern world personage – a jongleur and a troubador in one – not for a single community, but for thousands of cities and for the remotest cabins. To have wings for such a service is not merely to minister to more people directly; but is to carry them the human kindness of others and to bring these people into wider human relationships."[23]

The Real Things of Life

The news surrounding Will Rogers' response to his sister's death in 1925 binds together many of the values and qualities which his audience identified with Will Rogers the "private" man. One report may stand as a representative of the whole. "The Real Things of Life" begins with an explanation of Rogers' wealth and popularity as an entertainer and journalist. The major point of the article (and a very important one for Rogers' followers) is that no matter how successful, how far on top of the heap, Rogers proudly kept his spiritual roots in the soil of Oklahoma.[24]

11. A newspaper cartoon in appreciation for Rogers' humanitarianism. Reprinted in the *Journal of Popular Film*.

The articles about the death of Rogers' sister and his response to it emphasize two incidents. The first occurs while Rogers is entertaining a convention hall filled with ministers. As he delivers his planned comic lines, Rogers is overwhelmed by the thought of his sister's suffering and breaks into tears. With an immediate change of mood, Rogers asks the assembled clergy to pray for his sister, Mrs. C. L. Lane. Far from ridiculing Rogers' display of emotion, an admiring reporter wrote: "He could not hide his sorrow, nor would it have been more manly in him to suppress his tears."[25]

12. Rogers and Producer Eddie Dowling help open a park for immigrant children of Hester Street.

The second incident involves Rogers' response to a newspaper story which he saw while returning to Claremore, Oklahoma, to attend his sister's funeral. Perusing a state newspaper, he noticed a headline calling his sister "Mrs. C. L. Lane, sister of famous comedian, Will Rogers." Rogers' response was noted well because it reaffirmed his respect for rural America, even though he was himself a success in the new world of the city. After seeing the headline, he attempted to correct what he saw as a very false impression. Reflecting about the reverent, mourning crowds of country people, he demonstrated his respect for "The Real Things of Life":

> It's the other way around. I am the brother of Mrs. C. L. Lane, "The Friend of Humanity." And I want to tell you that as I saw all these people who were there to pay tribute to her memory, it was the proudest moment of my life that I was her brother. And all the honors that I could ever in my wildest dreams hope to reach, would never equal the honor paid on a little western hilltop among her people to Maude Lane. If they love me like that at the finish, my life will not have been in vain.[26]

Such a statement of respect for the values and judgment of small-town America had broad resonances in 1925. The revolt from the village had long before become a trendy cause in popular and serious literature; Sinclair Lewis added the word "Babbitt" to the American language in 1922 when his searing portrait of the Midwestern businessman was published; *soi-disant* sophisticated readers of H. L. Mencken's *American Mercury* (1924-1933) were learning to chortle over the strange and antiquated manners and morals of the "booboisie" of the American hinterland. This was indeed a period when "the midwest stood for all that was tedious, humdrum, and false about human existence."[27] Within this context of contempt for rural America, Rogers' newspaper audience was impressed by his emotional reaction to his sister's death. Unquestionably, Rogers' followers were probably reading at least some of the writings of Lewis and Mencken, but they were impressed (and perhaps reassured) by this incident. Clearly, Rogers had his feet in basic old American values, even though he was living in the urban world and earning one of the highest salaries in show business.

His audience may have made the same rise, but they feared that they had lost touch with a society that could value people for noneconomic virtues.[28] In contrast, Will Rogers had made the same passage to the new without losing touch with the old. His ability to bridge the gap (and their capacity to admire him for doing it) salved their consciences. As one Hollywood acquaintance summed up Rogers' unusual capacity to keep his feet planted in both realms, "Bill is perhaps the world's most widely travelled citizen with the hometown feeling completely untouched."[29] Thus, to a disturbed and mobile people, Will Rogers "represented something fundamentally honest

13. Will Rogers savored the simple things in life—in this case, homemade "fixins'" prepared by Opal Peters (Marguerite Churchill) in *They Had to See Paris* (1929).

in human nature, something which, in the hectic movement of the passing time, we seem to be in danger of forgetting and eventually losing."[30]

WILL ROGERS: A JOURNALISTIC STYLE

Because Americans imputed so many anachronistic (yet estimable) characteristics to Will Rogers, in their confusion they willingly turned to his newspaper column every morning for a dose of common sense. Rogers seemed to be uncorrupted by the fads of the period, and this exemption convinced people that he (unlike them) could look straight at the new and see whether or not the emperor had on a new set of clothes. Frequently (to the relief of his audience), Rogers saw that the emperor was naked.

The Old (the Essential), the New (the Inessential), and the Crash (a Judgment)

While Will Rogers is remembered today as simply a "humorist," his contemporaries were very much interested in Rogers as a moralist. The moralism of his social commentary was rendered in his humor as much by a dramatic technique which runs through it as by the actual words he used. The basic inner technique of Rogers' humor is implicit in the relationship which he articulates between himself as an observer and the modern world which he reports for us. The observer in Will Rogers' humorous journalism is always an "old boy" from Claremore, Oklahoma, who has been bypassed by the germs of fashion. We are always forced to assume that this speaker has some kind of contact with a core of uncorrupted, "natural" rural values. Because our speaker is pre-modern, pre-urban, he can see through many of the artificial problems which perplex urban man.

The society and leaders observed in Will Rogers' humorous journalism are usually associated with ideas, institutions, inventions, or problems new to the twentieth century. As Rogers' innocent eye scans the contemporary horizon, it focuses quickly on the exaggerated sense of self-importance which urban man is always guilty of claiming for himself. The lesson which Rogers tries to communicate is that men in cities, in corporations, and at the head of big governments and major political parties may have convinced themselves that they are important to the world, but our rural commentator who is closer to nature knows better. Since man's pride is the subject of so much of Rogers' commentaries, it should be underscored that the insights he presents are penetrating not because of his special intelligence, but by virtue of the perspective of the human comedy which his rural (and pleasantly backward) location gives him. Only in exceptional cases does a product of the twentieth century prove itself to be a match for a counterpart in the 1890s. We are told both explicitly (by argument) and implicitly (by metaphor) that the people at the turn of the century knew who they were and what they wanted, but that twentieth-century American man is pursuing a set of hollow and trivial goals.

Rogers' device of speaking for an older value system is especially obvious in the following criticism of Reno's infamous (and then shockingly new) divorce mill:

> Lawyers meet the trains and line up and holler out the same as porters do down South at depots for Hotels. They got lawyers there that can get you loose from an Octopus. Lots of the women buy . . . cottages . . . till their probation is over. Lots of them keep their houses there, and then use them when they come back on the next case. Some women have as many as four or five 'notches' on the same house, showing that they had got their man.[31]

The humor in this passage is created by the speaker's attitude: he is a curious innocent looking on in bewilderment. The moralistic judgment of this passage is implicit in the verbal pictures that are presented, especially in the metaphor of the female as gunslinger. A society in which such chaos reigns is obviously decadent and corrupt.

Surveying a modern civilization which produces so much that the institution of advertising has been needed to force people to consume, Rogers tartly observes that "one-third of the people in the United States promote, while the other two-thirds provide."[32] The judgment in this remark stems from Rogers' adherence to the older ethic of work and productivity rather than the goals of leisure and consumption so praised by the ubiquitous voice of advertising. To Rogers' mind, advertising was especially dangerous because it frequently convinced people to relinquish valid old truths that had been tested over years. Such a negative judgment is the buried irony of the famous phrase which became a sort of verbal signature for Rogers the journalist. While the phrase "All I know is what I read in the papers" led most of Rogers' daily articles, it did *not* mean what it literally said but precisely the opposite. Rogers despaired that the average middle-class American in his audience swallowed the reports of the press and the claims of advertising whole each morning along with their new vitamin pills. To his peril, it was the average American who knew only what he read in the papers. As a man who represented a fading value system, which had been forgotten by the mass media, it was Rogers' purpose to hold the perspectives and information of the opinion-*creating* newspapers up to the light of his older, tested truths.

While Will Rogers the humanitarian certainly did not gloat over the stock market's resounding crash and the subsequent economic depression, he did believe that the Depression confirmed the criticism which he had been delivering all through the 1920s. Although he expressed himself in homier language, his critique was not unlike that voiced by Edward Sapir. While Sapir

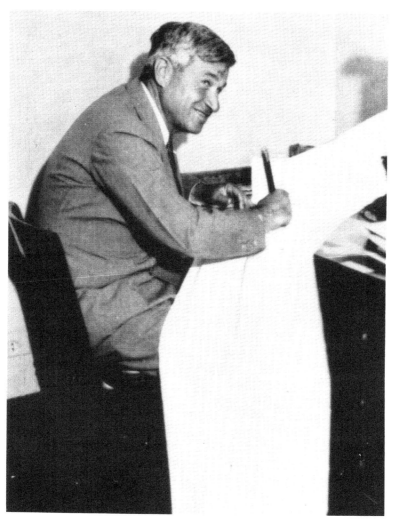

14. Rogers was a prolific writer but usually worked with less cumbersome instruments.

the academic explained that Americans were in a "spurious culture," Rogers summed up his criticism in the famous insight that "there ain't no civilization where there ain't no satisfaction, and that's what's the trouble now, nobody is civilized."[33] One quip by Rogers is particularly devastating: "Two hundred years from now, history will record: 'America, a nation that flourished from 1900 to 1942, conceived many odd inventions for getting somewhere, but could think of nothing to do when they got there.' "[34] His very famous observation that "America is the only nation to go to the poorhouse in an automobile" is a compression of this ironic criticism of the mindless worship of technology. As the Depression deepened, Rogers' vision grew darker, bordering on a very uncharacteristic despair. Shortly before his death, he wrote that "civilization is nothing but acquiring comforts for ourselves, when before civilization they were so hard they didn't need em. We still strive to put in another bath, when maybe our neighbors can't even put in an extra loaf of bread."[35]

Let Me Play with Your Problems

Because Will Rogers had faith that men could survive both their problems and their leaders, he was fortunately spared the kind of despair which the last quotation seems to reflect. For although he was a political commentator for most of his adult life, he believed that "history makes itself, and statesmen just drag along."[36] For some men, such a conclusion could be fatalistic, but in Rogers the message which is hammered home repeatedly is that we should not take our politicians, intellectual systems, or ourselves as seriously as we do—life is more fun and less taxing when we learn to see that man is not at the center of the universe. Rogers could remain aloof even during the crucial presidential election of 1932. In response to the exaggerated predictions of gloom by both candidates, Rogers retorted that "this country is a thousand times bigger than any two men in it or any two parties in it. This country has gotten where it is in spite of politics, not by aid of it. That we have carried as much political bunk as we have and still survived shows we are a supernation." Given this perspective, Rogers advised the candidates to take a rest and let the people make up their minds: "Get the world off your shoulders and go fishing. Then come back next Wednesday and we will let you know which one is the lesser of two evils."[37]

In the "playful" (versus the "moralistic") vein of his journalistic humor, Rogers seems to have appointed himself to be a translator of the new to the American people. In this role, he strives not so much to judge the new as to play with it as his audience looks on with admiration. On first inspection, many of these verbally playful articles seem superficial. After all, they formulate no solutions for the problems they discuss. Such an analysis misses the real point of these articles; in the articles, Rogers is not attempting to formulate answers so much as to give his audience a sense that the novelty discussed is not as awesomely complex and threatening as it might appear at first. Rogers' major goal in these articles is not to turn out stock answers to the daily headlines. He modestly wished to slow down their impact on the mind of his audience. If he could only juggle them long enough, the result would be that his audience could deal with them more sensibly. Some small sampling of these playful articles is necessary to counterbalance the impression that Rogers was strictly a moralist. In the following daily telegram, Rogers sends President Coolidge a mock warning about the popular tune "Valencia." It is on its way to poison the public mind of America: "My dear Mr. President: There will be a song hitting you now if it hassent already hit you. Do what you can to keep people from going entirely cuckoo over it. It is in exchange for 'Yes, We Have No Bananas,' and is called 'Valencia.' It ain't the Piece — it's all right — it's the amount of times they play it. Have Ear Muffs ready." This is the voice of a man who delights in the absurdities of popular culture.[38]

Rogers' capacity to make his readers laugh at their own frenetic involvement in change must have released psychological tensions. In one telegram that became famous, Rogers observed: "Give an American a one-piece bathing suit, a hamburger, and five gallons of gas and they are just as tickled as a movie star with a new divorce."[39] Here Rogers addresses himself directly to manifestations of the rapid changes in the moral, social, and physical environments: the one-piece bathing suit was considered to be a daring symbol of rebellion from Victorian prudery; the hamburger is the snack of a society which is in a hurry (and probably not exactly sure where it is going); the automobile is obviously a symbol of the new industrial civilization. The final, synthesizing line about the movie star with a divorce gives the description a special twist. The reader *does* feel guilty and confused about the rapidity with which his life is changing in all sectors, but he knows that he is not as fallen as the movie star. The inappropriate conjunction in this humorous comparison helps reassure the reader that he has not yet gone off the deep end, for all his movement away from the certainties of the 1890s.

To the obvious delight of his audience, Rogers would "play" with the most unplayful of problems. The growing combativeness in Europe and Asia was no laughing matter to Americans in the 1920s and 1930s. Rogers could not hold back, however, because he was driven to be the representative tester of the new: "Japan wants a 'Monroe Doctrine' with them playing the part of Monroe, 'doctoring' on China. Not only 'doctoring,' but operating."[40] Here is a line directed at events that were in the papers of the previous day. What Rogers succeeds in doing here is subtle, but essential to understanding the appeal of his daily articles. In a short space, he has summarized the nature of the threat. He then exaggerates the justifications of the belligerent so that they appear ridiculous and self-criticizing. Finally, he provides a summary judgment of the problem. When a typical reader of Will Rogers' daily article put down the newspaper, the problem was no less real to him, but it was certainly psychologically more manageable. With numerous messages of violence, war, and depression pouring into the press from all points in the world, people needed to laugh so that they could function. Rogers' humorous treatment helped insulate the shocks. As one of the townspeople says in *The Will Rogers Story* (starring Will Rogers, Jr.), "You don't tell us much, Will, but you sure do keep us laughing."

Speaking in his moralistic voice, Rogers could conclude about the Depression that it wasn't "Hoover, the Republicans, or even Russia that [was] responsible. I think the Lord just looked us over and decided to set us back where we belonged."[41] But for all his criticism, Rogers had a deep faith in the ability of the American people to adapt. To help them with their adjustments, Rogers undertook for himself the role of reducing massive, abstract threats in politics and society to manageable proportions. By making Americans laugh at Japan's Monroe Doctoring, he skillfully provided a catharsis for real and profound tensions. The common denominator which links Will Rogers' moralistic journalism to his playful journalism is his explicit and articulate discussion of the new and challenging in the contemporary setting.

WILL ROGERS ON TIMELY TOPICS

Aviation and the Influx of Machines

Sometime during 1920, while working on a film in Hollywood, Will Rogers was offered a ride in a studio plane. Former Army ace G. B. Manly made the short trip as exciting as possible with the hope of flustering the cowboy actor. As the pilot later recalled, Rogers "looked out over the edge of the careening cockpit and chewed his gum a little faster. When we came down, Will shifted his gum to the other cheek and remarked drily: 'Try anything once. Try some things oftener. When you goin' again?' "[42] Rogers had been bitten by an aviation bug. From that time on, the Oklahoma humorist jumped at every opportunity to fly. General James ("Jimmy") Doolittle believes that Rogers was characteristically excited by this new gadget: "I don't remember him refusing my call [to fly] if he didn't have anything else to do."[43]

During the 1920s, Rogers decided that the flying machines were more than novelties. They were needed for national defense to be sure, but they could serve a higher purpose: the challenges of flight could foster frontier values in an age of machines and "bunk." As spokesman for a point of view forgotten by the mass media, it was Rogers' self-appointed chore to test current fads, personalities, and events by frontier standards. The airplane was clearly symbolic of the new era of machines, but the inveterate passenger saw something more. The life-and-death struggles of pilots with elements of wind, fog, and darkness or such geographical barriers as oceans and mountains aroused his admiration. In fact, Rogers believed that this ocean of air above the American continent could serve as an inexhaustible testing ground for young Americans. He hoped that the airplane might constitute a new kind of transportation revolution, helping Americans to fly into the twentieth century without abandoning values of the nineteenth-century experience.

Rogers' response to the March 1928 decision to display Samuel Langley's flying machine at the Smithsonian Institution evoked his hostility to one form of Washington bunk. Rogers admired the Wright Brothers as individualists who succeeded in heavier-than-air flight against great odds. It appeared that Langley was to receive special recognition simply because he was an administrator at the Smithsonian: "Just read the Smithsonian Institution's explanation about the Wright flying machine. They say the trustees decided Langley's machine could have flown first but didn't. I could have flown to France ahead of Lindbergh, but I just neglected doing it. I had a lot of other things on my mind at the time."[44] Bureaucratic back-scratching was winning out over honest merit.[45]

The William ("Billy") Mitchell controversy was the quintessence of bunk. Rogers followed the developments closely, both because of his personal friendship with Mitchell and because he feared that government bunk might endanger national defense. On December 11, 1925, Rogers rode a train from Baltimore to Washington to attend the Mitchell court-martial. The journalist's presence caused a stir: the presiding officer, General Robert Howze, called a brief recess to receive Rogers, after which the commentator took a seat among the attorneys.[46] It was by means of this kind of research that Rogers knew more than what he "read in the papers."

Articles on the Mitchell affair stress the bunk of officials devoted to punishing a subordinate who had caused them severe public embarrassment. In an especially clever weckly article, Rogers invented a dialogue between the secretary of the army and one of his advisors. In this imaginary discussion, the underling suggests that a civilian jury be appointed to the Mitchell case in order to lift the onus of persecution from government shoulders. Being a master of bunk, Rogers' secretary of the army retorts: "That is all right, but suppose the jury takes Mitchell's part? Where will we be? They are liable to take aviation away from the army and navy and put it in the hands of a separate department. We must never let it get away from us, no matter how bad it gets."[47] It would have been difficult to fashion a more persuasive parody of government officiousness.

Early in the Mitchell debate, Rogers flew over the nation's capital with Brigadier General Mitchell. In a short article describing the sightseeing tour,

Rogers evoked an American hero who would not truckle to bunk. In the opening, Rogers established himself as a terrified passenger: "I did not want to see Washington by air. In fact, I never had any desire to see anything from the air."[48] On the other hand, the aviator faced the risks of flight with equanimity. Prior to takeoff, Mitchell asked Rogers if he used cotton to keep out engine noise, one of the hazards of flight; finding a bunk-related contrast, Rogers replied: "No, I only use cotton in my ears when I visit the Senate Gallery."

After the trip, Mitchell shared some shocking news with his passenger. For his outspoken stand on air power, Mitchell was soon to be demoted to colonel and transferred to a minor airfield in Texas. Rogers was sad for both personal and political reasons. The article concluded with a popular cultural parable against bunk: ". . . we had just flown over Washington's home, the Father of our Country, whose first claim to Fame was telling the truth about a Cherry Tree! But George wasn't in the Army then, and the Cherry Tree had nothing to do with our National Defense." Obviously, Mitchell was a nonconformist willing to sacrifice personal advancement for *res publica*.

Had Mitchell's aerial battles with storms and mountains given him such strength? Certainly Rogers described pilots as the last individualists in an era of conformity, Prohibition, and consumerism. These ex-army and navy officers were intelligent and tested professionals. What Rogers especially admired was the autonomy of the machine-mounted heroes: "They don't have to take off unless they want to. It's up to them. They are the last word. The company knows they will go if it's physically possible, and they let them decide."[49] Such independence was enviable in an era of assembly lines.

Lindbergh's flight blew a breath of fresh air into an era of bunk. The story of a "tall, bashful, smiling American boy" taking on the Atlantic Ocean alone, a frontier "where no lone human being has ever ventured before," seemed to give hope that America was still producing heroes.[50] A month after the Lone Eagle's flight, Rogers tried to identify the source of public excitement stirred by Lindbergh. "The reason that people have ate it all up this time is because it's the only thing that has been in the papers in years that was clean, and no dirt connected with it in any way. People hadn't read clean stuff in so long that they just went crazy over this."[51] There was still hope that young Americans could do more than play golf, drink gin, and drive recklessly.

Rogers promoted Lindbergh as a living embodiment of traditional values. An age of bunk needed such role-models: "This lad is our biggest national asset. He is our Prince and President combined. We only get one of these in a lifetime."[52] Press use of the name "Lucky Lindy" irritated Rogers because it detracted from the young hero's accomplishments.[53] In 1929, Rogers made his strongest criticism of the press: after their wedding, Charles and Anne Morrow Lindbergh eluded reporters. Disappointed newsmen accused

Lindbergh of ingratitude; after all, they felt they had created the popular hero. Rogers reprehended: this hero "was made by just two things—the Lord and a Wright whirlwind motor. Newspapers couldn't have flew him from one side of a razor blade to another."[54] Any other explanation was bunk.

Rogers often described pilots as machine-age cowboys. During a trip through Russia in 1926, Rogers met a Bolshevik with a trusty mechanical steed, "the funniest looking old chucklehead, shave-haired Russian boy that didn't look like he was over twenty. But say, Bob, that clown could sure rein that thing around and make it say uncle and play dead and roll over. He was an aviator."[55] The Fokker aircraft which ferried Rogers through Russia was personified as a skittish mount needing constant guidance from a skilled horseman: "This little plane seemed mighty small and jumpy to me, but this old Russian boy pulled the slack out of his reins, kinder clucked to her, and I want to tell you she left there right now. . . . He just give her her head, and didn't seem to pull up for rivers, railroad crossings, or mountains." While the image of a Bolshevik cowboy taming a mechanical Pegasus made amusing copy, the idea behind the comic image was serious: given youths like this pilot, men—rather than machines and bunk—could ride in the saddle.

Rogers frequently employed equine imagery. On his way to the Republican National Convention in 1928, America's "anti-bunk" candidate suffered two accidents. While Rogers was landing in Las Vegas, a wheel fell off and the plane turned over. Some hours later, the landing mechanism of a second plane broke during a landing in Wyoming. The Oklahoman could relate to the experience, even though machines seemed to buck very hard: "Once in a while, I've had a horse throw me where I've been underneath him and him topmost, but I've never been thrown like I was today. They're getting easier, however. The first spill wasn't so bad, and the second was almost a pleasure."[56] As always, such real, physical dangers contrasted with pitfalls back in the world of bunk. Of the Las Vegas crackup, Rogers reflected: "Wheel broke when she came down and turned over and lit on her back. I'm the first candidate to land on his head, and being a candidate, it didn't hurt the head."[57]

When Lindbergh began to take senators and congressmen for short flights, to win them over to aviation, Rogers congratulated the young hero for getting them "air broke."[58] Lindbergh married Anne Morrow in 1929 and then began a cross-country flight with his new wife. Rogers was pleased to see the couple as Westering pioneers: "See the Lindberghs are flying West. They have their camping outfit with 'em. If somebody lands in your back yard and you smell bacon frying, it won't be a soul but Annie and Charley. He is the first aviator to carry his own cook."[59] Despite the fact that this aviation couple traveled by machine, they appreciated the simple things in life. They obviously enjoyed getting away from the press and doffing their celebrity status: "You have never seen him at his best till you sit out in the pilot's seat by his side. When he has a plane in his hands, there is no careworn or worried look; that's when he is in his glory."[60] Once airborne, Lindbergh could forget the pressures of a bunk society.

Rogers especially admired the pioneering qualities of airmail pilots. These young men summoned the courage to confront elements of earth (mountains) and wind (storms) for a socially constructive purpose. Their dangerous work brought Americans closer together. Rogers admonished his readers to be grateful for the sacrifice: "When you get an air mail letter . . . you just ought to stop and think what a chance a half-dozen fine young men have taken with their lives to get that letter one or two days earlier."[61] Rogers found it difficult to overstate his admiration for these trailmakers of the air: "Boy, what pilots these air mail babies are. Lindbergh came from a great school."[62] As a contrast to this professionalism, elected officials in Washington—who should have provided living examples of civic heroism—were generating hot air, and this could be a problem: "They say hot air rises. And I guess it does. An airplane flying over the Capital the other day caught fire from outside sources."[63] Although Lindbergh and many clean young heroes had been disciplined by flight experience, the society of bunk was still dominant.

The airplane could bring societies closer together and promote better feelings among nations. Through personal example, Will Rogers taught this lesson, especially during his mercy tours.

Floods ripped through the Mississippi Valley in 1927, dispossessing thousands of farmers and covering many rural towns. Rogers wrote about the problem regularly. Even in the famous telegram which saluted Lindbergh, Rogers added a charitable suggestion: "What could be better to celebrate his arrival than another donation to 600,000 of our very own, that are not even fortunate enough to be flying over water, but have to stand huddled upon the banks and look into it as it washes away their lifetime's work."[64] In one highly publicized trip, Rogers flew to Louisiana to survey the damage. He asked the governor of Louisiana to put a plane at his disposal: "I want to get a look at first hand so when I speak on the flood, I can talk with authority."[65] (When Congress later convened a committee to study flood control, the airborne observer was called to testify.) Rogers played a number of benefit performances to raise money for flood victims. A special trip to Mexico (preceding directly a visit by Lindbergh) during the same year demonstrated that the airplane could help nations feel more neighborly.

When drought destroyed the crops of the Southwest turning the region into a Dust Bowl, Rogers showed that the airplane could speed up missionary procedures and allow one neighbor to help another. President Hoover would not commit public funds to alleviate the suffering because of his belief in free enterprise. Rogers refused to stand by: people were in trouble and immediate action—not more bunk—was needed. Rogers persuaded a

Texas company to supply him with a plane along with a famed former ace, Frank Hawks. Mounted aboard the loaned craft, the humanitarian galloped from state to state on his mission of mercy: he visited ten cities in Texas; he made at least eighteen stops in Oklahoma; and he stopped at five locations in Arkansas. Proceeds from his performances went entirely to the Red Cross: half could be used by the city in which he raised the money, while the other half was to be shared with impoverished rural communities.

Rogers dramatized his efforts in daily telegrams and weekly articles, stressing the contribution of both pilot and plane to the tours of mercy. An indelible impression was made on his contemporaries as a result of both the 1927 and 1931 trips. In a representative response, an editorial of the *Jacksonville Journal* (Jacksonville, Florida) tried to express the admiration of Americans for the symbolic actions of the Oklahoma humorist:

> Giving wings to most people does not add to their ability to be of benefit to the world . . . though it may increase their economic efficiency. . . . But when a genius such as Will Rogers got wings, he becomes a sort of superman, not by reason of a superiority of attitude, but by the multiplication of his contacts with human creatures who need a bit of cheer in their helplessness or weariness or misery. Like St. Francis, he is a lover not of mankind at large, but men as individuals. St. Francis used the "shabby expedient" of a rope to tie around his waist in this spiritual vocation; Will Rogers used it to humanize his philosophy. And the good he does in this world is increased by his mobility.[66]

This was more than a boost for aviation—it was a tribute to Rogers' living lesson that machines could serve human purposes.

Rogers regularly tried to portray the pure fun of flying, cowboy-style, across the aerial frontier: "It's like sitting astride a lively cloud and sailing over the earth with a marvelous, ever-changing mountain-top view beneath you."[67] The American continent revealed special beauties to those aloft: "In the east, you get the colorful panoramas of spring's tender greens and autumn's gorgeous foliage. Out west, you soar over magnificent painted deserts lonesome as the moon. . . . Then you strike a valley with pretty little ranches all along the edges, and feel as if you were back on earth again." In the article touting the pioneer efforts of Western Air Express, Rogers celebrated the sense of the open land which air flight conveyed: "Brigham Young might have seen more women than I have, but I have seen more of Utah today than he ever saw. Who said this country was all settled up?"[68] Flying provided a viewer with so many different perspectives that the beauty of the land seemed inexhaustible: "Even if you go over a country one way and come back by the very same route, the whole thing looks different to you. It's because you're seeing it from exactly the opposite angle. You will swear you didn't come that way before."[69] Such variety inspired awe. Night runs were even more exhilarating than day flights. Although an element of danger was added, an inexpressible feeling of transcendence was more than sufficient reward: "especially the thrill of sailing over a big lighted city at night. Below, you see hundreds of lighted rows of streets running in every direction, the dark outlines of the rivers and lakes, and the thousands of automobile headlights that dart around like bugs." Above every city — no matter how crowded — was a frontier ocean of air where young men and women could test their mettle, gain a sense of the power for good available in the machine age, yet return to an orderly society once the experience of flight was over. Americans needed both the challenge offered by the ocean of air as well as the orderly world created by technology: "When you swoop down out of the darkness into all this flood of light and efficiency — well, you'll just have to experience the sensation yourself, that's all."

In a weekly article written during the summer of 1929, Rogers described an endurance flight being conducted over a Los Angeles suburb. The article merits close examination because it indirectly addressed a broader issue: what kind of testing ground was the ocean of air, and how were America's young people rising to the challenge?

Rogers opened the article by describing the location of the test, Culver City, California. Although little known, it was an influential community: "all over the world, you hear about Hollywood, and hear of it as the home of all the films, when as a matter of fact there are more pictures made in Culver City than in all Hollywood. This Culver landed some of the biggest studios three years ago and they have grown bigger ever since."[70] As a representative American city, the open land of Culver was becoming crowded with studios, homes, and golf courses.

The endurance pilots were sons of local leaders: Paul Whittier was "a mighty fine young Pilot, son of a very wealthy family out here who were the founders of Beverly Hills"; one of the sponsors was "Young McAdoo, W. G.'s oldest boy." The entire Culver Field team consisted of young men accepting the challenges of a grueling endurance flight, even though they lived in one of the wealthiest communities in the United States.

Rogers detailed the dangers braved by the young men. Simply refueling the circling "Curtis Pigeon with an old Liberty motor" was fraught with peril. Passing the refueling hose between ships put the men on both crafts in danger: "If at any time during all these contacts it had ever touched the propeller it would have been all off." Other hazards made the endurance flight as much a test of character as of equipment: on one occasion, the refueling ship could not fly, and improvised means had to be devised to keep the ship afloat; at another time, when thick fog prevented the planes from finding each other, in a daring maneuver they linked up under the natural obstacle seconds before the endurance ship ran dry. These unexpected moments of difficulty forced the young pilots to draw upon resources of courage and flexibility; they were meeting the test of a frontier.

Living in an endurance plane was not unlike earlier forms of roughing it. Air sickness proved a debilitating factor, but "as time went along, they got stronger and more cheerful every day." The heat was so intense that "they didn't wear their clothes just run the ship in their underwear, with all the windows open." Sleep was allowed only briefly on an improvised inflatable air mattress. The conditions could not have been more primitive. Given Will Rogers' concern about American youth and frontier values, it is not surprising that the endurance flight heartened him: "It was a real kick to stand on that field and see them at the very moments that they were breaking the record, the longest any humans had ever stayed up." The rich boys had extended a frontier: with the assistance of their machines, they had stayed up even longer than "birds and fowl." Their accomplishment was a tribute both to character and to engineering.

The pilots over Culver Field were not unique. Young aviators in Dallas, Cleveland, and other American cities were testing their powers on the ocean of air. As a result, Rogers could be confident that leaders were being molded, leaders who could master machines and employ executive skills to explore new frontiers: "There is a whole lot more to this than just saying I will go up and break a record. It takes a lot of cooperation and work and much planning ahead." Those tested in the air could assume leadership roles in the technological society below. Fortunately, aviation assured that the age of bunk could still produce heroes: these men had the qualities of frontiersmen, but they were also skilled in making machines and organizations work toward constructive ends.

As machines became more sophisticated, more distant frontiers could be explored. Rogers envisioned American youths eventually mounting their mechanical steeds and riding off into outer space. Lindbergh had crossed the Atlantic; these future Lindberghs could conquer even greater obstacles: "Round June 22, 1950, here is what will be headlined in the planet Mars morning papers: 'A young man from a place called Earth flew in here yesterday. He had been in the air continuously for two months. He had some letters of introduction from the Chamber of Commerce from a place called Englewood, New Jersey. He asked to have his ship refueled as he is taking off for Venus in the morning.' "[71]

Will Rogers' fantasy was prescient. Ten years after the predicted date of 1950, John F. Kennedy called for Americans to dream of a "New Frontier." Like the 1920s, the 1950s had been an era of conformity and stagnation: postwar prosperity encouraged Americans to become soft. The American space program was launched on the premise that Americans needed to recapture the thrill of pushing back frontiers. Recently, Tom Wolfe has found heroic qualities – what he calls the "right stuff" – in our astronauts.

Wolfe's celebration of space exploration has become a bestseller because contemporary American readers share Will Rogers' concern about the effects of a closed society.[72] In the 1980s, we hope that young Americans will show the courage and resourcefulness Will Rogers saw exhibited over Culver City, California, in 1929.

International Politics

The United States emerged from World War I as a superpower confused about its global responsibilities and disturbed by its allies' lack of gratitude. Woodrow Wilson would be destroyed by the isolationist backlash of his own people, yet Europe seemed destined to be thrown back into conflict if the United States did not enter the community of nations as an active force. Will Rogers, in a number of articles, books, and short films, attempted to provide a humorous light on a subject he knew was not entirely a laughing matter. But laughter helped clarify a topic so often obscured by somber political rhetoric and inflated bombast.

A *Saturday Evening Post* assignment in 1926 serves as a representative foray by Will Rogers into the maelstrom of international relations. Other trips occurred before and after 1926, but his *Letters of a Self-Made Diplomat* constitute the quintessential Will Rogers vision; in later reports, only the names would change.

On April 15, 1926, Rogers had lunch with George Horace Lorimer, the famous editor of the *Saturday Evening Post*. The *Post* had recently carried a feature entitled "Letters of a Self-Made Merchant to His Son." Lorimer wondered if Rogers could write a special feature series of weekly articles which would take a similar approach to the pressing foreign policy issues confronting the nation, something along the lines of Mark Twain's famous travelogue, *Innocents Abroad* (1879).

As a writer, Will Rogers had a literary problem to overcome. To whom would the letters of this self-made diplomat be sent? Fortunately, a comedic technique developed by Rogers in the *Follies* suggested itself. It was Rogers' habit in the *Midnight Frolic* to call celebrities in the audience up on the stage or to address them as they sat with their friends. Always an energetic reader of newspapers, Rogers would refer to some business or political issue currently before the public, gently "roasting" the celebrity or giving "personal" advice on the issue, but always with an eye toward entertaining the audience present. Playing the role of public confidant had proven popular at the *Follies,* but experiments in print had yielded only mixed results. President Woodrow Wilson heartily responded to Rogers' counsel and frequently quoted the comedian to the press and to public audiences. Like a later president, Franklin Roosevelt, Wilson recognized that attention from Will Rogers could not hurt men in the public eye. Rogers knew that Calvin Coolidge was not as dour as the press portrayed him. He decided to make the president his pen pal. An advertisement for the *Post* series conveys the light tone of the letters.[73] A slender man, who is obviously President Coolidge, faces away from us. Into his ear, Rogers is whispering sage counsel about foreign affairs: "Now listen, Mr. Coolidge. This is between you and me . . . and the rest of the nation." The technique was simply a carryover from Rogers' *Midnight Frolic* show, except that now the audience numbered in the millions, for admission to this show cost only a nickel.

It should quickly be added that Rogers intended no disrespect toward the president. On the contrary, Rogers was a great admirer of Coolidge, whom he described as "a great politician. He looks further ahead than any of them." Choosing the letter format had more to do with literary considerations than political judgments. In writing letters rather than essays, Rogers could employ an informal and intimate style, emphasizing personal observations and feelings rather than abstractions. Hundreds of books had been written on the future of Europe by professors and pundits; Rogers needed a literary vehicle that would allow him to emphasize the human side of the story. Why not a series of letters from one rural man to another?

Will Rogers' tour of Europe and Russia would have the same lively pace which characterized his early spring transcontinental speaking tour. There was no fixed itinerary for the trip. Rogers was simply to wander according to impulse, provided that he sent back colorful and instructive copy. While the title of the series had been conceived in jest, the role which Rogers was to play was ambassadorial in a serious sense; he was performing a special service for the nation. There had been so many variant reports that perplexed Americans looked forward to reading his down-to-earth opinions.

At 12:30 on the morning of May 1, 1926, the *Leviathan* backed out of its berth in New York Harbor, carrying among its passengers Will Rogers and his fourteen-year-old son, Will, Jr. Six days later, the modern liner was next to a dock in Southhampton, England. After a week in London, father and son flew to Paris in a large new French airliner. It was a rough trip, and an airsick-prone devotee of aviation experienced one of the negative effects of flight. The next day, the Americans were on a train bound for Rome. When they stopped en route to visit the disarmament proceedings in Geneva, business almost came to a halt. As the *Tulsa Daily World* proudly reported: "Will Rogers, American Lariat Artist and 'Wise Cracker' bobbed up in the League of Nations Disarmament Commission session in the afternoon and attracted more attention than many delegates."

Dictator Benito Mussolini was the object of Will Rogers' trip to Rome. A "noninterview" between the representative from Claremore and Il Duce is one of the more enthusiastic moments of the *Letters of a Self-Made Diplomat,* for Rogers saw Mussolini's early work as constructive and beneficial to Italy. (It should be noted that this evaluation preceded by four years the excesses of Mussolini's foreign policy and that Rogers' views at this time were shared by many.)

While in Rome, Rogers was given an audience with the Pope. His letters give evidence that he saw many of Italy's masterpieces of architecture and painting while in the Eternal City. From Italy, Rogers sailed to Spain for an interview with another dictator, Miguel Primo de Rivera. The American democrat took pleasure in the traditionalism which he encountered in this country.

Within two weeks, Rogers was back in London preparing for a flight into Russia. Permission to observe the Communist experiment in social engineering had arrived while Rogers was in Italy. The *Saturday Evening Post* was as obliging in this case as it had been about the European tour and for the same reason. Because there had been so many contradictory reports by commentators, the American people would take pleasure in a Rogers treatment of the subject. The series was published independent of the European travelogue under a facetious title, *There's Not a Bathing Suit in Russia and Other Bare Facts.* Like the *Letters,* the series first appeared in the *Post* and was later published in book form.[74]

By mid-July, Rogers was back in London where he signed a much publicized contract with British National Pictures. The British were hoping to break Hollywood's monopoly on film comedy. While in London, Rogers found other ways to communicate with the British, while paying expenses. Almost as soon as he stepped off the plane from Moscow, he signed a contract with *Cochran's Revue,* a British imitation of Ziegfeld's *Follies.* In addition, he began to appear in a late night cabaret in a show similar to the *Midnight Frolic* which had made him so popular among New York's late night set. Finally, the Oklahoman made quite a stir when he went on the air in August "for the largest fee ever paid to a radio talker in this country" and then donated the fat check to a hospital charity.

Early September found Rogers in Ireland, delighting in the Irish landscape but again taking time to do benefits for charity. A tragic fire in Drumcollogher had killed many and seriously injured scores. Rogers immediately volunteered to perform at a theatre in Dublin, with all proceeds going to the sufferers. He raised $2,000 at the door, to which he added a contribution of $500. Rogers was fast transforming himself into an ambassador of goodwill. (In 1927, President Coolidge capitalized on this humanitarian image by sending Rogers on a goodwill tour of Mexico with Dwight Morrow and Charles A. Lindbergh.)

Mrs. Rogers, daughter Mary, and younger son Jim joined the humorist in early August. Will, Jr. was sent home; he had been away from his books long enough. After the comedian settled his family into comfortable quarters in Switzerland, he left for a hasty last reconnaissance, to include Greenland, Scotland, Wales, and Germany. On September 21, the entire family boarded the *Leviathan* for home.

As the *Leviathan* sailed back to the United States, Rogers could total up a number of accomplishments: he had plumbed the motives of the intellectual and political leaders of the new Europe; his travels had allowed him the opportunity to talk with average citizens, the "regular birds" of the continent; and he now had first-hand information about basic foreign policy matters. It was no longer true—as it had been during the war—that all he knew was what he read in the papers. His horizons had expanded and his insights had deepened; his observations in the future would be increasingly authoritative.[75]

The distance between the country bumpkin and the city slicker seems always to have tickled the American funnybone from Royall Tyler's eighteenth-century play *The Contrast* up to the television story of the "Beverly Hillbillies." Will Rogers put himself in the role of innocent abroad for both comic and serious purposes. He was aiming strictly for comedy when he described the difficulties of gaining entrance to the House of Commons. According to his tall tale, all doors were suddenly opened when he announced that he was from Claremore, Oklahoma. The letter goes on to report that not only was he given a seat immediately, but that the English were also very curious about Claremore's exemplary city government! Following Twain's example in *Innocents Abroad* (1879), Rogers played upon the theme of the superiority of the American landscape. His disdainful comparison of the Bay of Naples with American ports is only one example among many:

> Did you ever see the bay of Naples that you have heard and read so much about? Did you ever see the harbor in San Francisco? Well it makes the bay of Naples look like the Chicago drainage canal, and I am from Los Angeles, too. When even the harbor of Los Angeles with its growing barley fields, and its thriving subdivisions, if it had any water in it would be better than Naples. Why Houston stole a better harbor from Galveston than Naples is. It hasn't got the blue water that Naples has, but it will float an old tug full of cotton. Why Miami Florida if they ever cleaned those gin bottles out of that harbor of theirs would lay it all over the Mediterranean (p. 55).

The obvious point made by the loyal provincial was clear: he loved his country and refused steadfastly to be hoodwinked by Europe's pretensions.

But Will Rogers used the device of American innocence for serious purposes, especially in Rome. He was irritated by the claim that living among historic monuments automatically made Europeans more cultured than Americans. As a dedicated observer of the Washington scene, Rogers could deny this environmentalism without much difficulty: "Men in Washington you know yourself, Calvin, live where Washington and Jefferson and Hamilton lived," but their actions had clearly shown that "Association has nothing to do with culture" (p. 73). The much vaunted grandeur of the Roman republic made little impression on this professional critic of senators and congressmen. Rogers was more alert to the brutality of the Roman games than to the civic genius of the republic. Over the entire city, he sensed a dark cloud of accumulated sin, a history of human wrong which his own isolated, "innocent" nation had been exempted from experiencing: "Everything in Rome was stolen from somebody at some time. It's just a question of who's got it last" (p. 80). Curiously, Nathaniel Hawthorne, a very different sort of American visitor to Rome, had come to the same conclusion some sixty-seven years earlier.

Another serious idea emerged during Rogers' lighthearted discussion of American innocence. As he warned his president, Coolidge was "standing guard over the best little patch of ground in all the various hemispheres" (p. 81). The thought had broader meaning, including a corollary that the United States should stay out of European affairs in order to maintain its innocence. Europe seemed destined to quarrel and fight. Our self-interest therefore dictated a healthy distrust of any entanglements with the fallen continent.

As *Letters of a Self-Made Diplomat to His President* revealed, the issue of war debts owed to the United States was hotly debated on both sides of the Atlantic. In fact, Rogers noted that Treasury Secretary Andrew Mellon was visiting Europe, consulting with former allies about payment. There were two very different sides to the debt question. Most Europeans believed that they had paid an incalculable price on the battlefield. Many attributed the astronomical casualty figures to the United States for vacillating four years before joining the Allied cause. On the other hand, the average American saw the war debts as simply financial obligations to be honored by borrowers. As Rogers simplified the matter for his readers, it had come down to two plans: either the European (no payments) or the American Plan (partial payment). Using rhetorical irony, Rogers showed personal contempt for anything less than full payment in the following description of the French reception of a recent settlement:

> It seems that there is just some little minor difference or defect in the agreement with America. The change don't mean anything, but they want to have it put just right before passing on it. There is just some three 000—naughts—on the end of some figures that they want to have erased. It was probably just a misprint, and taking off just those three little figures will of course make no material difference in the main settlement (p. 86).

As with other judgments in his writings, Rogers analyzed the issue in terms of individual morality. The French Deputies might wish to assume a *nonchalant* attitude, but from Rogers' old-fashioned perspective, a debt was a debt. For millions of his readers at home who were experiencing the pangs of postwar inflation, such elementary thinking made good sense.

President Woodrow Wilson had entered the Great War with an ideal, one that at first attracted considerable enthusiasm. The president hoped that out of the peace settlement would emerge a League of Nations which could replace the international community under a rule of law. Nations, the argument went, could disarm when both a World Court and a League of Nations supervised international relations.

Rogers was a sanguine supporter of preparedness. Germany's conduct in World War I had proven to the Oklahoman that the ability to hurt an opponent was much more persuasive than arguments on paper. The inefficacy of President Wilson's many notes and telegrams to the kaiser just prior to America's entrance into the war seemed *prima facie* evidence that a nation best protected itself by supporting a powerful and mobile military establishment. Rogers' European tour was only to confirm this prejudice. While aboard the *Leviathan,* Rogers chuckled over the absurdity of sending military men to negotiate a disarmament agreement: "Can you picture these Army and Navy fellows being enthusiastic for disarming? Can you see Andy and Hilary voting a Battleship out from under themselves? It's a great move to passify the pacifists, but these are pretty smart old Birds and they know when those boats will come in handy." Any concessions made would probably be limited to antiquated equipment and weapons: "General Nolan and Major Strong say if they give up anything it won't be anything more than their Spurs" (p. 18). During their noninterview, Mussolini reinforced Rogers' sense of the futility of disarmament schemes. Rogers asked the Italian premier about the prospects for the Geneva meeting. Mussolini first laughed and then replied that "we disarm when England disarms on sea; when France in air and land. So you see we never have to disarm" (p. 68). Spain's ruler, Primo de Rivera, answered similarly. As Rogers reported to his friend Calvin, "I got the same laugh out of him I had out of Mussolini. He had the usual European reply: 'When everybody else disarms, I will disarm' " (p. 93).

The dictators had very little good to say about the fledgling League of Nations. Mussolini hinted that the organization would be unable to cope with a real emergency. Primo de Rivera told Rogers about the Geneva Conference's ridiculous treatment of Spain. Age-old national rivalries were heightened rather than restrained by the supposedly supranational organization: "Now, between you and I, Calvin, I have talked to everybody that I could possibly get to that I could understand in this whole trip, and they all feel the same about this League and Disarming and World Courts and all that stuff. They feel like England and France runs the whole thing and they don't want anything to do with it" (p. 93).

The final letter of the *Post* series distilled the many lessons learned during Rogers' four-month fact-finding mission. The question of America's image abroad could now be settled. While it was obvious that part of the animosity toward America could be linked to the debt question, Rogers espied deeper roots: "We don't stand like a Horse Thief abroad. Whoever told you we did is flattering us. We stand as good as a Horse Thief. They know what you were sore at them for" (p. 107). Europe's "regular bird" had disclosed a deeper motive than the recent money problem. The hate-America campaign was just a temporary fad, one that would disappear as soon as American aid was needed again. The truth was that Europe was an armed camp with every nation hating the others and summoning up memories of past grievances if current ones were not bilious enough: "If you can find me one Nation in Europe that has a real down-to-earth, sincere regard for any other Nation, I will jump out of the top of the Washington Monument" (p. 107). The specificity of Rogers' itemized list of grievances shows how much he had learned from his European tour: "Russia hates everybody so bad it would take a week to pick out the one she hates most. Poland is rarin' to fight somebody so bad that they just get up and punch themselves in the jaw. They can't make up their minds whether to jump on Russia, Germany, or go up and annex Lithuania. Turkey has been laying off three months now without any war, and Peace is just killing them. You can't even pass out of the south of Russia into Rumania. Bulgaria is feeding an Army and deriving no benefits from it whatever" (p. 109).

Rogers blamed conditions rather than human nature for these horrible portents of war. Principally, Rogers blamed geography and the spirit of nationalism. Pacifists were simply ignorant of these principles: "You let France change places with Canada, and Germany change places with Mexico, and England with Cuba, and Japan with Hawaii, and you would see if we would be so anxious to disarm" (p. 111). The fires of nationalism were so strong that Rogers saw little hope for the future: "Say, if I didn't have any more friends than some of these Nations have around them, I not only would not disarm, but I would get another Gun, and wouldn't only have a gun in each hand as I went to bed, I wouldn't go to bed—I would stay up and watch all night" (p. 111). Americans had helped shape these fatal conditions. To Rogers' mind, President Wilson's principle of self-determination of nations had only added more fuel to the fires of nationalism. In a short time, the result of arbitrary nation-building would lead to a "self-disintegration of small nations. You see, the more Nations you create, the more chances you have of war" (p. 112).

The final letter of the *Post* series contained a number of serious recommendations for President Coolidge. Rogers was very pessimistic about the efficacy of any action by the United States. Every major power was tottering as the result of internal upheaval: strikes were plaguing the British, while the French could not maintain a government in office for more than a few weeks, and often for only a few days. Many smaller powers were on the brink of revolution. The general tone of bellicosity on the Continent simply increased Rogers' pessimism. World War I and other recent examples of American intervention had shown that we were often blamed even though our intentions were good: "All we have to do to get in bad is just start out on what we think is a good Samaritan mission, and we wind up in the Pest-house" (p. 114).

It is important to note that Will Rogers' isolationism was thoroughly consistent. He did not advise detachment from European affairs only. He counseled total aloofness, and he decried the brand of imperialism practiced during the 1920s by his good friend Calvin. Our hemispheric diplomacy must be guided by the same principle of noninvolvement: "if Argentina, Brazil, Peru, Chile, or anyone else have any disputed territory, and they want to populate it . . . why let them go ahead and do it. What business is it of ours?" (p. 115). Rogers told his president to concentrate on domestic inequities. America would attract the friends it deserved by setting an example to the rest of the world: "It will take America fifteen years steady taking care of our own business and letting everybody else's alone to get us back to where everybody speaks to us again" (p. 115).

Until recently, "isolationism" has been more of a smear word than a legitimate foreign policy position. But the term does accurately describe Will Rogers' outlook, if it is properly understood. After thousands of miles of travel and hundreds of hours of talk, he simply concluded that no one — not even a well-meaning United States — could significantly affect the European conditions described in the *Letters of a Self-Made Diplomat*. The air was charged with national rivalries. Even the small nations created after the recent war were enthusiastically training pilots for the next conflagration. The League of Nations had failed to exert the elevating effect upon the international community which President Wilson had promised. With two oceans serving as geographical barriers, Rogers recommended that the United States devote its energies to improving domestic conditions, an activity that would produce tangible results. In a recent interview for the film *Will Rogers' 1920s,* Will Rogers, Jr. stressed that his father's position was positive, that it included a respect for the rights of other nations. This dimension of Rogers' isolationism is too easily overlooked:

> I think that Dad represented what we think of as fundamentally American at that time. He wanted us to be the most powerful country in the world and he wanted us to have a big Army and Navy and later a big Air Force, but he didn't want us to use it. He didn't want to see America go into Nicaragua, for example. He didn't want us to send the Marines into China. . . . He was very outspoken in that way. He was anti-imperialist; he didn't want us to interfere with other people's business. . . . He said, "I saw an odd thing. I saw a Marine in Washington." He took a lot of cracks at our expansionism.[76]

Certainly, Will Rogers was no xenophobe. The Oklahoman kept an open mind, recognizing that differing cultures should expect to see the world differently: "I am not the fellow to go to a Country and then start criticizing it from our angle at home. You have to look at a thing through their eyes to be fair." Rogers made an effort to apply this principle of cultural relativity in his analysis of Mussolini. He knew that the typical American view of the Italian leader was simplistic: "Well, you got to be in Italy to really understand this fellow. Now to us he looks like he was the Tyrant and the Dictator, and that he was always posing like Napoleon, and that he was going to get his Country into war any minute. Now that's our angle on him" (p. 65). But in context, Mussolini was only adapting to Italian conditions. In fact, Rogers tried to show that while Coolidge and Mussolini appeared to be very different kinds of political leaders, in many ways each was working for the same ends but within very different constitutional conditions:

He gets up in Public and tells Austria and Germany what to do. You have Kellogg send Mexico a note telling them what time to quit work that day. He comes into the House of Deputies over there and tells them the measures that shall be put through. You have five or six Senators for breakfast and the same thing happens.

You see, everyone of us in the world have our audience to play to; we study them and we try to do it so it will appeal to what we think is the great majority. Now Italy likes everything put on like a Drama; they like a show, they like to have their patriotism appealed to and spoke about. . . . Mussolini says a lot of things publicly that sound like boasting, but they are only meant for Home Consumption (p. 65).

It would be hard to imagine Will Rogers as a devotee of the Communist system, but he was willing to see the world through the eyes of the Russian intellectual, Trotsky, if only for a short time. Unfortunately, Trotsky was going out of favor, and Rogers was not allowed to speak with him. Speaking about the canceled appointment, Rogers reflected: "If I had met him and had a chat with him, I would have found him a very interesting and human fellow, for *I have never yet met a man I didn't like.* When you meet people, no matter what opinion you might have formed about them beforehand, why, after you meet them and see their angle and their personality, why you can see a lot of good in all of them."[77]

This was the first public formulation of a phrase for which Rogers would be long remembered, "I never met a man I didn't like." The statement in its full meaning should be seen as a counterbalance to the theme of isolationism which runs through Rogers' advice to President Coolidge. Will Rogers was certainly no mindless nationalist who supported his country right or wrong; nor did he ever adopt an irresponsible attitude toward the world community. Finally, Rogers was never misanthropic; his writings abound with humor about the joys of being a social human being. The saying which is inscribed at the base of his statues in Claremore, Oklahoma, and

Washington, D.C., is internationalist in the best sense. It means that below nationality, class, sex, religion, or politics there is a basic humanity which we must honor. Respect for this common humanity could serve as a foundation for a peaceful world community.

Such was Rogers' hope. But he was also keenly aware that men had great difficulty detaching themselves from their roles and the influence of ideologies. As he sailed back from Europe in 1926, he felt that the barriers of class and nationality had been constructed to insuperable heights. Thus, while Rogers hoped for mutual respect among nations, his *Letters of a Self-Made Diplomat* focused upon the actual state of affairs in Europe. Instability characterized both internal and external politics. Governments were toppling; the masses were turning to dictators to restore order. Rogers advised his president to cast his influence where it would do palpable good, in settling America's farm problem, in bringing a new tone to our nation's politics, in confronting honestly that legislative fluke, Prohibition. After America's recent experience with Vietnam and Watergate, many Americans are again advocating that internal rejuvenation should be given priority over our bumbling attempts to shape the destinies of distant nations.

But it was not necessary to share all of Will Rogers' conclusions to enjoy his articles for the *Saturday Evening Post*. Franklin D. Roosevelt was as internationalist as any American politician, but he could savor the combination of drollery and insight which he found in the *Letters:* "In addition to my deep appreciation of his humor, the first time I fully realized Will Rogers' exceptional and deep understanding of political and social problems was when he came home from his European trip in 1926. While I discussed European matters with many others, both American and foreign, Will Rogers' analysis of affairs abroad was not only more interesting but proved to be more accurate than any other I had heard."[78] Whether Calvin Coolidge agreed with all that his ambassador had to say was not as important as the president's much-publicized response when Rogers returned home. An official car was sent to bring the literary ambassador to the White House for an "official" report. Rogers was asked by the Coolidges to spend the night at their house. A literary device had become a reality! But there was more than poetic justice involved; it was only right that the pen pals should meet.

WILL ROGERS ON FILM: AN EVOLVING IMAGE

A scene from the (now lost) film *One Day in 365* (silent, 1922) is a convenient point to begin a discussion of Will Rogers' film career. Will is sitting in the sunroom of his beautiful house in Santa Monica Canyon, reading the newspaper. The headline reads: "REGARDLESS OF DISARMAMENT PLANS, THERE ARE RUMBLINGS OF WAR." Will looks up from his paper and says to Betty Rogers, "I guess the Republicans want another war, to show how much better they can run it than the Democrats." When he finally finishes reading the paper, he throws it down in disgust saying, "Same old junk—murder and divorce—the people who were divorced last year are being murdered this year."[79]

In this scene we are watching Rogers humorously combine the moralism and the capacity to "play" with elements of the contemporary world. It is of interest in our discussion of Rogers on the screen because its relevance to current events is atypical. Rogers played many parts on film, but the common characteristic of all of them was their removal from pressing contemporary issues. And the longer Rogers remained in Hollywood, the farther back into an Arcadian preindustrial past his characters moved.

Will Rogers made his first film, *Laughing Bill Hyde* (1918), while twirling his rope on the stage of Ziegfeld's *Follies*. Not surprisingly, he was cast as a cowboy in various melodramatic and comic roles. Rogers had real problems with his audience in these first films. New York critics who knew Rogers from the *Follies* brought an understanding of his humor to the films, and this preparation helped them to understand the silent film character. On the other hand, the general public was indifferent because it had not yet been properly exposed to this fresh breeze of air from the West. Records show that Samuel Goldwyn lost at least $40,000 on these early films.[80]

After a short time as a cowboy, Rogers developed a second film persona. Called "Jubilo," this figure is a rural clown, a perpetual loafer who floats through society getting himself into trouble and avoiding work whenever possible.[81] Jubilo is an eccentric figure whom we love despite his numerous flaws. He is distinctly unlike the late, philosophical Rogers persona: Jubilo can fall in love and even has a few (rather athletic) fistfights.

Rogers experimented with satire in two uproarious silent films. In *Doubling for Romeo* (1921), Rogers humorously spoofed the swashbuckling film romances of Douglas Fairbanks, Sr.: Rogers swings from chandeliers, holds off hundreds of opponents with his single sword, and captures the girl of his dreams. In the process, he takes advantage of the opportunity to expose the absurdities of the conventions of Hollywood's popular love pictures. In a second film, *Two Wagons—Both Covered* (1924), Rogers satirized the sententious epic of the silent era, *The Covered Wagon*—a kind of frontier *Ben Hur* of its day. As an authentic Westerner who had grown up with pioneers, Rogers relished this opportunity to mock those who spun romances about the settlement of the American West.

During Rogers' middle film period (1929–1932), he developed a fourth screen persona, one that would have been readily recognized by his daily readers. In these portraits of an innocent abroad, Rogers plays a simple down-to-earth figure (usually from Claremore, Oklahoma) who is forced to travel outside his provincial world to Washington *(Going to Congress,* 1924), New Orleans *(Handy Andy,* 1934), or Europe *(They Had to See Paris,* 1929). The innocent is usually forced out of his normal environment

15. An unusually natty Rogers ca. 1930.

by his wife, who usually aspires to be a sophisticated and "broad-minded" citizen of the twentieth-century city. In a few instances, some local political faction accidentally elects the innocent to Congress.[82] The humor in all of these films about the innocent abroad derives from the interplay between the central character and the corrupt people of the urban centers which he is forced to visit. In most cases, Will Rogers overwhelms the corrupted urban men by the sheer force of his ebullient personality.

In playing these roles as the innocent, Rogers began to show that he was more than merely a good actor. One reviewer discerned that Rogers tapped deeper, national themes: In speaking of Pike Peters (a character portrayed by Rogers in *They Had to See Paris,* 1929), the reviewer noted that "Will Rogers has become a national character, infinitely more characteristic of America than the grotesque figure of Uncle Sam. It would be an artistic and patriotic crime to let such a film character [that is, the innocent abroad] die."[83] The reviewer and his public were not disappointed, for *So This Is London* (1930) provided Rogers with the same kind of ironic contrast between solid provincial and an effete society.

America's new place in the international scene determined the strong response to Rogers in this role. While America had refused to enter the League of Nations, the facts of international life could not be denied — the United States was the most powerful nation in the world but was still unsure of its place and its role. Rogers' innocent abroad films gave Americans confidence and a sense of poise in the international setting. The messages of these films is always that older civilizations may have posted their claims to preeminence before the United States, but postwar realities obviously showed that the United States was the only country in the world whose spirit had not been broken by the experience of the Great War. As one discerning reviewer reported, Rogers not only gave Americans a confidence-inspiring self-image, but he also conveyed a better picture of American character and values to the outside world:

> There was always the quiet homely voice and the lovable smile to keep us in touch with the things we knew and understood. He was a Westerner talking to Westerners in a language and with an awkward grace readily comprehended. He was the epitome of the spirit of the West: open-handed, free and easy, loquacious, oddly philosophical, genuinely sentimental with a smile ever within reach — one of the boys. And we liked to think that this was the picture of us that he carried to other and far corners of the world, where people, not knowing us too well, were apt to think of us as uncouth and six-shooting.[84]

The advent of sound films effected a transformation in what Rogers could convey to his audience. Prior to sound, viewers missed much of Rogers' special humor if they were not prepared by a night at the *Follies* or exposure to Rogers' daily column. With sound, it was impossible to miss his mysterious, radiating humanity. Speaking of this power to project a lovable personality, a reviewer of Rogers' first talkie, *They Had to See Paris,* noted that "this picture changes all [the difficulties of communication in the silent films]. Rogers' shadow is almost a living thing. The wit is spontaneous and droll . . . the disarming humanness of the man envelops the screen, the orchestra and the auditorium with one surging feeling of brotherhood."[85]

What was now needed in the era of sound was the proper screen "vehicle" for the Rogers personality. Of importance in selecting that role was the awareness that the camera could supply much of the atmosphere for the Rogers persona, that Will Rogers in a film could say less and actually personify the values which had guided his "private" life and his journalistic commentary. The final Rogers films portray him as a small-town figure. He is no longer the cowboy, the clown, the satirist, or even the innocent abroad, but a very different symbol of a harmonious America before the turn of the century. He lives in the mythical world which Americans nostalgically projected back into the 1890s because of the pressures they felt themselves to be under in the 1930s.[86]

Actually, Rogers had experimented with the small-town role during the 1920s. One critic was extremely impressed by its possibilities, given Rogers' personality and style. In a review of *Jes' Call Me Jim* (1920), the critic noted the kinds of effects that would later be attributed to the Rogers of the later sound films — that he was not merely amusing his audience, but conveying a much needed message of brotherhood and a refreshingly positive perspective on human possibilities. In this way, Rogers was showing that his films performed a social function: "Will Rogers' . . . good natured personality seems to spread throughout the world a sense of happiness and kindness. I suppose a man like this, acting as he does before almost countless millions, does more good to this old earth than scores of preachers and philanthropists; able to reach more hearts than can be reached through any other medium."[87]

In *State Fair* (1933), Rogers came back to this role. Audiences, executives at 20th Century-Fox, and critics all recognized immediately that this was the ideal role for Rogers because it placed him "in a day when American village life was far more isolated than it is today."[88] Celebrating that "Will Rogers Restored Picture Themes to Provincial Subjects," a reviewer captured the essence of this universally positive response: "*State Fair* taught Rogers his *metier* and it taught the industry that pictures concerning inland, provincial characters were more appealing than penthouses and gun-spattered pavements." The reviewer concluded that Rogers' nostalgic pictures had tapped a "forgotten public" which "had lost interest in crime and so-called 'smart' films [and had] stayed away entirely from cinema."[89]

At least in the beginning, both the film critics and this "forgotten public" shared a common enthusiasm for these rural films. Some critics thought that they saw a "complete metamorphosis [in Rogers] from amusing philosopher into character actor."[90] Other critics saw that Rogers, after being a cowboy, clown, and innocent abroad, had finally stumbled upon the right character for the screen. But after the formula was repeated a few times, critics tired of the rural Rogers "vehicle." Ironically, while the film critics stopped applauding Rogers' films, the American public swarmed to them in ever-increasing numbers, and film rentals for Fox averaged about $2.5 mil-

16. Rogers talks with Al Smith's son in a rare case in which the Oklahoman
was overdressed for the occasion.

lion per film. The irony of this disaffection of the critics was that Rogers
had begun his film career as a darling of the critics but a box-office failure;
in these late films, Rogers was obviously appealing to real and profound
popular emotions, emotions that could easily be overlooked by a critic
interested in film as an art form. For the average viewer of these films did

not buy his or her ticket to see art, but for the psychological relief and fatherly support which Rogers seemed to offer.

If we ignore the artistic merits of the later films and keep a clear focus on the response of the viewer, we begin to see why Rogers refrains from commenting directly on current events. The world of the late Will Rogers films is purposefully insulated from contemporary strains and pressures. For this reason, the viewer's psychological "payoff" from these rural dramas was the opportunity to escape temporarily from the world of ethical confusion, depression, and impending war. In *David Harum* (1934), this place is called "Homeville," a term we will use hereafter to describe the nostalgic, preindustrial world which we find in all of Rogers' later films. Economic breakdown, the separation of a democratic society into rigid classes, and the professionalization of knowledge may exist in this world of the later films but in a special form. In Homeville, all of these threats are reduced to human proportions. They may challenge the wits of Homeville's citizens, but they never seem to be overwhelming.

Because the challenges to happiness and fulfillment have been reduced, the Will Rogers persona in Homeville can deal with them. (Rogers in these last films will hereafter be called "Uncle Will" because of his avuncular role.) In a few instances, Uncle Will enlists the aid of the threatened, but most often he is capable of solving the problems by himself. He is really more than just an inhabitant of Homeville: he is its superintending consciousness. Uncle Will has a special insight into the human heart. Because of this special power and because every problem in Homeville has a human face, Uncle Will is a master of this world.

The best metaphor for the perspective given the viewer of the late Rogers films is probably that of a telescope which we look through backwards. The result of looking at the world with this perspective is that everything appears smaller and therefore less challenging to the viewer. The remainder of this chapter looks closely at *David Harum* (1934), *Steamboat 'Round the Bend* (1935), and *In Old Kentucky* (1935) in an attempt to show how this miniaturizing process takes place in three specific cases.[91]

David Harum (1934)

The first scene of *David Harum* (1934) could not be more explicit about the function of the later Rogers films to transport the viewer back into a simpler past. Rogers plays a rural banker who has come to the big city of New York to visit General Woolsey, a banker on Wall Street. The Panic of 1893 has forced the general to close his doors. Consequently, the general is very curious to know how Uncle Will can remain open for business during times of "depression, unemployment and starvation."

David Harum's answer is hardly an answer at all. Its dramatic purpose is to accentuate the differences between the two worlds which these men inhabit: the general lives in the city which has proven itself to be out of balance; Uncle Will lives in the country where people may not be good, but the proximity of men to each other assures that they are always under control. Harum explains to the general: "Well, General, I go a long way on character, and after I've gone a long way on character, I check on collateral. Then I give 'em half of what they ask for."[92]

This statement says something about the volume of business which Uncle Will does up in Homeville. He knows everybody in Homeville, and he also realizes that it is "human nature" for borrowers both to pad their loan requests and to overestimate their ability to provide collateral. Fully aware that even his best clients will cheat, Uncle Will gives them half of what they request — which, ironically, is probably what they really need! The point of all this is that the urban banker is a victim of impersonal economic forces which he cannot control. David Harum's Homeville, on the other hand, is never affected by anything as abstract as twenty-one year periodic economic cycles. As David explains, the people of Homeville are not dependent on a fickle outside market for their prosperity. Because they are closer to nature, they are self-sufficient and can therefore "roll their own" in hard times.

The young male figure enters *David Harum* with troubles not entirely foreign to a 1930 audience. John Lennox's father recently committed suicide because of his heavy losses on the stock market. To compound John's problems, his calculating, urban fiancée has closed out their engagement as she would a savings account — there is no more money in it. John has been searching for a job in a city that has none to offer. But because this is the Panic of 1893 (and not the Depression of the 1930s) John has recourse to the country to renew his chances for a good life. General Woolsey cannot help John personally, but he makes arrangements for David Harum to take John into the bank up in Homeville. When John leaves the befuddled city for the stable, self-sufficient countryside, he remarks pointedly: "Thanks, General — I want to get away from the city and get to work."

Homeville is unlike the impersonal city because it has a superintendent of hearts. Uncle Will is there to assure that a money problem never becomes an obstacle to individual fulfillment. Because of Uncle Will's ever-present concern, the inhabitants of Homeville are rewarded on the basis of personal virtue rather than on the basis of the intelligence, class, or sophistication which the world may have given them.

John Lennox (as an urban man who must learn to get some roots back into "the real things in life") has severe initial difficulties with the primitive conditions of Homeville. On the stormy night of his arrival, he finds the kitchen of the local hotel closed, and he learns that, if he wants to use the tub, he must pay extra for such a luxury. Upstairs, he finds that the ceiling of his room leaks and that the broken pane in his window is not interfering with the play of the rain. The night clerk of the hotel informs John that the town's only carpenter will fix the window when his rheumatism improves — which will probably be never. The purpose of building up these

17. This photo from family life has the same avuncular tone of the late Rogers movies. Here Will poses with Will, Jr.

details of backwardness and inefficiency is to communicate clearly that we are living in a world where work is not the most important part of life, where people take their time because they are ignorant of the city's treadmill of ambition and selfishness. As a result of not being obsessed by the Protestant ethic, the people of Homeville are happy, even if they are unwashed and a little behind on conveniences.

Uncle Will (as David Harum) personifies Homeville's indifference toward work and money. The more we watch Uncle Will in this film, the more we conclude that he is liberated from all material concerns. In order of their priority, his worldly interests seem to be: horse trading; ring toss (played in his office with his pocket knife stabbed into the middle of his papers as a pole); and fishing. Uncle Will even has difficulty making it to his office at all on many days because of the chances for horse trades and conversation along the way.

If considered closely, the six horse trades in *David Harum* fit into the overall pattern of reduced threats that we find in Homeville. As explained by Uncle Will to his skeptical sister, the golden rule of the horse trade is "Do Unto Others What They Want to Do Unto You." Translated into the world of the 1920s and 1930s as a business ethic, this is precisely the doctrine of the survival of the most aggressive and dishonest which led to disaster. Yet, in the setting of Homeville, the false representation and shaping of the horse trades seem quaint and entertaining, for what is destructive in Hooverville can be transformed into humor in Homeville.

David Harum's business practices as a banker reflect his easygoing attitude, his charity, but also his power to see into the human heart. David Harum's opening lines teach us that human beings are neither good nor bad, but a little of each. Because they can easily go astray, they cannot be completely trusted; but because they are not completely evil, we should not be completely cynical.

The film also indicates that a small town is an ideal social unit because in a small town people have an opportunity to study one another over a long period of time. In sum, Rogers communicates to his audience that the small town is an ideal society, not because people act better there but because in a small town a better watch can be kept over a wayward human nature.

Uncle Will's behavior as a small-town banker reflects this basic philosophy. When an impoverished widow cannot keep up with the payments on her mortgage, Uncle Will discovers a "forgotten" bank account which clears her of debt. This tender act of charity is followed by an entirely different scene which demonstrates that, for all his charity, Uncle Will is no sentimentalist who can be outwitted by the worldly. Immediately after his scene with the widow, Uncle Will is confronted by a burly customer who arrogantly refuses to pay his loan on time, claiming that an improper signature of his co-signer makes him exempt from prosecution. Uncle Will looks out of the corner of his eye — he knew that this confrontation would come eventually—and slyly explains to the defaulter that he had obtained the proper signature earlier in anticipation of this ploy. The note must be paid. This revelation leads to a fistfight, and, although no one is hurt in the uproar, a significant message comes through: If you are angry in Homeville, you can actually identify and take a swing at your oppressor. This personalized environment which allows the individual to let off steam contrasts with the frustratingly complex world of Muley Graves in Steinbeck's *Grapes of Wrath*. Unlike that impersonal setting of land companies, banks, and distant corporations, the forces that operate in Homeville always have a human face and heart. As noted, Uncle Will's charitable spirit controls Homeville because he has special powers to see into the human hearts of his small town.

Uncle Will's inveterate matchmaking in these last films tells much about his concern for particular human hearts. Reviewers tired rather quickly of the Kent-Venable mating that is repeated over and over again in the late films, but the mass audience kept coming back for more. To understand the full effect of these love-matches, we must realize that everyone in the audience understood that Rogers was in no way interested in the young girls he helps to find their man. One reviewer summarized the audience's sense that Rogers was a sympathetic and comforting old man: "If ever a man was a father, it's Will. When Ann comes up to Will's bedroom [at the opening of *David Harum*] while he is dressing, there is no embarrassment. With any other actor, the audience might smirk and think naughty thoughts. But with Will, he is so much the father type, naughtiness occurs to nobody."[93] These romances are really of no interest in themselves, but they have a function in the later films. Just as marriages in nineteenth-century novels frequently have social and other significance, so the presence of separated young people in the late Rogers films is used to convey a deeper meaning. Simply put, the young lovers exist in these films so that Uncle Will can have something loving to do.

It is not difficult to decode the appeal of this element of the late films. Rogers' audience was living in a world that was growing increasingly *im*personal. As a result of intellectual and economic strains, not only community feeling, but also the small loyalty demanded by the nuclear family was becoming exhausted. The appeal may have been sentimental, but an image of such a man as Rogers was very much needed by his audience to counterbalance this drift toward depersonalization. In a treacherous world which seemed to be out of control, here stood a sympathetic personality, completely unselfish, concerned with warding off harm rather than amassing power. Viewers of the late films were shown lovers who were separated because of financial differences *(David Harum)*; the law's delays *(Steamboat 'Round the Bend)*; the dishonesty of a spoiled rich boy *(Life Begins at Forty)*; and the covetousness of city folk *(In Old Kentucky)*. Fortunately for the young lovers, in all these cases democratic Uncle Will is present to help.

He manipulates the people of Homeville (and even the weather) so that these barriers can be surmounted. The result is that the young people finally recognize that they are just human beings and that the differences which seemed so insuperable are really artificial and flimsy when weighed against the inner promptings of the heart. As a result of all this matchmaking, Rogers comes to represent a disinterested spirit of brotherhood. And while this message is transmitted in the later films through a flimsy set of conventions, the ultimate effect upon the audience is to demonstrate that we Americans still have the capacity to transcend our materialism and our growing class barriers.

Our superintendent of hearts frequently calls into play some forms of *deus ex machina* to extricate him and his friends from the predicaments in which they find themselves. The most absurd of them all (from *In Old Kentucky)* is worth relating for its unreality and its appeal. Grandfather hires a rainmaker to salt the clouds so that the track will be wet during the climactic race. When the rainmaker's standard concoctions fail, he ties a bundle of dynamite to a cluster of balloons and hopes for the best. When the balloons fail to lift the dynamite, the bundle slams into a water tower near the finishing stretch, completely flooding the track. Because the track is flooded, the Martingale horse, Blueboy, comes from behind at the last moment to win the race. His victory ends all of the personal difficulties and family feuds with which the viewer has become familiar during the film. Only in Homeville, the land of wish-fulfillment, can such a *deus ex machina* grind out its answers without complaints from the audience!

Here the theme of the use and abuse of power enters in a coded form. We have already indicated that Uncle Will is the benevolent dictator of Homeville. Always a critic of men who aspired to hold power, how does Rogers on the screen avoid the abuses he found in others? Here the contrived conclusions of the films find their meaningful (and comforting) place. Certainly, most of the films achieve their happy endings in this way: In *Judge Priest,* Uncle Will persuades his Southern jury to acquit his client by playing "Dixie" outside the courtroom window at the right moment; in *Steamboat 'Round the Bend* a race, which eventually joins the lovers and saves an innocent man's life, is won because an unexpected supply of patent medicine (with a high alcoholic content) is discovered at the last minute to be useful as a high-energy fuel; *In Old Kentucky* ends with a horse race in which the track becomes providentially muddy. In every case cited, Uncle Will sees to it that all the love knots are tied and that society's conflicts are resolved—but always without an overt display of power. Uncle Will always gives us the impression that he has somehow transformed power into love. Unlike political and business leaders outside the theatre, he has the gods on his side. In all of the late films, the viewer is encouraged to identify with the young lovers, to experience their (temporary) sense of tension and unfulfillment, but then gradually to be rewarded by the tutelary deity of Homeville,

Uncle Will. The viewers who succumbed to those love stories may have been guilty of taking an emotional holiday, but we can understand their deep need for such an escape when we consider the world that awaited them outside the theatre. In these hours of escape, the viewers could smile at the pleasing notion that John Lennox and Ann Madison are married at the conclusion of *David Harum*. The viewers could applaud John and Ann's decision to remain in Homeville rather than return to the city. Unfortunately, the viewers could not lean on Uncle Will's comforting spirit, nor could they stay in the protected landscape of Homeville; they had to go home when the lights went on.

Steamboat 'Round the Bend (1935)

What has been said about Homeville and Uncle Will applies to the Rogers persona and the community portrayed in *Steamboat 'Round the Bend* (1935).[94] *Steamboat* drops Uncle Will into a characteristic *fin de siècle* setting: the main title is followed by a montage showing a paddle wheeler steaming down the Mississippi; the river is broad and the banks are lined with timber. Just in case viewers might be inattentive to details of rustic *mise-en-scène,* descriptive titles clearly identify that we are back in Homeville: *"Time: 1890s . . . Place: The Mississippi Valley."*

At the bow of the *Pride of Paducah,* we listen to an orotund evangelist (Burton Churchill) who claims to be "The New Moses." By means of a dissolve (indicating a short passage of time), we move slightly aft where we find "Doctor" John Pearly (Will Rogers) selling patent medicine of high alcoholic content. Contrasts could not be more extreme: The New Moses preaches against Demon Rum and Sloth; Doc Pearly promises that his Pocahontas remedy will exempt consumers from work, "especially at plowing time." Viewers should expect that all characters in this nostalgic tale will be equally eccentric and that the action will contain similar implausibilities.

After selling his entire stock, Doc Pearly climbs to the bridge of the ship to talk with Captain Eli (Irvin S. Cobb), master of the *Pride of Paducah*. In a series of unscripted lines, the two aging humorists introduce the action. Captain Eli learns that Doc Pearly has purchased "an old mud scow" which he plans to name the *Claremore Queen*.[95] When Captain Eli claims that he will beat him in the annual steamboat race to Baton Rouge, Doc Pearly takes up the challenge: a bet is made, winner take all. Captain Eli then drops Doc Pearly and his engineer, Efe (Francis Ford, brother of the director), at a jetty. A short distance away is the deserted *Claremore Queen,* a backwheeler in considerable disrepair.

Plot complications are soon introduced. After sundown, Duke (John McGuire) comes aboard secretively, bringing with him a "swamp girl" named Fleety Belle (Anne Shirley). Doc Pearly is dismayed to learn that Duke has recently killed a man while fighting for the "honor" of this ragamuffin. When Doc Pearly hears that the homicide was in self-defense, he counsels Duke to surrender in order to clear himself. Duke follows this sensible advice, but an ill-tempered judge condemns the young man to be hanged. Duke's only hope is that Doc Pearly will find the New Moses, sole witness to the fight, before the scheduled hanging. The law's delays and the challenge of the elements provide Doc Pearly, in the persona of Uncle Will, with a number of opportunities to work his magical powers.

In *Steamboat,* as in the other late films of Will Rogers, plot complications are never as important as atmosphere. Early in the film, Duke finds that even the jails of Homeville are hospitable. When Doc Pearly and Duke present themselves to Sheriff Jetters (Eugene Pallette), they are received as friends seeking lodging. The agent of law and order throws Duke the keys, inviting his "guest" to select any jail cell that looks comfortable. During Duke's incarceration, the prison guards permit other domestic functions expected in Homeville: Duke and Fleety Belle conduct a lovers' tryst, while a chorus of black prisoners serenades them with a mellow rendering of "There's No Place Like Home." Prior to Duke's departure for execution at Baton Rouge, the sheriff and his family do their best to provide the young lovers with a proper wedding. That the sheriff's sermon is ungrammatical and unnecessarily emphatic about the phrase " 'til death do us part," and that his daughter can only play "Listen to the Mockingbird" as a processional, only contribute to the quaint atmosphere. Affirmation of authority so pervades the mood of this segment that Duke refuses to escape when Fleety Belle plucks a rifle from the sheriff's hands.

Doc Pearly's attempts to find the New Moses become more desperate as the time for Duke's execution approaches. When the *Claremore Queen* heads toward Baton Rouge, Fleety Belle and Doc Pearly become embroiled in the annual steamboat race. Fortunately, the *Claremore Queen* happens to pass a landing where the New Moses is declaiming against booze. Drawing on his cowboy skills, the favorite son of Claremore lassos the prophet and drags him aboard. The evening watch also finds use for the improvised lasso: in an effort to conserve fuel, Doc Pearly ropes a capstan on the stern of the *Pride of Paducah*; with a tow line firmly affixed to the bow of the *Claremore Queen,* Doc Pearly is able to bank his fires. Not until the next morning does Captain Eli discover ("Holy jumpin' catfish") that he has been pulling a competitor all night.

During the closing miles of the race, the *Claremore Queen* runs so low on fuel that the New Moses proclaims, "Nothing will save us now but the power of prayer." Recapitulating the contrasts of the opening scene, we discover that not prayer, but the potent power of Pocahontas will bring victory over the *Pride of Paducah*. Bottles of Doc Pearly's long-forgotten patent medicine are cast into the flames: humorously, flashes from the wonder-working elixir are shown spurting from the twin smokestacks of the vessel, propelling the *Queen* at unwonted speed. Throughout the excitement, black comedian Stepin' Fetchit, cabin boy for the *Queen,* expostulates while others stoke the fires that will bring victory. A concluding reaction shot of Captain Eli shows us that he has been completely overwhelmed by this *deus ex machina.*

Although completely devoid of verisimilitude, this conclusion has the virtue of tying up a number of loose plot elements: Duke is exonerated moments before his scheduled execution; Stepin' Fetchit gets the victory cup; and, most important, boy gets girl. In the final shots of *Steamboat 'Round the Bend,* Doc Pearly lounges on a "back porch" aft of the *Claremore Queen*'s pilot house, smoking one of Captain Eli's favorite cigars. Our avuncular protector deserves his rest: he has resolved the discord around him, and life in Homeville will return to its normal placidity.

In playing the role of Captain Eli, Irvin S. Cobb probably assumed that audiences would bring a knowledge of his Kentucky regional style to a viewing of *Steamboat 'Round the Bend.* It would have been difficult for a contemporary to be ignorant of Cobb: his articles were syndicated in the daily press, and scores of his stories had found their way into the pages of the *Saturday Evening Post* and other magazines. Will Rogers' fans would have seen *Judge Priest* (1934), a film that had been adapted from a story by Cobb.[96] Whatever the reasons, a marvelous anecdote conveys the insouciance of the two major actors as they approached the shooting of *Steamboat.* Here is Cobb's memory of the first meeting between the two regional writers and their young director, John Ford:

So we went out to make *Steamboat 'Round the Bend.* We had a grand director, John Ford, an emotional Maine Yankee-Irishman, one of the authentic geniuses of the movies. The first morning of "shooting," Will and I were to have a scene together.

"Do either of you two gentlemen by any chance happen to have the faintest idea of what this story is about?" inquired Ford, with his gentle, Celtic sarcasm which can be so biting.

"I don't for one," confessed Rogers, and grinned sheepishly. "Something about a river, ain't it? Well, I was raised at Claremore, Oklahoma, where we don't have any rivers to speak of, so you might say I'm a stranger here, myself."

"I thought so," murmured Ford, who had directed Rogers before. "And I don't suppose, Mr. Rogers, you've gone so far as to glance at the script?"

"Been too busy ropin' calves," admitted Rogers. "Tell you what, John, you sort of generally break the news to us what this sequence is about and I'll think up a line for Cobb to speak and then Cobb'll think up a line for me to speak and that way there won't be no ill feelin's or heart burnin's and the feller that kin remember after it's all over what the plot is about — if there is any plot by then — gets first prize, which will be a kiss on the forehead from Mister John Ford."

As heaven is my judge, that is how we did the scene, with Ford sitting by, as solemn as a hoot owl.[97]

Director John Ford had good reasons for being so indulgent: what these two regional figures said was not as important as what, in the accents and colloquialisms, they *represented.* Cobb and Rogers were simply more important as relics of a bygone era than as actors playing roles. For this reason, the script was designed to be little more than a framework within which these regional humorists could be seen and heard. The Fox Studio was alert to the monetary rewards for such hokum. The American audience was actively interested in seeing more "family films," and Fox was eager to please. Both the general audience and the critics were in agreement about the appeal of films about Will Rogers' "Homeville"; "audiences thanked him for his contribution to clean, family diversion. The more analytical saw him as a social factor and a godsend to a stagnant theater."[98] Thus, there were solid economic reasons for allowing Rogers and Cobb to clown on the set.

During location shooting near Sacramento, California, Rogers and Cobb continued their repartee on one of Rogers' regular Gulf radio broadcasts.[99] Audience expectations as to the characters' "innocence" can be extrapolated from the following radio dialogue. Rogers and Cobb here portray themselves as men from the heartland who have succeeded in Hollywood without becoming tainted by it:

Rogers: Do you feel yourself kind of going Hollywood in any way? You know, we all kinda do. It kind of gets us down there. Do you feel yourself doing that?

Cobb: Well, I find that I am talking to myself, and worse than that I am answering back. And I have been cutting out paper dolls at odd times.

Rogers: Saying your own yesses?

Cobb: Yes, I'm living in a yes-man's land, which is worse than no-man's land was during the war. I haven't worn slacks yet. I'm still sticking to my first wife. I guess I haven't gone Hollywood.

Rogers: Do you find this censorship that Will Hays has got in on us now, does it kind of interfere with you, sort of cramp your emotions in any way?

Cobb: Well, I notice as a result of Will Hays' campaign they no longer talk about putting a tax on raw film.[100]

The role of innocent had dual functions: over the airwaves, Cobb and Rogers posed as innocents abroad in America's most liberated city; in *Steamboat,* John Ford was doing his best to establish them as innocents at home in a simpler, rural past.

The love-match between Duke and Fleety Belle takes up a considerable amount of screen time early in *Steamboat,* but, as the film progresses, we discover that the most significant emotional tie in the story is the filial bond between Doc Pearly and the swamp girl. Doc Pearly is at first scornful but gradually discovers that she is "a spunky rascal." The last of his doubts are dispelled after a confrontation with her "people" from the swamp. In the wake of this test of character, Doc Pearly supplies Fleety with a feminine costume in place of her rags, making her a true "Belle." Throughout subsequent attempts to save Duke, Doc Pearly and the young girl work together as a father-daughter team.

If her function in the film is properly understood, Anne Shirley performed admirably as Fleety Belle. Proponents of women's liberation could easily brand the character as just another clinging vine since she is transformed into womanhood with the help of a man (Doc Pearly), and she seems to require masculine guidance. Another view would stress her function as an alter ego for viewers. Like many in the Depression audiences for *Steamboat,* Fleety Belle is poor, an outcast longing to be valued for her inherent worth. An accident of birth may have labeled her a swamp girl, but we have the opportunity to learn that she is really a sincere and sensitive young person who needs help.

A close observer of the Depression era and Will Rogers' role in it might venture a few additional speculations. Like the audience, Fleety Belle needs the guidance of a kindly uncle or father figure. This protector must be above personal or selfish concerns. How much alike Will Rogers and Franklin Roosevelt were in the eyes of theatregoers cannot be determined; but it is certain that many who have studied films of the era agree with Andrew Bergman that movies of the 1930s conveyed "that the federal government was a benevolent watchman, that we were a classless, melting pot nation."[101] Certainly, the Homeville movies communicated a sense that American character (as embodied by Will Rogers) was sustaining the spirit of the Fleety Belles and the Dukes of this world. And the "forgotten public," viewers who had suffered economic setbacks or had felt the stigma of class, could find reassurance through Uncle Will that the American Dream was still viable.[102] With regard to the performance of Anne Shirley, it seems clear that she was not merely conforming to a screen stereotype, but was also serving as a developed symbol representing the needs of a weak and confused nation.

Executives at Fox pictures seemed to understand that anecdotes about Rogers' off-screen benevolence toward Shirley were good for the picture. According to a release repeated endlessly in the press, Rogers allowed the novice to steal scenes from him. Supposedly, Rogers took John Ford aside one day and told him that "I'm gettin' the star's billin' and drawin' down the star's salary, but the star of this picture, man or woman, is the one that can steal it. Come on, John, and have a heart — give the kid a chance."[103] Whether this "real life" scene came from reality or from the Fox publicity department does not really matter: either way, we have proof that there was an appetite for vicarious participation in the protective influence of Will Rogers. Scenes in the pilot house of the *Claremore Queen* concretize this theme of benevolence: both Will Rogers and Anne Shirley wear hats inscribed with the word "Captain"; both share the wheel of the ship, a traditional symbol; there is even a bit of bussing from time to time. An involved viewer of these moments of tenderness could interpret that Uncle Will is helping us to steer a course through difficult times, and that he is concerned because our normal hopes and desires have been thwarted by impersonal forces.

In Old Kentucky (1935)

In Old Kentucky brings together the rural-urban conflict explored in *David Harum* with problems of the heart found in *Steamboat 'Round the Bend*—all within a Homeville setting of the Middle South.[104] The story brings two very different families into conflict.

The Martingales are an out-at-elbows rural family whose very special horse, Blueboy, is coveted by a neighboring gentleman farmer and his daughter (the Shattocks). Somewhere in the past, a piece of property was added illegally to the Shattock farm, initiating a feud between the two families. Uncle Will in this setting plays a horse trainer, Steve Tapley, who is especially concerned about the boy and girl who are separated by the feud.

The style and behavior of the Shattocks symbolizes that the city is encroaching upon the countryside. Grandpa Martingale becomes the center of controversy because he is still angry about the stolen piece of land. He aims his shotgun at the Shattock automobile whenever it passes the Martingale house. But Grandpa never fires. Viewers quickly learn that Grandpa is an eccentric old man who is really quite harmless. Nevertheless, because they are city people, the Shattocks know how to call the impersonal force of the law into play. They file a complaint against Grandpa, with the hope that legal pressure will force the Martingales to sell their horse, Blueboy.

As Steve Tapley, Uncle Will is hard pressed to avert a tragedy. After all, he is a mere horse trainer in this film and therefore lacks the social leverage which was his when he was David Harum, Homeville's only banker. Nevertheless, Uncle Will lives up to the occasion because in Homeville (unlike Hooverville) character, and not money or social position, is the source of power. For this reason, a social inferior like Uncle Will who can see into the human heart can gain complete control. With his insight into the darker regions of the human heart, Uncle Will can anticipate the ploys of the Shattocks as they attempt to buy (or steal) Blueboy; with his more tender concern for individuals, Uncle Will can ensure that Nancy Martingale and Lee Andrews are eventually matched.

As in *David Harum,* so here, Homeville brings threats to manageable proportions. For example, we note almost immediately that class divisions exist. The Shattocks exhibit the worst characteristics of the American rich: they dress according to the latest fashion; they have an affected accent which has obviously been learned; they have themselves chauffeured around Homeville in an enormous Packard touring car. In distinct contrast, the

Martingales are unaffected citizens of Homeville: Grandpa still dresses like a farmer; young Nancy is always in a loose sweater and riding clothes; and when the Martingales travel, they either bounce along on a buckboard or ride on their fine horses. At their farm, the Shattocks have hordes of retainers, while the Martingales do their own work.

In *In Old Kentucky,* Rogers takes the opportunity to comment on the new woman. Her superficiality and artificiality are contrasted with the virtues of Nancy Martingale, a woman of older America. While Ms. Shattock is identified quickly by her dress, her accent, and her snobbery as the bitch that the new woman has become, Nancy Martingale shows herself to have feelings for animals (always a cardinal virtue in Homeville). Nancy also knows enough to rely on Steve because she seems to recognize in him both a confidant and guardian angel.

A scene in which Uncle Will visits a dress shop in the city most effectively contrasts the life-styles of the urban Shattocks and the rural Martingales. A kickoff dance at the local country club has been planned for the night preceding the big race. Knowing that Nancy cannot afford a dress for herself and aware that she must be at the dance to meet her young man, Uncle Will decides to take direct action. In this scene, Rogers tries to develop at some length the distance between the sensibility of an older, rural America and the worldliness of the contemporary American mentality that is reflected in women's fashions. The store owner who greets Uncle Will speaks and acts more like a madam of a bordello than a saleswoman. From the beginning, she and Uncle Will operate under a misconception: he wants a modest dress for his young employee; the manager of the dress shop thinks he wants something spicy for a mistress. While Uncle Will is muttering to himself in a corner, the madam parades out six or seven models who line up behind him half dressed (or half undressed) in diaphanous nightgowns and peignoirs. When Uncle Will turns around to see what has been brought out, he is shocked. Averting his eyes, he apologizes profusely for stumbling into the ladies dressing room! When the confusion is finally cleared up, Uncle Will buys a white, high-necked, long-sleeved dress which is more consonant with his old-fashioned ideas about women. Predictably, on the night of the dance, Arlene Shattock is wearing one of the low-backed, clinging gowns which made Uncle Will blush. The lesson is obvious—in her covetousness and in her dress, Arlene has shown herself to be all that is bad about the new woman. On the other hand, Nancy Martingale shows herself to be an old-fashioned girl who knows that she must rely upon the guidance and strength of the men around her.

In Old Kentucky miniaturizes the problem of the professionalization of knowledge, a twentieth-century development which Rogers spoke about frequently in his columns. Rogers was extremely suspicious of professional or school-trained experts, for he suspected that they frequently ascribed expertise to their work when none really existed.[105] Whether bogus or not, the idea of the world becoming too complicated for the average man to understand was very much on the minds of Rogers' audience.

Dr. Lee Andrews enters Homeville as a representative of professional learning. Whereas Uncle Will becomes a trainer by working with horses, Dr. Andrews has taken copious notes in the classrooms of Kentucky's new agricultural and mechanical college. Within the setting of Homeville, Uncle Will quickly subdues this symbol of complexity. Not only does Lee show complete respect for the old-fashioned trainer, but also the young doctor is entirely dependent upon Uncle Will in his love-match with Nancy Martingale.

In Old Kentucky thus presents (and reduces) the problems of a society breaking down into rigidly isolated classes, of a new morality and a new woman, of the professionalization of knowledge. All of these unsettling developments are presented in such a way that we do not see them as clear demonstration that our world is becoming increasingly perplexing and violent. Instead, our response (like our response to Will Rogers' "playful" journalism) is one of reassurance—Uncle Will's presence on the screen has lessened their impact upon us. Throughout, the most important factor is that the environment and the people in Homeville are entirely malleable under the workings of the spirit of Uncle Will. Millions of Rogers' fans must have watched such resolutions of conflict with satisfaction. They must have been impressed by what one contemporary reviewer noted was Rogers' power "to set right all the troubles of the impulsive people around him."[106]

Given a sympathetic understanding of the forces affecting Americans in the 1920s and 1930s, it is difficult to deny them their need to love such a symbolic man. He meant so much to his people in a time of change and deprivation because he presented them with an image of what Americans had been told to believe was the best in their national character. In preserving this image of humanity and love, Rogers was making no small contribution to the sanity of Americans in a world rushing toward international violence. A reviewer of *In Old Kentucky* hit upon some of the essential positive factors of Rogers' contribution as man and as film image. These later Homeville movies reassured Americans (especially frenzied New Yorkers) "about the solidity and innate common sense of this country." While the reviewer granted that Rogers was probably playing "himself," he felt compelled to add that as a representative figure, Rogers supplied welcome reassurance in an era of bad news: "Will Rogers has a curious national quality. He gives the impression somehow that this country is filled with such sages, wise with years, young in humor and life, shrewd, yet gentle," Most important for the reviewer, "He is what Americans think other Americans are like."[107] After the erosion of values in the 1920s, after the economic disaster of the 1930s, Americans were indeed fortunate to have such a public person to keep a hopeful image of American values and optimism bright.

NOTES

1. File Box No. 14, Will Rogers Memorial and Museum, Claremore, Oklahoma; hereafter referred to as File Box No. 14.

2. William E. Leuchtenburg, *The Perils of Prosperity: 1914–1932* (Chicago: University of Chicago Press, 1958), p. 213.

3. Samuel P. Hays, *The Response to Industrialism: 1885–1914* (Chicago: University of Chicago Press, 1957), p. 190.

4. Leuchtenburg, *The Perils of Prosperity,* pp. 178–203.

5. Ibid., p. 158.

6. Ibid., p. 169. The *locus classicus* for the absurdities of popular culture in this period is Frederick Lewis Allen, *Only Yesterday: An Informal History of the 1920s* (New York: Harper and Row, 1957).

7. Edward Sapir, "Culture, Genuine and Spurious," in *Culture, Language, and Personality,* ed. David G. Mandelbaum (Berkeley: University of California Press, 1968), p. 97.

8. Ibid., p. 101.

9. Leuchtenburg, *The Perils of Prosperity,* p. 14.

10. "Chatting with the Editor," *Western Canada Radio News,* Fred Stone Scrapbook No. 3, Will Rogers Memorial and Museum, Claremore, Oklahoma. Most of the contemporary responses to Rogers the man and film image in this chapter have been taken from the numerous 2′ x 3′ scrapbooks collected and preserved by Robert and Paula Love of the Will Rogers Memorial. Whenever possible, the article's title will be given along with scrapbook and page numbers. Many of these fascinating popular reactions are unidentifiable in any other way.

All of these scrapbooks have been microfilmed and are on deposit in the University Library, Oklahoma State University, Stillwater, Oklahoma 74078. Hereafter they will be referred to as Memorial Scrapbooks, Fred Stone Scrapbooks, or Homer Croy Scrapbooks.

11. Thornton Sargent, "Will Outwits the Scxy Fellows," Memorial Scrapbook No. 24, p. 152.

12. Ada Peterson, "Via Long Distance," Memorial Scrapbook No. 14, p. 47.

13. Memorial Scrapbook No. 24, p. 36.

14. Memorial Scrapbook No. 20, p. 17.

15. Anon., "An Ideal Home," Memorial Scrapbook No. 20, p. 17.

16. "The Movies," *Beverly Hills Script,* Memorial Scrapbook No. 8, p. 204.

17. "Will Rogers for President," Memorial Scrapbook No. 15, p. 62. (Will Rogers became involved in a mock campaign for the presidency in 1928.)

18. Memorial Scrapbook No. 24, p. 152.

19. "On the Set with Will Rogers," Memorial Scrapbook No. 1, p. 13.

20. "His Last Precious Days with Will Rogers Recalled by Irvin Cobb," File Box No. 14.

21. "Dr. Bull," Memorial Scrapbook No. 1, p. 31.

22. Memorial Scrapbook No. 16, p. 1.

23. "Simple Life and Kindly Manner Marked Life of Will Rogers," Fred Stone Scrapbook No. 11.

24. "The Real Things of Life," *Lincoln (Nebraska) Star,* April 24, 1925, Memorial Scrapbook No. 25, p. 43.

25. "Manly Sorrow," *Iowa City Press-Citizen,* April 19, 1925, Memorial Scrapbook No. 25, p. 43. Other articles in the Memorial Scrapbook from newspapers in Kansas City, Missouri, and Memphis, Tennessee, echo this story.

26. "Manly Sorrow," p. 43.

27. Leuchtenburg, *The Perils of Prosperity,* p. 156.

28. For an idealization of the rural town as a place where human beings are honored for their character rather than their power, class, and the like, see John Donald Wade, "The Life

and Death of Cousin Lucius," *I'll Take My Stand* (New York: Harper and Brothers, 1930), pp. 265–301.

29. Rochelle Hudson, "On the Set with Will Rogers," Memorial Scrapbook No. 1, p. 14.

30. "Chatting with the Editor," *Western Canada Radio News,* Fred Stone Scrapbook No. 3.

31. Will Rogers Memorial Manuscripts; also found in Donald Day, ed., *The Autobiography of Will Rogers* (Boston: Houghton Mifflin Co., 1949), p. 146.

32. Will Rogers Memorial Manuscripts and Day, *Autobiography,* p. 85.

33. Will Rogers Memorial Manuscripts and Day, *Autobiography,* p. 221.

34. Will Rogers Memorial Manuscripts and Day, *Autobiography,* p. 226.

35. Will Rogers Memorial Manuscripts and Day, *Autobiography,* p. 365. The spelling in this passage has been left untouched.

36. Will Rogers Memorial Manuscripts and Day, *Autobiography,* p. 323.

37. Will Rogers Memorial Manuscripts and Day, *Autobiography,* p. 298.

38. Will Rogers Memorial Manuscripts and Day, *Autobiography,* p. 128.

39. Will Rogers Memorial Manuscripts and Day, *Autobiography,* p. 325.

40. Will Rogers Memorial Manuscripts and Day, *Autobiography,* p. 310.

41. Will Rogers Memorial Manuscripts and Day, *Autobiography,* p. 234.

42. Scrapbook No. 24, p. 41, Will Rogers Memorial and Museum, Claremore, Oklahoma.

43. KTUL-TV, Tulsa, Oklahoma, *Videotaped Interview with General James Doolittle,* November 5, 1979. This interview is available at the Will Rogers Memorial.

44. "Will Rogers Criticizes Smithsonian Airship Stand," *Daily Telegrams of Will Rogers; The Coolidge Years, 1926–1929, The Writings of Will Rogers,* Series III, Vol. 1 (Stillwater: Oklahoma State University Press, 1978), pp. 186–187. Hereafter cited as *Daily Telegrams, 1926-1929.*

45. The response by Rogers was characteristic, although his facts were wrong. It was true that the Langley machine was placed on exhibit; however, no one — least of all Samuel Langley — was attempting to obscure the accomplishments of the Wright Brothers. For a discussion of the Langley machine as experimental craft and tourist attraction, see Archibald Black, *The Story of Flying* (New York: McGraw-Hill, 1940), pp. 41–46.

46. Will Rogers Chronologies, Will Rogers Memorial, Claremore, Oklahoma. Every day in the life of Will Rogers is covered by this resource. Since 1938, fascinating (and, to the scholar, invaluable) details about Rogers' day-to-day activities have been accumulated and recorded.

47. "Mitchell's Back and Coolidge Is Letting Nature Take Its Course," *Will Rogers' Weekly Articles: The Harding/Coolidge Years: 1922-1925, The Writings of Will Rogers,* Series IV, Vol. 1 (Stillwater: Oklahoma State University Press, 1980), pp. 370–371. Hereafter cited as *Weekly Articles, 1922-1925.*

48. Will Rogers Memorial Manuscripts and Day, *Autobiography,* p. 113. The two quotations that follow are from this article of May 10, 1928, pp. 113, 114.

49. As quoted in Carl Stearns Clancy, "Aviation's Patron Saint," *Scientific American,* October 1929, p. 285. Hereafter this important contemporary view of Rogers will be cited as "Aviation's Patron Saint."

50. "No Jokes from Rogers Till Lindbergh Arrives," *Daily Telegrams, 1926-1929,* p. 90.

51. "Let's Keep Lindbergh Out of Vaudeville," *Will Rogers' Weekly Articles: The Coolidge Years, 1927-1929, The Writings of Will Rogers,* Series IV, Vol. 3 (Stillwater: Oklahoma State University Press, 1981), p. 37.

52. "How to Reward Lindbergh: Ideas from Will Rogers," *Daily Telegrams, 1926-1929,* p. 91.

53. "Calling Lindbergh 'Lucky' Arouses Will Rogers' Ire," *Daily Telegrams, 1926-1929,* p. 96.

54. "Press Is Told to Hold Its Tongue," *Will Rogers' Weekly Articles: The Hoover Years, 1929-1931, The Writings of Will Rogers,* Series IV, Vol. 4 (Stillwater: Oklahoma State University Press, 1981), p. 342. Hereafter cited as *Weekly Articles, 1929-1931.*

55. *There's Not a Bathing Suit in Russia and Other Bare Facts,* ed. Joseph A. Stout, Jr. (1927: rpt. Stillwater: Oklahoma State University Press, 1973), p. 25. The quote that follows is from the same volume, p. 26.

56. As quoted in "Aviation's Patron Saint," p. 284.

57. "Will Rogers' Own Version of the Airplane Accident," *Daily Telegrams, 1926-1929,* p. 220.

58. "Rogers Glad That Lindbergh Took Prize from the Marines," *Daily Telegrams, 1926-1929,* p. 191.

59. "Will Rogers Compliments Lindbergh and Fletcher," *Daily Telegrams of Will Rogers: The Hoover Years, 1929-1931, The Writings of Will Rogers,* Series III, Vol. 2 (Stillwater: Oklahoma State University Press, 1978), p. 43.

60. "Will Rogers Takes a Flight with Lindbergh As His Pilot," *Daily Telegrams, 1926-1929,* p. 130.

61. "Airplanes, Ladies and Politics," *Weekly Articles, 1929-1931,* p. 183.

62. "Will Rogers Chases Wolves on His Flight Back Home," *Daily Telegrams, 1926-1929,* p. 140.

63. "Weekly Exposure Dishes Up the News," *Weekly Articles, 1922-1925,* p. 186.

64. "No Jokes from Rogers Till Lindbergh Arrives," *Daily Telegrams, 1926-1929,* p. 90.

65. Memorial Scrapbook No. 15, p. 80.

66. "Simple Life and Kindly Manner Marked Life of Will Rogers," Fred Stone Scrapbook No. 11. The quotation that follows also comes from this article.

67. As quoted in "Aviation's Patron Saint," p. 285. The quotation that follows is from the same article, p. 285.

68. "Will Rogers Chases Wolves on His Flight Back Home," *Daily Telegrams, 1926-1929,* p. 140.

69. As quoted in "Aviation's Patron Saint," p. 285. The two quotations that follow are from this article, p. 285.

70. "Staying Up in the Air: Aviators Have Got the Birds Beat for Endurance," *Weekly Articles, 1929-1931,* p. 45.

71. "Mr. Rogers Peers into the Future and Sees Inter-Planet Flier," *Daily Telegrams, 1926-1929,* p. 182.

72. *The Right Stuff* (New York: Farrar, Straus, and Giroux, 1979). The differences between Tom Wolfe's "right stuff" and what Will Rogers hoped would be inculcated by flight cannot be explored here. It is not surprising that each observer discovered a different ethic among aviators of his time. Tom Wolfe is a student of colorful trends, whereas Will Rogers strove to study and to influence national morale. By 1965, Wolfe indicates that "the era of America's first single-combat warriors . . . had gone, perhaps never to be relived" (p. 436). Another fad was exhausted.

73. The *Post* articles were later collected and published under the title *Letters of a Self-Made Diplomat to His President,* which recently appeared as Series I, Volume Six of the Oklahoma State University *Writings.* Hereafter the volume being examined in this article is referred to as *Letters of a Self-Made Diplomat.* All parenthetical notations refer to this volume in *The Writings of Will Rogers* series.

74. *There's Not a Bathing Suit in Russia and Other Bare Facts* (1927) has been reprinted as Series I, Volume Two of *The Writings of Will Rogers.* Subsequent citations are from the Oklahoma State University reprint.

75. Information for this survey of Rogers' movements was culled from the numerous chronologies, datebooks, and scrapbooks in the vault of the Will Rogers Memorial.

76. *Will Rogers' 1920s: A Cowboy's Guide to the Times* (Los Angeles: Churchill Films, 1976).

77. *There's Not a Bathing Suit in Russia,* p. 52. Italics in the original.

78. Memorial Scrapbook No. 14, p. 32.

79. Memorial Scrapbook No. 8. The Will Rogers Memorial and Museum has a large collection of Rogers' film scripts.

80. "Series R" Goldwyn Contracts, December 29, 1923, indicate that Goldwyn lost $40,102.23.

Most biographers of Will Rogers claim that Rogers was a "failure" in silent films but a "success" once sound was introduced. In terms of box-office receipts this is true, but Rogers' biographers also believe that he was a poor actor in these films. *New York Times* film reviews indicate that Rogers' earliest silent films were very much admired by those who understood Rogers' style of humor. The real problem for Rogers was to make the nation aware of that style. This he did from 1922 onward as a public person, public speaker, and syndicated journalist. Rogers became such a powerful film image precisely because of the associations which viewers brought with them to the theatre.

81. Some of the films of this persona are *Jubilo* (1919), *Jubilo Jr.* (1924), *Too Busy to Work* (1923), *Honest Hutch* (1920), *Boys Will Be Boys* (1921), *The Headless Horseman* (1922), *Fruits of Faith* (1922), and *Don't Park There* (1924).

82. Some of the films of this persona are *Strolling Through Europe with Will Rogers* (episodes) (1927), *Going to Congress* (1924), *A Truthful Liar* (1924), *A Texas Steer* (1927), *They Had to See Paris* (1929), *Lightnin'* (1930), *So This Is London* (1930), *Young As You Feel* (1931), *Connecticut Yankee* (1931), *Ambassador Bill* (1931), and *Business and Pleasure* (1932).

83. Memorial Scrapbook No. 8, p. 204.

84. "Chatting with the Editor," Fred Stone Scrapbook No. 3.

85. *Beverly Hills Citizen,* September 19, 1929, Fred Stone Scrapbook No. 11.

86. In this final role, Rogers plays a variety of small-town figures: in *State Fair* (1933) he is a farmer anxious to see his pig take first prize; in *Dr. Bull* (1933) he is a small-town doctor who is resistant to new-fangled ways; in *David Harum* (1934) he is a small-town banker who is more interested in fishing and horse trading than gain; in *Handy Andy* (1934) he is a small-town druggist who runs amuck when he tries to become part of the leisure class; in *Judge Priest* (1934) he is a small-town judge in the post-Civil War South; in *County Chairman* (1935) he is a frontier politician in Wyoming about the time that Wister's hero, the Virginian, would have been settling down to make his bundle; in *Life Begins at Forty* (1935) he plays a small-town newspaper editor with his hand on the pulse of the community; in *Steamboat 'Round the Bend* (1935) he is an avuncular captain of a renovated steamboat, *The Claremore Queen*; *In Old Kentucky* (1935) tells the story of the world of the Kentucky Derby before the syndicate moved in.

87. Memorial Scrapbook No. 20, p. 37.

88. Homer Croy Scrapbook No. 24, p. 90.

89. John Rosenfield, Jr., "Screen Loses Star at Peak of Influence," *Dallas (Texas) News,* August 17, 1935, Memorial Scrapbook No. 5.

90. Memorial Scrapbook No. 1, p. 46.

91. The desire to look back at a simpler past is not new in American thought. In the 1970s, people were looking back on the good-old 1950s, forgetting in the process the atomic bomb, air raid drills, the Korean War, and the rampage of Senator Joseph McCarthy. In the 1860s and 1870s, Harriet Beecher Stowe held her inverted telescope up to the religious and social history of New England and discovered the nostalgic and peaceful towns she describes in *Oldtown Folks* (1869) and *Poganuc People* (1878). Still earlier, Royall Tyler wrote probably the first work of nostalgia in *The Contrast* (1787), a play about a country squire and his man in the corrupt city of New York.

92. Quotations from *David Harum* (Fox, 1934) are drawn from viewing notes supplemented by a shooting script and may, therefore, be subject to errors of detail. *David Harum* is rented by Films, Incorporated (Archive Collection, Wilmette, Illinois, office) and by the Museum of Modern Art.

93. "Daddy of Us All," Memorial Scrapbook No. 24, p. 48.

94. Quotations from *Steamboat 'Round the Bend* (20th Century-Fox, 1935) are drawn from viewing notes supplemented by a shooting script and may, therefore, be subject to errors of detail. *Steamboat 'Round the Bend* is rented by Films, Incorporated (Archive Collection, Wilmette, Illinois, office).

95. Audiences in the 1930s would have noted the aging of these two syndicated humorists: Rogers was fifty-five and Cobb was fifty-nine. Also apparent to audiences would have been the significance of the ship names: Paducah is a city located on the Ohio River where it joins with the Kentucky; and Claremore is the major city of Rogers County, Oklahoma, where Will Rogers was born and where the Will Rogers Memorial and Museum now stands.

96. Cobb tells his story in an autobiography entitled *Exit Laughing* (New York: Garden City Publishing Co., 1941). Like Rogers, Cobb saw himself in the tradition of Mark Twain, for his regional humor as well as for his journalistic commentary on the times.

97. "His Last Precious Days with Friend Will Rogers Recalled by Irvin Cobb," File Box No. 14.

98. Rosenfield, "Screen Loses Star at Peak of Influence," Memorial Scrapbook No. 5, p. 27.

99. Contrasts between Rogers' journalism and his films could be no better illustrated than in this broadcast. While *Steamboat* takes us away from contemporary events, the nationwide radio program addressed such issues as unemployment, a proposed California state tax on the movie industry, prejudice against Indians, the Civilian Conservation Corps (CCC), and the national debt.

100. Gulf Radio Broadcast, May 19, 1935. Both tapes and transcripts of these broadcasts are available at the Will Rogers Memorial.

101. Andrew Bergman, *We're in the Money: Depression America and Its Films* (New York: New York University Press, 1971), p. 149.

102. Students are invited to explore the relationship between American heroes of the period (on screen, in real life) and the ability of traditional institutions to weather those troubled years. A more extended version of the above quote from Bergman might stimulate discussion and writing: "Movies of the Thirties made a central contribution toward educating Americans in the fact that wrongs could be set right within their existing institutions. They showed that individual initiative still bred success, that the federal government was a benevolent watchman, that we were a classless melting pot nation."

103. "Cobb Bares Secrets on Film Lot," *Tulsa Daily World,* September 5, 1935.

104. Quotations and details from *In Old Kentucky* (20th Century-Fox, 1935) are drawn from viewing notes supplemented by a shooting script and may, therefore, be subject to errors of detail. *In Old Kentucky* is rented by Films, Incorporated (Archive Collection, Wilmette, Illinois, office).

105. In a day in which Madison Grant's *The Passing of the Great Race* (1916) was still accepted by the public as a work of social science, Rogers' suspicions were not entirely unwarranted.

106. Memorial Scrapbook No. 1, p. 31.

107. Review of *Life Begins at Forty, New York Sun,* File Box No. 14.

3

THE VISION OF WILL ROGERS: AN INTELLECTUAL MONTAGE

In filmmaking, an intellectual montage brings together disparate images in rapid succession in an attempt to evoke ideas. Similarly, this chapter collocates terse, pungent comments by Will Rogers on a variety of issues with a goal of evoking his world-view. Every remark is followed by commentary about content and style. The commentary is supplied to encourage the reader to conduct his own studies rather than to provide exhaustive analysis.

The last two items are reprints of comments by Rogers on his comedic technique. Since they are constantly referred to, but are difficult to obtain, it seemed unfair not to reprint them in this bio-bibliography.

PROGRESS BRINGS AN END TO THE SIMPLE LIFE

The Passing Frontier

Up here attending the beautiful Santa Barbara fiesta, showing the life in California before Fords, movie salaries and realtors in knee-breeches made a Coney Island out of the State.

P.S. The weather was not unusual.[1]

Will Rogers is out on the American road, surveying contemporary developments and providing commentary on the meaning of what he sees. In this daily telegram, Rogers employs a frequently used "then and now" device. The frontier simplicity of an earlier time is contrasted with the most vulgar example of urban excess, Coney Island. Rogers and his audience seem to agree that California was—as it still is—on the cutting edge of social change: Fords, the movie industry, and rising property values are adduced as evidence of precipitous change. In *Two Wagons—Both Covered* (1924)—a Rogers parody on a famous silent epic, *The Covered Wagon* (1923)—pioneers are attacked by "Escrow Indians" as they reach the Pacific Ocean. For this slapstick scene, the ferocious land agents are dressed in the knickers mentioned here.

Rogers always employed an intimate style, writing as one friend to another. The "P.S." here attempts a reversal of the usual postscript comment. Although lighthearted, a serious judgment lies below the surface of this report.

Murder, Too, Has Progressed

This murderer out here, Hickman, confessed, so that means a long-drawn-out trial. It's going to be a fight to a finish between the alienists and the photographers.

American murder procedure is about as follows: Foul enough to commit a crime, dumb enough to get caught, smart enough to prove you was crazy when you committed it and fortunate enough to show you was too sane to hang.[2]

The trial of John Hinckley, Jr. in the spring of 1982 touched off a movement to limit the use of the insanity plea. In the early days of 1928, William Hickman was tried for murder in a highly publicized courtroom battle. Rogers claimed to be "the only writer to refuse newspaper offers to cover the Hickman trial" (DT for February 3, 1928). There was simply too much attention devoted to the event, and the prospect that Hickman's insanity plea might prevail disturbed Rogers.

The second paragraph of this daily telegram performs the quintessential Will Rogers service: it boils complex issues down to simple language, supplying a description all could understand. Use of such elemental words as "foul" and "smart," together with intentional grammatical errors, evokes the serious notion that any common sense person could see through Hickman's tissue of fictions.

HENRY FORD, THE AUTOMOBILE, AND MACHINE CULTURE

Put a Ford in the Driver's Seat?

Democrats are the middle-of-the-road party, Republicans are the straddle-of-the road party, so I hereby nominate Mr. Henry Ford for President and christen the party the all-over-the-road party.

In the first place it is too bad he is so competent: that's the only thing that will beat him. Mr. Ford is a good friend of mine, and years ago he overlooked a suggestion that would have made him immortal. That's when he went over to Europe to stop the war. I wanted him to take the girls we had in the Follies, and let them wear the same costumes as in the shows and march them down between the trenches. Believe me, the boys would have been out before Christmas!

He has made more money than any man in the world by paying the highest wages; yet he don't even manufacture a necessity. Neither would you call it a luxury; it just kinder comes under the heading of knick-knacks.

I was in his home last year and happened to ask him that in case of stiff competition just how cheap he could sell his car. He said, "Will, by controlling the selling of parts, I could give the cars away." He said, "Those things will shake off enough bolts in a year to pay for themselves. Why, the second year, that's just clear profit."

People think that Dr. Coué was the originator of auto-suggestion. Mr. Ford is! He originated auto-suggestion.

He just recently lowered the price fifty dollars. That's done to discourage thievery.

He is the first man that ever took a joke and made it practical. So let's let him take this country, maybe he can repeat. He should make a good political race, he carries two-thirds of this country now. There is no reason why there shouldn't be a Ford in the White House; they are everywhere else.

He is the only man that could make Congress earn their salary. He could start a bill through, and give each one something to tack on to it, and when it comes out, it would be ready to use. He is the only man that when Congress started stalling, could pick up the hood and see what was the matter with it.

Some are against him because he don't know history. What we need in there is a man that can make history, not recite it.

Now if Mr. Ford will just take another one of my suggestions, he can be elected. If he would just make one speech and say: "Voters, if I am elected, I will change the front on them!"[3]

This mock nomination of Henry Ford for president is used in the documentary film *Will Rogers' 1920s* because it shows another typical Rogers device, the use of a current issue or name in popular culture to discuss other seemingly unrelated developments. For the contemporary reader, the various references to politics, technology, and religious fads—all within the context of a mock public address—must have lightened the burden of thinking about all of the subjects mentioned. Henry Ford's special application of mass production, his attempt to pay high wages, and his refusal to change body styles for many years are all treated in relation to other issues. Crank panaceas are not ignored. In this case, Ford's Peace Ship Mission is obvious, but the last line about changing the radiator is a less easily discernible satire of campaign promises which never come true. Congress is criticized for inefficiency, while the recent Wilson presidency is found wanting. "What we need in there is a man that can make history, not recite it." In referring to Émile Coué, a Theosophist whose following included Herbert Croly of *The New Republic*, Rogers is using a pun. Although the pun is considered the lowest form of humor, it was a staple for nineteenth-century American humorists.

This speech is a delightful potpourri of people, theories, and events of the day. Ford is shown as part of the times, yet somehow superior to them by virtue of his demonstrable accomplishments — in contrast with healers, congressmen, and presidents. The device of the nomination address pokes holes in political oratory, for inventors produce without oratory.

Birthday Salute to a "Big Wheel"

We hadn't any more than got rid of the birthday of Italy's greatest man than here our headliner has one. Henry Ford is 66 years old today. He has had more influence on the lives and habits of this nation than any man ever produced in it.

Great educators try to teach people; great preachers try to change people but no man produced through the accepted channels has moved the world like Henry Ford. He put wheels on our homes. A man's castle is his sedan. Life's greatest catastrophe is a puncture. Americans don't fear the Lord as much as they do the next payment. Everybody is rushing to go somewhere, where they have no business, so they can hurry back to the place where they never should have left.

So good luck, Mr. Ford. It will take a hundred years to tell whether you have helped us or hurt us, but you certainly didn't leave us like you found us.[4]

Used in *Will Rogers' 1920s*, this mock birthday salute to Henry Ford takes a more serious look at the great inventor's influence. Through hyperbole, Rogers tries to show how much the typical American's world has been transformed by the automobile. Pride in property has shifted from the domicile to the family car, bringing about a ridiculous obsession with the machine in the driveway. The automobile has given Americans a mobility that might not be entirely good for them, drawing them physically — and perhaps morally — away from established ways of life, to include the habit of thrift. The entire presentation revolves around a pun on "movement." In his conclusion, Rogers reflects the ambivalence which many Americans felt in the new era of automobility.

From Farm to Feedlot?

A farm in the country is judged now by how many blocks it is away from a filling station.[5]

Rogers warns that farmers are becoming dependent for their values and prosperity upon the spreading industrial way of life symbolized by the automobile. The serious, censorial message is conveyed by particular images rather than by abstractions, a characteristic Rogers device.

MACHINES THAT FLY: A SIGN OF HOPE FOR A FALLEN AGE?

"First Machine Was Ever in There"

I got the real kick of my life out of aviation today. Left western Kansas and flew down to Oklahoma and landed right on the old ranch I was born on. First machine was ever in there. When I was raised, I never thought there would ever be anything faster than a horse got in there.

I ask you and plead with you again, you luncheon clubbers, will you please paint the name of your town on top of your building? I will pay for the paint if you will do it. We were lost today, and all the towns in Kansas had no names we could make out till we got to Bartlesville, Okla., who had their name out.

Are you ashamed of your town?[6]

Here the familiar "then and now" metaphor, a prevalent device to question the present, is employed to celebrate technology. Rogers was sanguine about the frontier qualities fostered by aviation: although seated in a machine, the aviator was in constant struggle with the basic elements and, through that struggle, was toughened and ennobled.

Rogers' pleas for civic groups to paint the names of cities on roofs — like many other public suggestions made in jest — resulted in a great number of paint bills arriving by mail! Still, the fact that the middle-class businessman is addressed is a significant indication of the typical Rogers reader.

The telegram hints at a synthesis which aviation seemed to promise: it might be possible to continue the advance of technology without losing the pioneering character which made America great. There might be a way of avoiding moral decline evidenced by such events as the Hickman trial and other dark events of the day. As Rogers related in another aviation-oriented telegram, the Lindbergh hero worship had at least turned the spotlight of media attention to something wholesome: "Of all things that Lindbergh's great feat demonstrated, the greatest was to show us that a person could still get the entire front pages without murdering anybody" (DT for May 23, 1927).

The True Spirit of St. Louis

No attempt at jokes today. A slim, tall, bashful, smiling American boy is somewhere out over the middle of the Atlantic Ocean, where no lone human being has ever ventured before. He is being prayed for to every kind of Supreme Being that has a following. If he is lost it will be the most universally regretted single loss we ever had. But that kid ain't going to fail, and what could be better to celebrate his arrival than another donation to over six hundred thousand of our very own, that are not even fortunate enough to be flying over water, but have to stand huddled upon the banks and look into it as it washes away their life-time's work. They didn't even have enough to buy a paper to know that he had gone. Nothing would please him better than for you to help them in his honor for he comes from the banks of the Mississippi, and he knows what it can do.[7]

This telegram conveys the same warm tone which comes across in the late feature films—a tone of concern for one's fellow man. Here Rogers admires the achievement of Lindbergh as a daring American hero, but he immediately brings the sentiment of admiration to bear on the needs of other Americans, those suffering from the catastrophic flood of 1927. He concludes by relating the plight of the little people of the Mississippi Valley to the lofty achievements of the boy from St. Louis: there is a greatness of achievement, but there is something greater—our responsibilities to those in need.

It would be possible to find the admiration for Lindbergh or the appeal for the flood victims in the writings of many, but this peculiar combination—radiating as it does a deep national feeling blending pride and responsibility—is peculiarly Rogers.

PROSPECTS FOR PEACE: THE PANACEA OF ARMS LIMITATIONS

Europe's Army-Navy Game

The Disarmament Conference in Geneva adjourns just at the only time when it was about to agree. Now they will go home and study on it and return with their usual propositions. France will want England to sink their navy. England will agree to France sinking their army. Both will want Germany to sink her remembrances, and all three agree on Italy sinking Mussolini.

Asking Europe to disarm is like asking a man in Chicago to give up his life insurance. We can't preach "good-will," but if we lived in Europe among those Hyenas we would be in war before we got our grip unpacked. While we are having Washington Days and Lincoln Days, let's have a "Thank the Atlantic Ocean Day."[8]

Will Rogers not only read about disarmament conferences, but he also attended the Washington (1922) and Geneva (1926, 1931) meetings where the delegates received him as a celebrity. Rogers understood that the participants had good intentions, but his close observation of the European scene revealed too many long-standing quarrels. If nations were willing to disarm, it was only in terms of equipment which had been superseded by newer gadgets: "It's like holding a traffic conference and just discussing the limiting of horses and buggies" (DT for December 23, 1929). Here, in a very brief compass, Rogers shows the essential self-interest which lay behind the various proposals. The first paragraph builds to a "topper" punchline about Mussolini, blending the issue of deadly weaponry with the threat posed by dynamic totalitarian leaders. The second paragraph makes a humorous reference to news about gang wars in Chicago and then ends with an essential Rogers point on U.S. foreign policy: our geographical position was such as to exempt us from the quarrels of Europe. As a journalist, Rogers regularly unveiled the realities behind rhetoric. Not distinguished leadership — celebrated by "Washington Days and Lincoln Days" — but the large Atlantic Ocean was the source of America's exemption from the fallen ways of Europe.

The Power of Songs

Lots of people don't know the difference between the two songs of America and England — "Columbia, Gem of the Ocean" and "Rule Britannia, Britannia Rules the Waves." Here is the difference: "Britannia Rules the Waves," is a fact; "Columbia, Gem of the Ocean," is just a song.[9]

Will Rogers was worried that Americans were giving away too much at disarmament conferences, creating a basis for future tragedy: "Wars don't diminish our navy. It's peace that's so devastating. When we were attacked by the disarmament conference we had even our lifeboats shot from under us" (DT for February 2, 1927). In this observation, Rogers makes a serious point of playing with song titles. Using the trivial to describe the significant here yields humor along with insight; clowning triggers thought.

EUROPE — A POWDER KEG

Europe's Ball Game

The Balkan nations have gone into a huddle. It looks like Bulgaria's ball on Rumania's ten-yard line. Poland was penalized ten yards for being offside against Lithuania. Mussolini is the triple-threat man of the game. It will all wind up like the last one, just another incompleted war. They will have to bring it back and line up again.[10]

Here Will Rogers employs a technique frequently applied to domestic and foreign topics, the pose as a sports announcer who seems to be talking about events in popular culture but is actually concerned with more important developments. The sports metaphor implies that this is a game which all know how to play, that the cycle of hatred and destruction will be recycled with every new season. In fact, the statement that "They will have to bring it back and line up again" rings less humorously the more it is thought about.

GUNBOAT DIPLOMACY AND THE ARROGANCE OF POWER

Gringoism

We say that Diaz is the properly elected president of Nicaragua, but Brazil, Argentine, Peru, Chile, Mexico, Ecuador, Costa Rica, Cuba, Guatemala, Colombia, Uruguay, Paraguay, all those say that the doctor is the properly elected president. It's funny how we are the only ones that ever get anything right. I'd rather be right than Republican.[11]

The Mayor

As someone growing up in Indian Territory, Will Rogers was quick to see the actions of government from the point of view of the people abused by power, especially—during the era of what has been called "Gunboat Diplomacy"—the perspective of those south of the Rio Grande. In 1927 and 1931, Rogers traveled to Mexico, Central America, and South America on goodwill and humanitarian tours; as a result, he had direct knowledge about Third World developments.

The effectiveness of Rogers' condemnation of American intervention into Latin American politics comes from the accumulation of names. The many nations listed were in support of "the doctor," Juan Sacasa, but American arrogance was blind to the obvious. The final sentence further underscores the triumph of political rhetoric and self-interest over obvious facts. Signing as "The Mayor" is an allusion to Rogers' then-recent experience as an honorary mayor of Beverly Hills who had been unseated by a special act of the California legislature. Small or large, the games played by American politicians were very much alike: they protected selfish interests rather than representing the general will.

When Is a Marine Like an Entertainer?

I like this part of Mr. Coolidge's message best: "both parties in Nicaragua were pleased with the outcome of their election and have asked for the marines again next time. But I did not commit myself." Yes, I think I would let Hoover contract 'em for that one.

The marines will certainly be tickled to know they can get booking four years ahead. They have always just had to pick up little wars from day to day. Now they can kinda look ahead and plan, and have a permanent address.

If they satisfied both parties after election, I believe the Democrats will sign 'em up right here at home, for the November, 1932, follies.[12]

Here is a typical Will Rogers opening, based on the notion that all he knew was what he read in the papers. After citing a quotation from the papers, Rogers shows the absurdity of its implications. The second paragraph develops a metaphorical parallel between the marines and a condition Rogers knew from personal experience, the plight of an entertainer in search of regular work. Advanced "booking" will help the marines to plan their interventions ahead rather than rushing from country to country haphazardly. Rogers further stresses the absurdity of the notion by reminding Americans that their own political processes are not entirely orderly: what works well for satisfied customers in banana republics might just as well be tried at home. Calling U.S. presidential elections "follies" undercuts the entire process; in both foreign and domestic politics, there are real motives, usually selfish, which determine the actions of men. These selfish motives were rising to the surface, and Rogers, in his next day's telegram, was not optimistic: "We are at peace with the world because the world is waiting to get another gun and get it loaded" (DT for December 5, 1928).

Machines in the Garden

I see where our bombing planes down in Nicaragua bagged fifty natives yesterday.

The natives put up a pretty good fight. They threw rocks and knives at the planes, but our forces were too cunning for them. They wouldn't fly low enough to be hit.

Strategy has won many a war and it may pull us through this one.[13]

The ability to sympathize with "backward" (that is, in the material sense) peoples informs much of Will Rogers' commentary. It seems hard to believe that his Indian background did not give him the perspective to construct a portrait of a brutal industrial power misusing its technology.

A Selfish Determination

See by the papers today that the Philippines wanted just to vote to see if they wanted independence. But we told 'em "No, you can't even vote to see if you want it or not, and furthermore we urgently request that you don't even be seen thinking about it."

What was that slogan the whole country was shouting just exactly ten years ago today? Does this sound like it, "Self determination of small nations."

Yours for memory.[14]

A silly public statement is quoted verbatim, followed by a common sense evaluation. In this case, the object of satire is the hypocrisy of Americans who had recently sacrificed blood and treasure for a principle of "self-determination." Rogers avoids using the word "hypocrisy"; instead, he evokes the notion by showing American inconsistencies.

POLITICAL FIGURES: CALVIN COOLIDGE

Coolidge is Choosey

When a word comes out and you don't know what it means, you rush to old man Webster. But when one comes out and even Webster don't know what it means, why our only chance to learn what it means is to ask the man that used it, but when he only replies "it means what it means," why we are not any better informed than we were at first. So we just have to wait till something happens that makes him divulge his secret.

Well, in Kansas City three weeks from Tuesday it happens we will learn for the first time on any stage if "choose" means "yes," "no," "maybe," "I can't tell yet," "who knows," "search me," "probably," or "perhaps."

I claim that it means "will" under proper pressure, so don't argue; just wait three weeks.[15]

Many observers, including Will Rogers, believed that Calvin Coolidge would run for a second term in 1928; however, it seemed probable that the incumbent president wanted to be drafted rather than appear to seek office. In this observation, Rogers plays verbally around the ambiguous statement by Coolidge who announced that he did not "choose" to run. Rogers points ahead to the Republican Nominating Convention in Kansas City where events will cut through rhetoric. As in so many comments by Rogers, language is pictured as misleading — in this case intentionally — while events are real. People may say many things about their goals, but what they actually do is what matters.

POLITICAL FIGURES: ALFRED E. SMITH

No Inquisition This Week

If you want to read one of the only real straightforward statements ever issued by a politician, read Al Smith's, out today.

He explains that if elected President all Protestants would not be exterminated; that even a few of the present Senators would be retained, including Tom Heflin; that the Knights of Columbus would not replace the Boy Scouts and Kiwanis; that mass would not replace golf on Sunday morning, and that those who were fortunate enough to have meat could eat it on Friday.

It's no compliment to a nation's intelligence when these things have to be explained.[16]

The Old Burgomaster of Beverly.

In 1928, Alfred E. Smith's Catholicism constituted an insuperable barrier between the New York politician and the White House, a barrier that was less formidable thirty-two years later when John F. Kennedy sought the highest office. In this ironic evocation of Smith's problem, Rogers uses a device similar to his quotation-reaction formula which we have seen so often. In this case, Rogers paraphrases a public statement, intentionally exaggerating it to emphasize the fallen tone of American politics: "It's no compliment to a nation's intelligence when these things have to be explained."

The language of the summarized statement greatly exaggerates. Instead of mentioning that Protestants might receive less patronage, Rogers uses the word "exterminated." Rogers then cleverly snipes at the hypocrisy of anti-papists by describing Sunday as a day for golf rather than religious worship. The allusion to meat has a special twist: people are obsessed with religious ideology rather than with fostering a healthy economy. Instead of signing off as "Mayor of Beverly Hills," as he so often did during 1927, Rogers closes as "Burgomaster," a sign of sympathy for the foreign-born. In the case of Al Smith, the sympathy was more than a pose: Rogers and Smith were personal friends.

POLITICAL FIGURES: HERBERT HOOVER

When Seconds Count . . . .

The White House fire burned quite a while due to the following: When Mr. Hoover discovered that "some kind of condition existed" he sent out letters inviting all the Fire Departments in Washington, and when they arrived appointed them on a commission "to investigate, and recommend remedies." They did investigate, and on account of there being no prominent business men on the commission, they turned in their report fairly quick. "We find a fire does exist, and in keeping with the spirit of every amendment, recommend nothing but water to extinguish it."

Of course, by this time the house had burned down, but it was nevertheless gratifying to Mr. Hoover, for it was the first commission that he had ever appointed in his life that had really ever turned in a report. So he figures that loss of the building well worth it. It will renew his faith in commissions.[17]

In the early days of Herbert Hoover's administration, Will Rogers was sympathetic to the dilemma of the new president. Rogers felt that the public asked too much of one man: " . . . we never had farm relief in all our history, but we look to him for it . . . women think he will wash their dishes and look after their babies" (DT for March 6, 1929). After giving the president three months to come to grips with a worsening Depression, Rogers joined many observers in losing patience. There were simply too many social and economic problems requiring direct action for government to conduct business as usual.

Hoover's faith in commissions troubled Rogers. The success or failure of Prohibition legislation had been examined exhaustively by the Wickersham Commission. After two years of work and a cost of $2 million, the commission came up with the obvious conclusion that there was not total satisfaction with the Eighteenth Amendment. The Depression simply could not wait on commission reports. To convey his position, Rogers here uses news of a recent White House fire to discuss the national emergency: a sharp contrast is developed between a pressing existential need—a fire is raging and needs to be extinguished—and the delays of the presidential commission process. Solutions, not palaver, were what Rogers wanted; his was the spirit of direct justice and action.

POLITICAL FIGURES: FRANKLIN D. ROOSEVELT

Smith Finally Reciprocates

Al Smith unanimously nominated Franklin D. Roosevelt today for Governor of New York.

Roosevelt will always be remembered as the man that any time as many as three persons met, either in conference or convention, would arise and nominate Al Smith for President. You could just wake him in the middle of the night and he would start to nominating Al.

His nominating days over, he is now going to take up politics seriously. He is a Roosevelt by blood, but a namesake politically. If he had retained his splendid qualities and stayed with the Republican end of the family, he would have been President, but I doubt if he could have retained those qualities and been Republican.[18]

Will Rogers was a personal friend of both Alfred E. Smith and Franklin Roosevelt; if for no other reason, he followed their careers because they so often appeared in the Ziegfeld *Follies* audience. Rogers knew of Roosevelt's presidential ambitions; as a result, he enjoyed roasting FDR for nominating Smith at the 1924 and 1928 Democratic conventions.

Drawing from the news, Rogers cites a recent and unusual event: for a change, Smith has nominated Roosevelt! The remainder of the commentary roasts Roosevelt for playing second fiddle so often. The second paragraph ends depicting Roosevelt as a somnambulist who compulsively nominates Smith. The third paragraph explores a new chapter in Roosevelt's career, making an initial assessment of his potential.

Stylistically, the power of the comments comes from Rogers' assumed intimacy with the public figures. Alfred E. Smith is simply "Al"; the family and political aspects of Roosevelt's career are treated with equal familiarity. In talking about great men as "regular fellows," Rogers performed an ambassadorial role. Letters from Smith and Roosevelt in the Will Rogers Memorial reveal that the New York politicians reveled in this kind of playful attentiveness.

PROHIBITION: LAWS AND REALITIES

A Double Standard

Jim Reed says prohibition will not be the issue with the Democrats, and, as usual, Jim is right.

How are you going to make an issue of it? The drys want it in the Constitution and it's in there.

The wets want a drink and they get it.

So what's all the argument about?[19]

This statement shows Rogers pulling a fact out of a news context, and thereby distorting it to suit his own rhetorical needs. The "Jim Reed" mentioned in the first paragraph with such familiarity is Senator James Reed of Missouri who, in the statement referred to, was trying to stress that the Democrats would base their platform on the need for farm relief. In making his statement, Senator Reed was attempting to indicate that Prohibition had to be considered a less important issue during an agricultural depression. Because Rogers had other comic uses for "Jim's" public statement, he gives it a different twist.

Prohibition was synonymous with hypocrisy, creating a gap between precept and practice which Rogers despised. Here Rogers evokes the notion rather than spelling it out. The drys have made their point by passing the Eighteenth Amendment; on the other hand, bootleggers have learned to circumvent the law. The final sentence is more judgmental than it might first appear: Rogers implies that Americans are normally happy when what is said and what is done do not coincide. The concluding rhetorical question has strong negative implications.

AMERICAN POLITICIANS

The More Things Change . . . .

Just finished taking scenes here in Washington for a movie of the old stage play of Hoyt's, "A Texas Steer." It was the story of a man elected to Washington on bought votes. We are bringing it up to date by not changing it at all. In the stage version he didn't know what to do when he got in Congress. That part is allowed to remain as it was. He used to play poker more than legislate. That's left in. There was a little drinking among the members at that time. For correct detail in our modern version that has been allowed to remain in.

Yours for Government buy the people.[20]

These comments on *A Texas Steer* (Richard Wallace, director, First National Films, 1927) mock the familiar magazine coverage of a new film in which a producer, director, or writer explains how a story has been changed to bring its film version up-to-date. Humor is generated by working against the typical approach of such pieces, stressing the lack of changes needed because the rules of the game in Washington have changed so little. Legislators still buy votes ("Government buy the people"), they still come to Washington unprepared and unmotivated for their serious work as leaders, and they still ignore many of the laws they enact. (Unfortunately, no prints of *A Texas Steer* have been found.)

This daily telegram provides a good example of how Rogers used his ongoing activities as an entertainer as a springboard for social commentary.

THE FARMER'S PLIGHT

How Do You Spell Relief?

One thing about farmers' relief: It can't last too long, for the farmers ain't got much more to be relieved of.

A farmer knows.[21]

Cocklebur Rogers

The rural persona exploited by Will Rogers in his show business and journalistic ventures was more than a mask: throughout the 1920s, he constantly reminded urban Americans that a depression had already begun on the farms of the land. Here, as an Oklahoma "Cocklebur," Rogers writes of the desperate conditions just as Congress was considering legislation that would affect farmers. Rogers again employs the pun: "relief" meant assistance to farmers, but Rogers speaks of the farmers being "relieved" in the sense that crops, property, and pride were being taken away by bad times. Printed during congressional debates over the issue, this is clearly a case where Rogers attempted to influence legislative action.

Not all help should come from above. As Rogers noted a few days later, farmers needed to revamp their ways: "Rotation of crops and less automobiles will relieve them whenever they decide to try it" (DT for February 14, 1927).

THE HUMANITARIAN STRAIN

Homeward Bound

On my way home to Oklahoma. What's happier, especially if people have forgot what you used to be?

Flew over hundreds of miles yesterday and saw the advance guard of 700,000 people returning home. Home to what? To a great, big, flat mud-hole. No houses, no barns, no fences, no plows, no seed, no work, no stock, no stoves. What a home-coming!

Also yesterday received personal telegram from John Barton Payne, the head of the Red Cross, America's great possession, in which he made this amazing statement:

"We are still a million and a half short of our quota."

Remember that there has been a new quota set for you in the last week, so get busy. What did we rescue them for? So they would have the pleasure of starving later?[22]

Rogers' contemporaries deeply appreciated his numerous humanitarian efforts. In an era of big government and impersonal institutions, Rogers stood out as someone who went out to study conditions and then acted. As a contrast, he sarcastically described Congress as waiting "until the night they adjourn and then pass a resolution against another flood" (DT for January 23, 1928).

This passage contains a number of Rogers ploys. First, he is at the scene of the suffering, watching the events and commenting on them in personal terms rather than through statistics. He is flying home for a family reunion, an event that makes even more poignant the dispossession of families returning to ruined farms and towns. Rogers reduces the suffering to specific details: "No horses, no barns, no fences, no plows, no seed, no work, no stock, no stoves." Although in the field, he claims to be in contact with men of national stature who are addressing the problem. In fact, the director of the Red Cross has sent Rogers a personal telegram. Finally, Rogers exhorts his audience to further acts of charity. This statement evokes a profound sense of social and moral responsibility. Viewers of Rogers' later films would be informed by such insights about the humanitarian spirit behind the screen image.

DEPRESSION SPOKESMAN

"The People Are Not Asking for Money, They Are Asking for a Job"

Now don't get mad and start turning off the radio, I am not advertising anything! If the mouth wash you are using is the wrong kind, you will just have to keep on using it, and I don't know what cigarette will drag in your Adams Apple — unless you lay off apples.

Mr. Owen D. Young, and Mr. Gifford asked me to annoy on this program. You just heard Mr. Gifford, the biggest "Hello" man in the world, a very fine high-class man, but what a job he has got. Mr. Hoover just told him: "Gifford I have a remarkable job for you, you are to feed the several million unemployed." "With what?" says Gifford. "That's what makes the job remarkable; if you had something to do it with, it wouldn't be remarkable."

And Young, Owen D. Young. You know Young, he is the originator of the "Young Plan," the original "Young Men's Temperance Union," "Young's Meat Markets," "Young Kipper," and was the first democratic child born of white parents in Youngstown, Ohio.

The Young Plan was that every nation that owed each other should pay what they could, but somebody came along with an older plan than the Young Plan; in fact it is the oldest plan there is — it was that nobody pay anybody anything! So that being such an improvement over Young's Plan, why it's the one Europe is working under now.

Well, Mr. Young called me up and asked me to talk on this program. I told him I was very particular who I appeared with and who would be the other speaker. He said would Mr. Hoover be all right? I told him I would think it over. So I did, I looked everything up about him, and inquired, and found that after discounting about two thirds that the Democrats said about him, found I had nothing much to lose by appearing with him, so I took the chance. So if we do all right today, there's liable to be a new team on the radio. I told him not to get Mr. Coolidge in it; he would be selling some insurance.

Mexico's President is about to resign, Spain's resigned, Chile has had a crate of 'em lately, so that leaves Mr. Hoover the "dean of Presidents." Mr. Hoover has done some splendid work for us laterly. He rounded up the bankers and told 'em if they wanted to continue to get 8 and 10% from the yokels they better start letting out some dough without the security of a right eye and three ribs. He told 'em to melt some frozen assets. A frozen asset is just a banker's mistake; anyhow he sent 'em home renewing notes.

So now things are different, everybody is holding their own, in fact that's just what's the matter with the country, everybody is holding their own and won't let go!

We used to be told that depression was just a state of mind, but starvation has changed that impression, depression is a state of health, it's moved from the mind to the stomach, and it ain't really depression either, it's just a return to normalcy. We are just getting back to earth and it don't look natural to us anymore. We are back to twobit meals and cotton underwear, and off the $1.50 steaks and silk underrompers. The trouble with us in America is we are just muscle bound from holding a steering wheel, the only place we are callused from work is the bottom of our driving toe.

Now everybody has got a scheme to relieve unemployment, — there is just one way to do it and that's for everybody to go to work. *"Where?"* Why right where you are! Look around, you will see a lot of things to do: weeds to cut, fences to be fixed, lawns to be mowed, filling stations to be robbed, gangsters to be catered to. There is a million little odds and ends right under your eye that an idle man can turn his hand to every day. Course he won't get paid for it, but he won't get paid for not doing it. My theory is that it will keep him in practice in case something does show up. You can lay off so long that you can lose the habit, so keep practicing so work won't be a novelty when it does come. You eat just as much loafing as you do working, in fact more, you got more time.

The trouble with us is today we are in such bad shape that it takes us all day to tell about it, we keep yawning and yapping for the good old days of 26, 27, and 28. Well we might just as well wake up, for those "Cuckoo" times are not coming back anymore. How we all escaped a lunatic asylum during that time is more than we know now. We paid a dollar down on everything under the sun that anybody had to sell. I had a fifty cent equity in every lot in America.

Now here we are worrying and reading in the papers about a hundred different problems that they got us all excited and making us believe they amount to something. This country has just one problem: it's not the balancing of Mr. Mellon's budget, that's his worry not ours; its not the League of Nations, that you read a lot about; it's not the silver question. Not a one of these problems mean a thing in the world to us, as long as we have seven million of our own out of work that's our only problem, and to arrange it so that a man that wants work can get work, and give him a more equal division of the wealth the country produces. Now if our big men in the next year can't fix that, well they just ain't big men, that's all. What does all this yapping about disarmament amount to, compared to your own people that haven't worked in two years?

What does prohibition amount to if your neighbor's children are not eating? It's food, not drink is our problem now. We were so afraid the poor people might drink, now we fixed it so they can't eat. Is Japan's and China's troubles more to us than our bread lines? We got more wheat, more corn, more food, more cotton, more money in the banks, more everything in the world than any nation that ever lived ever had, yet we are starving to death. We are the first nation in the history of the world to go to the poorhouse in an automobile!

Our potters fields are surrounded with granaries full of grain. Now, if there ain't something cockeyed in an arrangement like that, then this microphone in front of me is a mousetrap. It's simply a case of getting it fixed, all the feed is going into one manger, and the stock on the other side ain't getting any of it, but we are better off than all those other nations that are hard up. They haven't got all this. We got it but we don't know how to split it up.

I guess we will get it fixed, for everybody is aroused and thinking on it. We been so busy in the last few years getting radios and bathtubs and facial creams, and straight eights, that we forgot to see if we had any bacon and beans.

Now a miracle can't happen and all these people get a job over-night. It's going to take time, so they must be fed and cared for perhaps all winter; everyone of us that have anything got it by the aid of these very people. There is not an unemployed man in the country that hasn't contributed to the wealth of every millionaire in America. The working classes didn't bring this on; it was the big boys that thought the financial drunk was going to last forever, and over-bought, over merged, and over capitalized. Now the people are not asking for money; they are asking for a job, but there is no job. Towns and cities can't say they haven't got the money, for the same amount of money is in the country as when these folks had their share—somebody's got it. Last winter we didn't realize the need, but this winter we got no excuse, its been shown to us all summer. I have said for the last two years that things would pick up in '32. Why, because it's an election year and the Republicans always see to it that things look good on election years. They give us three bad years and one good one, but the good one is the voting year. Elections are always just a year too late for the Democrats.

Now don't wait for the Government to feed these people. The taxpayer is feeding now about one-fourth of the people. I'll bet you that every town and city comes through. I have seen lots of audiences and heard lots of appeals, but I have yet to see one where the people knew the need, and the cause was there, that they didn't come through. Even Europe who hates us and thinks we are arrogant, bad mannered and everything else, but they will tell you that we are liberal, doggone it, our folks are liberal. I don't know anything about "America being fundamentally sound" and all that after dinner "Hooey" but I do know that America is "fundamentally generous."

I want to thank Mr. Gifford and Mr. Young—and especially Mr. Hoover—for the honor of being allowed to appear on the same program with him. There is not an unemployed man in America tonight that has worried as much, or taken this situation to heart, as much as our President. I know that he would rather see the problem of unemployment solved than all the other problems put together. He has had a long, tough, hard pull, and for every town and every city to get right out and raise their funds would make him mighty happy and happiness hasn't been a diet with him and he is a very human man. I thank you. Goodnight.[23]

For most of the 1920s, Will Rogers was a flip commentator on the ridiculous developments of an optimistic boom era—an H. L. Mencken dressed in bib overalls. During the late 1920s and early 1930s, a different kind of commentator emerged, a Will Rogers who applied his intelligence to healing wounds of the body politic, attending to them with a salve of concern and laughter.

This "Unemployment Speech" (October 22, 1931) opens with an admission that even the big men of the country are at a loss about how to deal with the economic collapse. Rogers' ambivalence is obvious: after saying what he can about President Hoover's relief measures, he reminds his listeners that the 1920s were unrealistic times, expressing this notion through humorous imagery: "We are just getting back to earth and it don't look natural to us anymore. We are back to twobit meals and cotton underwear, and off the $1.50 steaks and silk underrompers." The remainder of the statement attempts to peel away false issues which surround the critical problem of the Depression, the need for work.

Will Rogers' 1920s (Churchill Films, 1976) uses a recorded version of this talk to stress Rogers' sense of the paradox of the American tragedy. Instead of describing the situation as a disproportionate relationship between supply and demand, he boils the paradox down to a "Cockeyed arrangement." Rogers appeals desperately to the goodwill and fellow feeling of his audience; still, there is a sense that no workable solution is in sight. Certainly, the grieving — but inactive — president described has little to offer.

Rogers was trying to boost morale in this talk. He avoids economic arguments, trying instead to tap the spiritual resources of the nation: "I don't know anything about America being fundamentally sound and all that after dinner 'Hooey,' but I do know that America is fundamentally generous." The president's image obviously worries Rogers. Hoover is humanized — we have seen "Ambassador" Rogers do this for Ford, Smith, Roosevelt, and countless other figures of the period — but the image is still of a leader stymied by unexpected challenges. Unfortunately, there seems little consolation in knowing that Hoover "is a very human man."

Regulations and Leaf Raking: Making Sense of the NRA's "Goofey Ideas"

You are running a little shop or business. They come to you and tell you you got to let your man off earlier; then in addition hire another man. Now you are going to say "Hire another man? Don't need the one I got; only keeping him because he's been with me a long time. And he's got a family. I could let him go and do all the work myself and then sleep half the time. What is this — a joke, a gag or something? The whole idea sounds goofey to me." And by golly, you come to think of it, the idea is kind of nutty. Hiring somebody when you don't need them, and yet the speakers keep telling you what it will do for you to sign up and the benefits will start rolling in. Why, listen to them, the whole thing sounds like Santa Claus, but Santa Claus don't come in August or September. Santa Claus comes about four months from now, and that is just when this thing is going to come. Never mind what the orator told you; the orator never has to guarantee his speech; if he did we would have no oratory.

Already folks are complaining that they are following the NRA to the letter, but their business is showing no extra business, trade. That's because they have been misled. Speakers have not told them the whole scheme is like a crop; you can't plant it one day and start reaping the next; you can't hire a man one week and expect him to spend his salary back with you the next. It is going to take a few months for all these thousands and millions of small pay checks to reach your business. No, Santa Claus is not going to be with us till about the usual time this winter. It is going to be mighty hard on people trying to live up to this extra expense. Banks have got no help. The government helped them out; now, they got to help the people. And please don't run in and raid some little fellow's store because he has no Eagle painted on his chest. Talk to him; perhaps he could not get the money to call for this added expense that he was called on to spend. It's going to take money and it's going to take a little patriotism before this whole thing works out. The war ran for years. You knew it couldn't end the next day, and the war did not affect half as many people as this thing affects. This thing sounds goofey, but it's absolutely sound. We don't have to know much economy to know that if everybody is working we would have prosperity. If we had prosperity everybody would be working, but we waited four years for prosperity, but we could not have it because nobody was working. So, there is one case where we absolutely know which comes first — the chicken or the egg. We know that work must come before prosperity and that is what this whole scheme is. I was in Washington last week and I had several talks with General Johnson and also had quite a chat with our President, Mr. Roosevelt, all on this NRA. The President told me of various big financiers who had been in there. They were all down in Washington last week on the Code. He told me of one capitalist. He told this capitalist, "Why in your coal fields you have people living in coke ovens;" "Yes, that is right, Mr. President; I am very sorry for that, but I have an obligation to my stockholders;" and the President told him, "Yes but your stockholders are not living in coke ovens, and the right of a man to work is more important than the right of a man to dividends." And then the President said to me, "Some of these men cannot realize conditions have changed since the times when their fortunes were made. It's hard to show them (not all of them, thank God!) that by spending $2,000,000 now they can get $50,000,000 back."

I tell you folks, I came away from Washington last week with the idea that the little fellow had got somebody in his corner in Washington. I don't mean the Administration is against big business. There are hundreds and thousands of big ones entering into this thing with enthusiasm, and with their money and their whole hearts; but for the first time in years the big man comes to Washington the same as the little man. If this Administration ever goes under, it should have written on its tombstone: "Perished through trying to give the little fellow a square deal."[24]

By summer 1933, the New Deal had launched a multitude of programs to confront the Great Depression. In his Blue Eagle Drive Speech (August 27,

1933), Will Rogers made one of a number of contributions to the Roosevelt administration, in this case, on behalf of the National Recovery Administration (NRA) whose proud symbol was a famous Blue Eagle. Many of the devices used for humor in the 1920s are mustered here to communicate a serious, persuasive message.

The NRA plan to hire more people in order to increase purchasing power ran against the common sense of small business men. (Republicans grumbled about "make work.") To confront prejudices against such a plan, Rogers admits that "the idea is kind of nutty"; however, he goes on to explain why NRA guidelines and codes will make sense in the long run. To do so, Rogers reaches for popular culture metaphors — the planting of seeds, expectations of Santa Claus — to drive home a message about patience. Rogers is not afraid to invoke the idea of patriotism. In his well-established role as ambassador for the average man, Rogers has spoken with General Hugh S. Johnson, NRA's chief, and with President Roosevelt. He assures his listeners that these leaders are battling against entrenched interests "to give the little fellow a square deal." With such an administration on their side, American citizens might be able to weather bad times.

This Will Rogers evinces a seriousness seldom shown during the 1920s. All would mourn for him in 1935, an avuncular national figure devoted to helping his countrymen across the hard places.

WILL ROGERS ON HUMOR: TWO LOCI CLASSICI

Much of the existing scholarship on Will Rogers' comic strategies focuses on two brief articles, portions of which are duplicated here. "The Extemporaneous Line" (1917) and "The Wit of Will Rogers" (1919) are early comments by Rogers on his style of comedy. Note, however, how early these comments were made. Any comprehensive study on Will Rogers will need to include the insights suggested by Chapters 2 and 3 of this biobibliography.

The Extemporaneous Line
By Will Rogers

The question that every guy asked who used to come to interview me was "Did you really come from out West?" I got so tired of hearing it that I used to tell them: "No, I'm from New Jersey, but don't you tell anybody." The next question invariably would be "How did you get on the stage?" Say, anything can get on the stage. Its keeping them off that's hard. A fellow can be the champion soup eater and if he can locate a manager that will set him up behind a bowl, and tell him to go to it — if he can keep the audience amused and the soup holds out — why he's on the stage.

Of late all I am asked is "Who writes your stuff and where do you get it?" And the surprising answer is: The newspapers write it! All I do is to get all the papers I can carry and then read all that is going on and try to figure out the main things that the audience has just read, and talk on that. I have found out two things. One is that the more up-to-date a subject is the more credit you are given for talking on it, even if you really haven't anything very funny. But if it is an old subject, your gags must be funny to get over.

The first thing is the remark you make must be founded on facts. You can exaggerate and make it ridiculous, but it must have the plain facts in it. Then you will hear the audience say: "Well, that's pretty near right."

Lots of good subjects have been in the papers for days and I can't think of a thing on them. Some of the best things come to me when I am out on the stage. I figure out the few subjects that I will touch on and always have a few gags on each one, but the thing I go out to say may fall flat and some other gag I just happen to put in out there goes great. For instance, here is an example: "Mr. Edison is perfecting a submarine destroyer. Well they say he only sleeps three or four hours out of the twenty-four. That gives him plenty of time to invent." That was only a little laugh, but I used it to show the audience that I had read about the invention which had only been announced that day. It happened that at this time New York cafes were closed at one o'clock so I casually added to the remark my sudden thought: "Suppose Mr. Edison lived in New York and Mayor Mitchel made him go to bed at one o'clock, where would our invention come from?" And that was a big laugh.

This illustrates my work. I have to have my idea—all extemporaneous speakers do—but my laugh comes quickly and apparently out of no where.

Another thing I read, was that submarines could not operate in the warm Gulf Stream—so I said: "If we can only heat the ocean we will have them licked." That didn't get much of a laugh, and I was kinda stuck—but I happened to add, "Of course, that is only a rough idea. I haven't worked it out yet." This last went big and covered up the other.

I was talking of the income tax and how hard it hit our girls in the show, and just happened to mention, "A lot of them have figured out it would be cheaper to lay off."

I start on a subject and if it is no good then I have to switch quick and lots of times when I come off the stage I have done an entirely different act from what I intended when I went on. Sometimes an audience is not so good and my stuff that night may not be very good, so it is then you see the old rope commence to do something. It gets their mind off the bum stuff I am telling and as I often say to the folks in the show, I reach away back in my hip pocket and dig up a sure fire gag, as I always try to save some of my best gags just like a prohibition State man will his last drink.

In the two and a half years I have been with Mr. Ziegfeld in his *Follies* and *Midnight Frolic* where we play to a great many repeaters, I have never done the same act two nights. I have always changed parts of it and in the *Frolic* a great many times I have done an entirely new act.

Another thing, I think I do the shortest act of any monologue man and that recommends it. On the Amsterdam Roof I never do over six minutes and in the *Follies* nine or ten, generally eight.

Picking out and talking about distinguished people in the audience I use quite a little, but never unless I know them personally and know that they will take a joke as it is meant. The late Diamond Jim Brady I always spoke of, as I knew him and he always seemed to take an interest in my little act. Once at a big banquet Mr. Brady recited a little poem which he had written himself. I learned the piece and shortly afterwards one night when he was in the audience I did his poem. This made a great hit with Mr. Brady. My best one on him was "I always get to go to all the first nights, yes I do. I go with Mr. Brady. He sits in the first row and I stand at the back and if anybody cops a diamond I am supposed to rope 'em before they get away with it." He was certainly a wonderfully fine man.

On opening night of the *New Midnight Frolic,* Lieut. Vernon Castle had just returned from France and was then with Mrs. Castle. Vernon and I had played polo together and he is a regular fellow. I walked over to them, shook hands and said: "Here is one old Tango Bird that has made good," and then I told about how Fred Stone and I got Vernon a bucking horse once and that was where he got his idea of aviating. I said: "Vernon, we worried about you when you were out there at the front, but not half as much as we worried about Irene in the pictures. Boy you don't know what war is, you should see what your wife has been giving them in Patria."[25]

Will Rogers learned that his humor was most successful when based on stories in the newspaper, issues on the mind of his audience. Exaggeration of the facts would then convey desired humor and insight. Both in oral presentation and in writing, Rogers built line atop line until he achieved a "topper." Each step was only slightly humorous, but the sequence taken as a whole could be hilarious. Anyone who has seen and heard a Johnny Carson monologue knows that these combined techniques still work well with American audiences.

Originality and novelty were important Rogers techniques. He wrote his own material, and his work on Ziegfeld shows required constant turnover of lines because New Yorkers came back to the *Follies* or the *Midnight Frolic* as often as three times a week. Will Rogers turned this problem to his own advantage, roasting public figures in the audience. Later, as a journalist, he would apply this "roasting" technique to national figures out in his considerably larger reading audience.

Brevity was the soul of the Oklahoman's wit. Because the Rogers style never expanded beyond units larger than the paragraph, this chapter has intentionally selected passages from the short daily telegrams. Larger works are usually no more than an assemblage of telegraph-length insights.

The Wit of Will Rogers
By George Martin

"It was during the first week I was ever on a regular stage — down at Keith's old Union Square, which was the big New York vaudeville theatre in those days. I only had a roping act then. The idea of using any talk hadn't occurred to me.

"During the first week I had a trick where I threw two ropes at once and caught the horse and rider separately. Some actor told me I ought to announce it, as the audience didn't know what I was going to do. I didn't think up my speech beforehand. I just stopped the orchestra and said:

" 'Ladies and gentlemen, I want to call your sho'.nuff attention to this next little stunt I am going to pull on you, as I am going to throw about two o' these ropes at once, catching the horse with one and the rider with the other. I don't have any idea I'll get it, but here goes.'

"Well, they laughed. And, believe me, I was mad when I came off. I thought I hadn't said anything for them to laugh at, and I told the manager I was *through*. It was quite a while before I would open my trap again on the stage; but the other actors and the manager kept telling me to do it the same way again. And that's how I got to putting talk into my act. As it panned out, it was the luckiest thing I ever did; but I can't claim much credit for grabbing *that* chance. It took all my friends to *drive* me to it.

.   .   .   .

"One day my wife said: 'Why don't you talk about what you read? Goodness knows! You're always reading the papers!'

"So I started to reading about Congress; and, believe me, I found they were funnier three hundred and sixty-five days a year than anything I ever heard of.

"Now here's the point: if I had been in a regular show where they have a different audience every night, I wouldn't have had to change my stuff; but on the roof we got a lot of repeaters each night, and a man won't laugh at the same joke more than once. So that was what made me dig. I would read the papers for hours, trying to dope out a funny angle to the day's news, and I found that they would laugh easiest at the stuff that had just happened that day. A joke don't have to be near as funny if it's up to date.

"So that's how I learned that my own stuff, serving only strictly fresh-laid jokes, as you might say, goes better than anything else.

"I use only one set method in my little gags, and that is to try and keep to the truth. Of course you can exaggerate it, but what you say must be based on truth. And I have never found it necessary to use the words 'hell' or 'damn' to get a laugh, either.

"Personally, I don't like the jokes that get the biggest laugh, as they are generally as broad as a house and require no thought at all. I like one where, if you are with a friend and you hear it, it makes you *think,* and you nudge your friend and say: 'He's right about that.' I would rather have you do that than to have you laugh—and then forget the next minute what it was you laughed at.

"We played for President Wilson last fall, and I used one joke which he repeated in his Boston speech on his return from France. He said:

"As one of our American humorists says (up to that time I had only been an ordinary rope thrower), 'Germany couldn't understand how we could get men over there and get them trained so quick. They didn't know that in our manual there's nothing about retreating! And when you only have to teach an army to go *one way,* you can do it in half the time.'

"And still a lot of folks think it's pretty soft for a cowboy to get paid for stuff like that. But did you ever figure that lots of comedians go through a whole year with one act? But because I have set myself this job of trying to give them something new, they won't stand for old stuff from me, as they will from lots of others, because I'm expected to keep up with the times. And I tell you it is sure hard digging."

. . . .

Perhaps you've noticed that all this stuff is short. Three lines is the limit. Rogers tells twenty jokes to the other fellow's one. Most monologue men tell eight or ten stories. Rogers will average about forty in the same time.

Being brief somehow gives the impression of intelligence, and folks do admire intelligence. Brevity and clarity show that you have *thought,* and that you know what you're about.

Another good trick of Rogers, which applies to business as well as it does to clowning, is to make capital out of what the other fellow says and does. He plays one man off against another. In his Peace Conference stuff, kidding the present incumbents, he said the Kaiser seemed to be about as popular in Germany as a Democrat in the next Congress. Of course the Republicans all clapped. Then he said:

"All right, I'm goin' to 'tend to you Republicans in about a minute." Then he said:

"Of course you heard about 'em takin' a Republican with 'em to Paris. But you ain't heard nothin' about his *landin',* have you? They just took that guy along to *argue* with on the way over."

The best examples of how he makes capital out of what the other fellow says, are in his after-dinner speaking, of which he has done quite a bit in the last few years. He always likes to follow another speaker — never to lead the program. And the more serious the speech he has to follow, the better Rogers likes it.

He was once invited to address the Traffic Club of Chicago. It was a very serious meeting. The war was just over and those men wanted their railroads back. Seven burning and bitter speeches preceded Rogers', and just before he was introduced the meeting passed a long and fervent resolution to be sent to Washington, demanding that the railroads be returned. Then he was introduced.

"Folks," he said, "shortly before the coronation of the late King Edward, six pickled Irishmen — one a ditch digger, two hod carriers, a truck driver and a couple of bricklayers, met in the back end of a saloon in this town to decide whether they'd permit the coronation ceremonies to proceed. Next to that, I consider this the most momentous occasion in the history of Chicago."

That was his way of telling them that it didn't make a darned bit of difference whether they demanded the railroads back or not. It took a minute for it to sink in, but it got a laugh, and then applause, and before he went on everybody was happy.

Another time he was addressing the Rotary Club of Columbus. The man ahead of him represented the Methodist Centenary Celebration they were going to have in Columbus, and he was giving them all the details, telling how many thousands of this and how many hundreds of that they were going to have; how they were bringing wonderful things from all over the world, and about the parades and meetings, and the hundreds of thousands of Methodists who would be on hand. But when Rogers got up, his first remark was:

"It's a terrible thing for the saloons of this town that they'll have to close just before this great gathering of Methodists.

"But there are other terrible things. This man says there'll be one band of eighty trombonists—it's almost impossible to listen to *one,* but think of *eighty!* A trombonist is like vice—he ought to be segregated.

"And he says there'll be seventy thousand preachers. Can you imagine it—seventy thousand preachers? Why, you can hardly keep awake listening to one. What will seventy thousand of 'em do to you?"

Rogers believes it's a good thing to know something about a man before you decide what line of talk to give him. If you don't do that, you don't get his interest, and you can't do business with a man if you don't have his interest.

For instance, he never talks about politics to a Broadway crowd. Folks there have their heads full of girls and food, he says. Most of them don't know whether the Peace Conference has met yet. But if Gladys Fluffy Ruffles were a delegate, they'd know that. And all an audience of sporting men would know about it would be if Jack Dempsey were sent along.

The smartest all-around man in this country, according to Rogers, is the man who works all day and has to ride thirty minutes on a street car to get home at night. He reads the newspapers. He knows what you're talking about.

But he considers the best customer he's got is Woodrow Wilson. He says he is the average man developed to the nth degree and with an unusual lot of brains to boot. The best five nights he ever had, he says, were the nights he played to the President. And Washington is his best town because, he says, folks in Washington are so well informed about what's going on.

But you've got to be careful, even with a smart audience. One man's mind is sharper than another's, and you must be able to estimate how deep you can make your stuff and still get it across to him.

As an instance of this, one night when Rogers was playing and the President was in the audience, he got to talking about Lord Northcliffe, who had just been offered a place in the Ministry by Lloyd-George. He said:

"I see where Lord Northcliffe refused the Air Ministry today. I guess he figured it was easier to tell how to run this war than it was to help run it."

The audience clapped and yelled, and Rogers thought he had a peach of a gag. The next night, when the President wasn't there, he pulled it again and it didn't get a ripple. Rogers couldn't understand it. So when he came off he said something about it to the manager.

"Why, Bill," said he, "that's easy. I was watching your work last night and I saw what happened. The President was the only man in the house that got you on that gag. He commenced to laugh and then he got up and leaned out of the box and clapped. The crowd didn't make a move till then; but when it saw what he did, it followed suit, not because it got the joke, but just to prove that it was as smart as he was."

Folks are that way. The little fellow will take his cue from the big one almost every time. Maybe you can sell the big fellows and get the little fellows to follow through, but you can't always have the big fellows around when you're making a sale, and Rogers would rather sell the same first-class goods, but do it in a way *all* understand.

That gag was good. That was the trouble. It was too good. And in selling a product, any sales talk that's over the average man's head is no go.[26]

Sometime during the vaudeville years, Mrs. Betty Rogers noticed that people were as interested in the frontier twang as they were in the artifacts of cowboy life. It would not be long before Will Rogers exchanged his physical lariat for a verbal one, roping issues and great men with his gift of wit.

In an interview with George Martin, Rogers stresses the factual basis for his humor: "strictly fresh-laid jokes, as you might say, goes better than anything else." Not only a basis of fact, but providing an insight below the surface events was important: the laugh should clarify contemporary issues. Rogers knew who would be the best audience for topical humor. High society groups could not follow him, and show business people were often indifferent to the Oklahoman's barbs. The ideal Will Rogers reader was "the man who works all day and has to ride thirty minutes on a street car to get home at night. He reads the newspapers. He knows what you're talking about." This was the average American for whom Rogers served as jester and unofficial ambassador.

Unique to Rogers — some feel because he was impartial, while others suggest that it was his entertainer's need to please — is the technique of playing groups against one another, pointing at the weaknesses and excesses of all parties. No student of Rogers has been able to provide a satisfactory rationale for this dualistic approach. What was there about this social commentator's philosophy which prevented him from becoming a partisan, especially when the Depression called for messages of conviction and commitment?

In this regard, there is as much mystery as humor in Rogers' confession of political faith: "I am a member of no organized political party — I'm a democrat."

NOTES

(These endnotes identify the Rogers passages quoted. In most cases, they are daily telegrams and are found in *The Writings of Will Rogers* under the date given. The local editor usually formulated a headline for the entry, too often something like "Will Rogers Says." For the sake of this chapter — which seeks to evoke interest in Rogers' style and insights — I have created my own "headlines" for all entries.)

1. Daily telegram for August 12, 1927. Daily telegrams are hereafter cited as DT, followed by the appropriate date of release.

2. DT for January 26, 1928.

3. "Timely Topics," an early recording of 1922. Will Rogers Memorial, Claremore, Oklahoma.

4. DT for July 31, 1929.

5. DT for August 2, 1927.

6. DT for May 2, 1928.

7. DT for May 21, 1927.

8. DT for May 9, 1929.

9. DT for July 28, 1927.

10. DT for November 28, 1927.

11. DT for January 11, 1927.

12. DT for December 5, 1928.

13. DT for July 19, 1927.

14. DT for April 8, 1927.

15. DT for May 21, 1928.

16. DT for April 19, 1927.

17. DT for December 27, 1929.

18. DT for October 3, 1928.

19. DT for September 27, 1927.

20. DT for August 31, 1927.

21. DT for February 12, 1927.

22. DT for January 3, 1927.

23. Transcription of Will Rogers' Radio Program, "Unemployment Speech," October 22, 1931. Text is on microfilm and in the manuscript collection, Will Rogers Memorial, Claremore, Oklahoma. The radio address was also published as "Bacon and Beans and Limousines," *The Survey,* November 15, 1931, pp. 185, 219. More recently, it has been included in *Radio Broadcasts of Will Rogers, The Writings of Will Rogers,* pp. 65–67.

24. Transcription of Will Rogers' Radio Program, "Blue Eagle Drive Speech," August 27, 1933. Text is on microfilm and in the manuscript collection, Will Rogers Memorial, Claremore, Oklahoma. Along with a few other radio broadcasts for which there are transcriptions, this program was *not* included in the Oklahoma State University collection, *Radio Broadcasts of Will Rogers.*

25. *Theatre,* July 1917, p. 12.

26. *The American Magazine,* November 1919, pp. 34-35, 106-110.

4

A BIBLIOGRAPHICAL
ESSAY ON PRIMARY AND
SECONDARY SOURCES
FOR THE STUDY OF
WILL ROGERS

PRIMARY SOURCES: **THE WRITINGS OF WILL ROGERS** *(1967-1983)*

Sometime during the late 1960s, Robert Kamm, president of Oklahoma State University (OSU), Paula and Robert Love, of the Will Rogers Memorial, Odie Faulk, of OSU's History Department, and others conceived an ambitious goal: to republish the existing books by Will Rogers and to collect otherwise disparate writings by the great Oklahoman, thus making the insights of the state's great man conveniently available to research libraries. Those who initiated the movement to publish *The Writings of Will Rogers* firmly believed that scholars of the first three decades of the twentieth century needed these essential documents of America's cultural history.

Through the good offices of the Oklahoma Historical Society and with financial assistance from the state of Oklahoma and individual donors, the publication efforts began. Theodore Agnew (OSU History Department) was the first director of the Will Rogers Project from 1967 to 1972. During this formative period, considerable spade work was accomplished; this basic research and organization would later prove to be of constant benefit.

In 1972, Joseph Stout, Jr. (OSU History Department) assumed the position of director and was soon joined by an assistant director, Peter Rollins (OSU's English Department). James Smallwood (OSU History Department) became the director in 1976 and was joined by a new assistant director, Steven Gragert, who became the director in 1981. The turnover of OSU personnel has reflected an ambivalence toward the project on the part of the university's scholars. Although the Will Rogers publication efforts have been of high quality, there has always been hesitation. The fear was that local and national peers might not approve of such provincial expertise.

Fortunately, the efforts of the Will Rogers Memorial Commission, the Will Rogers Memorial Staff, and other friends of the project have compensated for what might have been lost due to a lack in project staff continuity. Special help came from Will Rogers, Jr., who has been a constant source of inspiration. As the Will Rogers Publication Project brings its work to a close in 1983, the state can take pride in the effort: a set of twenty-two volumes of edited, annotated writings of Will Rogers, together with transcriptions of selected radio programs. The twenty-third volume, a topical index to the entire twenty-two volume set, will complete the publication efforts. The state of Oklahoma, the Oklahoma Historical Society, and Oklahoma State University should be congratulated for preserving and publishing such important documents of America's cultural history. (For narrative details about the formation of the Will Rogers Project, see Stout [1973].)

Series I of *The Writings of Will Rogers* consists of books that were printed during Rogers' lifetime. Dates provided refer to the first printing of the work followed by the date of the OSU publication. *Ether and Me, or Just Relax* (1927/1973) was a humorous spinoff from a serious medical emergency. While on tour in 1927, Rogers became ill with what was later diagnosed as gall bladder problems. His reflections originally appeared as a series of articles for the *Saturday Evening Post;* they capitalize on the event to highlight the differences between "then and now." (See Chapter 3 for a discussion of this comedic device.) Such topics as movies, religion, medicine, politics, and contemporary music are all sewn into this story of an operation and its aftermath. *There's Not a Bathing Suit in Russia and Other Bare Facts* (1927/1973) reports a side trip to Moscow during a European excursion in 1926. First issued as a *Saturday Evening Post* series, this book makes the most of Rogers' brief glimpse inside the USSR. Rogers was preoccupied by the subjects of aviation and preparedness for the next war; he also ventured some interesting observations about the Soviet experiment. He obviously enjoyed playing the role of an American innocent abroad in such an exotic setting.

In 1922, Rogers began a weekly article series which would be distributed by the McNaught Syndicate until 1935 when Rogers' death called the fun to a halt. Thirty of the early efforts were issued in book form under the title *The Illiterate Digest* (1924/1974). Topics considered are as varied as the Oklahoman's interests: personalities such as Woodrow Wilson, Henry Ford, Warren Harding, and a host of congressmen take their place with discussions of America's changing social mores. *The Illiterate Digest* was probably the most substantial bound publication of Rogers' lifetime, matched only by *Letters of a Self-Made Diplomat to His President* (1926/1977). The *Letters,* like so many of Rogers' longer efforts, first appeared in the *Saturday Evening Post* as a series of epistolary comments on European conditions sent to an exalted pen pal, the president of the United States. It seems only fitting that President Coolidge invited Rogers to spend his first night back from the trip at the White House. (For more on this trip and the book that resulted, see Chapter 2.)

Two short volumes conclude Series I of *The Writings of Will Rogers*. Both *The Cowboy Philosopher on the Peace Conference* (1919/1975) and *The Cowboy Philosopher on Prohibition* (1919/1975) are collections of one liners from Rogers' comedy routines at Florenz Ziegfeld's *Follies*. Although most of the material is underdeveloped, those interested in the evolving style of Will Rogers will take an interest in the ways in which the early Rogers penetrated through complicated issues to reveal hidden human truths: the Versailles Conference symbolized all that was wrong with foreign entanglements; Prohibition was a favorite topic because it symbolized the tensions of an America confused about precipitous change. Series I of *The Writings of Will Rogers* contains a total of six volumes, with indexes for *The Illiterate Digest* and *Letters of a Self-Made Diplomat*. Since the other books are relatively short, the lack of indexes is not a serious problem and will be remedied when a cumulative index is published.

The remainder of *The Writings of Will Rogers* consists of materials never bound together before, although many of the more pungent quotations have been anthologized by such popularizers as Donald Day (1949, 1950, 1952) and Brian Sterling (1976, 1979, 1982). (In every case, the *Writings* is to be preferred to the sloppy and profit-oriented works of commercial writers.) *Convention Articles of Will Rogers* (1976) provides an important thread of reflection concerning the presidential election process. Rogers attended all of the Republican and Democratic conventions from 1920 to 1932; much of what he had to say about the function of such events in American society is still applicable in our media age.

The *Conventions* volume is the only book of Series II. Its natural companion is part of Series V: *"He Chews to Run": Will Rogers' Life Magazine Articles, 1928* is a delightful volume, perhaps the most consistently literate and humorous volume of the entire *Writings*. In 1928, Rogers was offered to the American people as an alternative candidate to the official party choices. *Life Magazine* devoted extensive spreads to the mock campaign, all of which have been collected in this book. In addition to articles by Rogers, there are tongue-in-cheek contributions by Robert Sherwood (*Life*'s editor), Judge Ben Lindsey, Henry Ford, Robert Benchley, and a host of other public figures. The enormous fun everybody had in promoting the "bunkless candidate" radiates from every article. The campaign between Hoover and Smith had so many nasty overtones that the Rogers involvement must have provided readers with a refreshing change of pace.

Series III of *The Writings* assembles the daily telegrams of Will Rogers in four volumes covering the Coolidge, Hoover, and Roosevelt years, 1926–1935. During this period, Rogers turned out a very pithy comment every day. This "daily telegram" was syndicated by the McNaught Syndicate and reached some 40 million readers across the land. Betty Rogers later recalled that the telegrams were the journalistic venture which Rogers most enjoyed. Over the nine years of their production, Rogers was given an opportunity to hook a barb into almost every conceivable public figure and every significant—and, occasionally, insignificant—public issue. Each volume of the *Daily Telegrams* is annotated and indexed, with the four-volume cluster comprising an impressive total of 2,817 telegrams. Many of these colorful efforts at compression still delight.

From 1922 until 1935, Rogers wrote a syndicated weekly article which was carried by many of the same newspapers that picked up the daily telegrams. Series IV of *The Writings* collects these longer efforts in six volumes. Each volume is indexed, providing researchers with topical access to the some 1,800+ pages of wit and wisdom by an extremely busy, "lazy" man. Not all of the weekly articles are better or more insightful than all of the daily articles. There is considerable overlap between the two, however, and the larger format gave Rogers a better opportunity to develop his ideas.

In addition to the *Life Magazine* articles (discussed above in relation to convention matters), Series V of *The Writings* assembles a variety of items. *More Letters of a Self-Made Diplomat* (1983) contains observations along lines found in the earlier volume with a similar title. They reflect Rogers' continuing interest in Latin American affairs; in addition, they register the reactions of a mature Rogers during an extended tour of the Far East in 1932. No survey of Rogers' foreign policy notions would be complete without a consideration of these writings, assembled in bound form for the first time.

"How to Be Funny" and Other Writings of Will Rogers (1983) brings together a number of important minor essays. Obvious topics are politics (Democrats, elections, officeholders), Prohibition, and many other subjects considered in the daily and weekly articles. More important are such essays as "The Extemporaneous Line" and "How to Be Funny," for they unveil a number of devices which Rogers consciously employed as a humorist. It is impossible to properly appreciate the self-conscious artistry of Rogers' work without exposure to these revealing discussions. (See Chapter 3 for some discussion of these articles.)

For many, Will Rogers was a radio voice, an aural companion perhaps even more familiar than the author of the famous "Fireside Chats." Series VI of *The Writings* collects transcriptions of important radio broadcasts of the 1930s. Rogers made twelve broadcasts for E. R. Squibb and Sons during the spring of 1930. From 1933 to 1935, he was the star of "The Good Gulf Show." *Radio Broadcasts of Will Rogers* (1983) includes these programs as well as an important single broadcast made in 1931 for the Organization of Unemployment Relief. Major contemporary personalities (Charles Lindbergh, the Prince of Wales, Dwight Morrow, Henry Ford), the reigning presidents (Calvin Coolidge, Herbert Hoover, Franklin Roosevelt), foreign and domestic policy matters (disarmament, Prohibition, the Depression, and "plans"), and the delight of popular culture are all fair game for the wit of Will Rogers. An index to this volume facilitates research. It should be noted that many of the Gulf Broadcasts are on tape at the Will Rogers Memorial and that many of the records currently available on the market draw from "The Good Gulf Show." The Gulf programs were recorded on aluminum discs, a rather unwieldy medium to be sure, but one that has not deteriorated much over the years. Anyone interested in the manner in which Rogers spun his magic must turn to these recordings and to his sound motion pictures.

Almost every volume of *The Writings of Will Rogers* has an index. All of the volumes also have detailed annotations for the personalities and issues alluded to by Rogers; these notes were designed for the general reader, but they are often helpful to the scholar. In sum, the scholarly apparatus of *The Writings* helps frame, define, and make more useful the materials collected in the twenty-two volume set. The Will Rogers Publication Project will terminate after *A Cumulative Index to The Writings of Will Rogers* is produced. This index, the work of Steven K. Gragert, will facilitate access to the entire *Writings.* As the final volume of *The Writings* goes on the shelves of America's university libraries, an ambitious goal of Robert Kamm, Paula and Robert Love, Odie Faulk, and many others will be fulfilled. When studies of the first three decades of the twentieth century are written in Boston, in Berkeley, and in Ann Arbor, the wisdom and insight of Will Rogers' journalism will be available. For some writers, the materials will confirm insights already reached; on the other hand, it seems clear that the right Will Rogers daily or weekly article in the hands of the right scholar may help us to gain a fresh perspective on who we were and who we have become. While Rogers was not a generalizer like Alexis de Tocqueville or James Bryce, the existence of *The Writings* provides an enormous quantity of particular observations from which important generalizations can be made. It is hoped that scholars will exploit this wonderful contribution of American culture studies for its wisdom without forgetting that Rogers delivered his observations in the spirit of transcendent jest.

Writings Not Published by **The Writings of Will Rogers**

"The Worst Story I Have Heard Today" was Will Rogers' first attempt at a daily column. Because the material was often borrowed and because some of the ideas in these stories are not considered to be in good taste today, the articles were not published in *The Writings.* The articles were released on nearly a daily basis from May 25, 1925, until January 15, 1927. The McNaught Syndicate distributed the series; it was supplanted by Rogers' *Daily Telegram,* a format more authentically his. Each article for "The

Worst Story" series was in the vicinity of 250 words, and each joke had a punch line saved for the last sentence of the piece. Unfortunately, Will Rogers' "Worst Story" articles often lived up to the series title.

SECONDARY SOURCES: SOME BIOGRAPHICAL APPROACHES

The memory of Will Rogers does not suffer for the lack of biographies. Local authors seeking to celebrate his Oklahoma roots, journalists seeking to earn a daily wage, family members wishing to set the record straight, fellow actors and entertainment folk with a nostalgic mission to evoke their friend, and dedicated scholars seeking to earn their degrees or to renew the focus on Rogers have all contributed their mite to the biographical effort. None of the existing biographies has synthesized all of the facets of the great Oklahoman—chiefly because of a combination of a lack of original and print materials (now no longer a problem) and because of the strong prejudices which the authors brought to such projects. This survey will take a topical approach to the mass of biographical studies.

Stressing the Regional Roots

Many biographies attempt to describe and explain the childhood influences on Will Rogers. The worst of these is by C. W. "Dub" West, *Will Rogers, Oklahoma's Gift to America* (1979). West is a local historian who seeks to show how the hometown boy made good. As a result of the local interests, Rogers' visits to Fort Gibson and Muskogee are given as much prominence as his far more important film career. The stated occasion for the unkempt volume was the Will Rogers Centennial, "to pay tribute to 'Oklahoma's Gift to America,' especially featuring his Cherokee heritage and his love for Oklahoma and its people" (p. 96). Fortunately, the centennial included other efforts. An especially chauvinistic study is Margaret Axtell, *Will Rogers Rode the Range* (1972), a book written so that "youth yet unborn may in their days to come, better know and always remember a once beloved cowboy who thrilled their ancestors as philosopher, humanitarian, humorist" (viii). The book surveys Rogers' entire life, with constant reference to his roots in the dust of cowboy country. Axtell's book is almost totally derived from existing sources; she merely adds an ingredient of gushy Western chauvinism. Both the works of West and Axtell are examples of the Rogers mystique rather than legitimate studies.

Two local studies stand out for their research. Ellsworth Collings in *The Old Home Ranch* (1964) provides an excellent model of local history. He traces the settlement of the Cherokee nation, the rise of Clement Rogers and his "White House," and the transition from cows to plows as the range was subdivided into farms. Even the removal of the great house from the rising waters of Lake Oologah to its current location at a state park is traced with meticulous detail. Like other Western studies, *The Old Home Ranch* is heavily colored by regional chauvinism; still, it is a work not to be ignored by anyone interested in Rogers' formative experiences and environment. *The Will Rogers Country* by Noel Kaho supplements the Collings study of immediate influences. Strangers to the complexity of Indian politics will observe that politicians did not need to travel to Washington to learn about political intrigue. Far from being noble savages living in some placid relationship with nature, the Cherokee Indians were in constant political turmoil — either within the tribe, or against the Osages, or in the increasing entanglements with the federal government. Kaho's early history of Claremore provides specific details about the world which Clem Vann Rogers and his contemporaries shaped for the next generation. The early chapters of the book are the most valuable; the story becomes increasingly clouded by civic pride and purple prose as it approaches the present.

The least pretentious regional study of Will Rogers is by Spi Trent (with the help of Eugene Brewster), *My Cousin Will Rogers: Intimate and Untold Stories* (1938). Unfortunately, "intimate" meant something different in 1938 than it does today; as a result, Trent's story is a series of humorous anecdotes by Rogers' companion in cowboy days. While the diction grates after about fifteen pages — Brewster, a New York writer, strove for excellence in Hee Haw prose — the anecdotes concerning Rogers' behavior in times of leisure and stress, 1890-1908, can be found in no other source. When a truly insightful biography of Rogers is written, it will interpret the personal information in this book.

A few of the celebratory biographies are worthy of serious consideration. David Milsten's *An Appreciation of Will Rogers* (1935/1976) was published in the year of Rogers' death, but had been under way for quite a time previous to the tragedy. As a result, it is packed with contemporary interviews and opinions. The regional slant of the book helps Milsten to appreciate the elements of Southwestern life which fed into Rogers' philosophy, especially in relation to his awareness of social and economic developments during the 1920s and 1930s. On the other hand, the book is definitely an "appreciation" rather than an objective study and suffers from long passages of purple prose in which Rogers is compared with various "brilliant sons of the republic" who have "stalked across the annals of history . . . [etc.]" (p. 2). Inexplicably, a book by Milsten bearing another title is merely a reprint of his *appreciation* with cosmetic changes only.

The View from Broadway and Hollywood

Published with unseemly haste after the fatal airplane crash of 1935, *Our Will Rogers* (1935) by Jack Lait has the virtue of looking at Rogers from the perspective of someone who worked in show business. Unfortunately, this virtue is more than compensated for, in a negative way, by a host of factual inaccuracies. Pluses like Lait's detailed description of how Rogers moved into the sound era as a film star are canceled by minuses such as reports that Rogers fought in the Boer War or an obsessive emphasis on the dangers of flying, a focus obviously designed to hold the attention of the 1935 audience. The photographs of this volume are excellent; they may be the most important historical contribution of the volume. As part of a series of "Little Big Books" for 20th Century-Fox, Jerome Beatty produced *The Story of Will Rogers* (1935), a publicity man's best effort at instant research. A few of the Hollywood details — if they are true — might prove valuable to the student of Rogers as part of the movie colony.

Sixty days after Rogers died, P. J. O'Brien raced into print with *Will Rogers, Ambassador of Good Will, Prince of Wit and Wisdom* (1935). The result was a "life and letters" volume with interpretations and quotations hurriedly assembled. O'Brien received criticism from the Rogers family for the inaccuracies of his work. O'Brien would not be the last commercial vulture to pick at the legacy of the great Oklahoman.

The only literate biography by a show business person is Homer Croy's *Our Will Rogers* (1953). Homer Croy was a writer of fiction who did well in Hollywood first as an adapter of his own works and later as a screenwriter with 20th Century-Fox. Croy worked with Will Rogers on *They Had to See Paris* (1929), Rogers' first sound film and an adaptation of a novel by Croy. Later, the writer and actor were in contact at various degrees of intensity for the following films: *So This Is London* (1930), *A Connecticut Yankee* (1931), *Down to Earth* (1932), and *David Harum* (1934). There were many opportunities for Croy to observe both the public image and the private reality of the famous actor.

Croy approaches the problem of the "public" versus the "private" Rogers in the most intelligent discussion I have found on the subject. In *Country Cured* (1943), Croy speculates that Rogers built a public image for himself and then felt obligated to live up to that image: there was no separate, private man; there was only the public persona, Will Rogers. The only other writer to consider this question with sensitivity is Samuel F. Roach (1972) whose dissertation attempts to explain the tension of Rogers' identity crisis under the scornful eye of a father who saw few virtues in a show business career. Clem Vann Rogers' displeasure may have motivated Rogers to become the special kind of showman he was, a person who fulfilled a civic role as well as provided entertainment. Much more interpretive work needs to focus on this area of Rogers studies.

Homer Croy conducted hundreds of interviews in preparation for *Our Will Rogers* (1953). Many of his sources were in their twilight years: someone should go back into the interview notes to see what additional information can be yielded. Such a search seems justified because the Croy biography is crowded with fileopietism; it is possible that matters of fact were dropped when they did not fit into Croy's predetermined picture.

The Most Important Biographies

There is a small cluster of biographies which contain the most reliable and insightful information about Will Rogers. Because each of these was written with an awareness of previous studies, a chronological approach seems appropriate.

With the editorial assistance of Richard Adamson and with counsel from Irvin S. Cobb, Betty Rogers produced a loving biography of her husband, *Will Rogers: His Wife's Story* (1941/1979). Betty Rogers was a sophisticated woman of the same upper-class origins as her husband; qualities of grace and taste shine through her smiling appreciation of a husband who obviously never quite grew up. Mrs. Rogers' biography is indispensable for a sense of the flow of Rogers' career and contains factual information which until recently could not be obtained elsewhere. It is not surprising that the book places Mrs. Rogers in an influential role at critical junctures of her husband's career; she helps him when he needs to get a daily article going, or when he needs the right scripts for his film career, or needs to be told to come home to enjoy the success of his first sound film. Rogers' own statements on the subject reveal that Betty Rogers had a strong influence over him. When asked if he would run for the office of governor of Arkansas, Rogers replied: "I already have one governor, Betty." She kept the home together and the children parented in a family from which the father was absent for long periods. It is likely she had less influence on Rogers than she asserted.

A tone of affection and nostalgia runs through Betty Rogers' overview of her husband's life. Every idiosyncrasy is seen as endearing; every event or social interaction is viewed from the best possible angle. Rogers emerges from the story a saint — without a flaw and never meeting men he didn't like. The story is as much a tribute to a widow's love for her husband and his memory as it is an investigation of the great man it depicts. I have read the biography many times and often refer to it for specific facts concerning Rogers' life; still, the glow which pervades the document jeopardizes its credibility. None of the gritty insights available in Croy's biography — such as Rogers' testiness about criticism — surfaces here.

Donald Day was a professional writer who devoted a considerable amount of time to the study of Will Rogers, much to his profit. In 1949, Day issued an anthology of Rogers' published and unpublished writings. Called *The Autobiography of Will Rogers* (1949), the book is still the only synoptic one-volume collection of Will Rogers' writings arranged in a chronological sequence. During the next three years, Day packaged the same material in different formats (1950, 1952); in addition, he and his wife produced a children's biography. A full study, *Will Rogers, A Biography,* was issued in 1962. Written for the general reader, packed with quotations from the *Autobiography,* most students agree that Day's book is little more than a tossed salad of information from Betty Rogers' biography dressed with colorful Rogersisms. Although the book quotes Damon Runyon's statement that Will Rogers was "America's most complete human document," little attempt is made to provide any interpretation of the document.

As its title indicates, the dissertation by Reba Collins, "Will Rogers: Writer and Journalist" (1967), is not strictly a biography, but its focus on pivotal moments in his career makes it worthy of discussion with the biographies. In her survey of the literature, Collins concludes that Donald Day "no matter how good his intentions . . . managed to bring confusion and distortion that is being compounded through reprintings" (p. 42). The dissertation makes a painstaking effort to pinpoint when Will Rogers began his writing career (Croy claimed it was 1919; Day 1922; and Collins earlier), and to explain how the career evolved. Collins concludes that Will Rogers had forged a distinctive style as early as 1916, a style that included such characteristics as familiarity, timeliness, and toppers—all items which Rogers scholars have pointed out, but in relation to later documents. Collins further asserts that Rogers did not need coaching from the McNaught staff or anyone else. He had developed his particular brand of humor as a "columnist of the theatre," and it was merely a matter of setting the same ideas in the same form of expression to the printed page.

The body of Collins' dissertation focuses upon various literary forms: the syndicated columns (Chapter V), the magazine articles (Chapter VI), and books (Chapter VII), and miscellaneous efforts (Chapter VIII). The Rogers style is discussed at length in Chapter IX, but nothing new is added to the insights already available in the writings of Jeannette Tandy (1925), Walter Blair (1942), E. Paul Alworth (1958/1974), and others. The dissertation is strongest in the early chapters where some original insights about Rogers as a young writer are made; also, the thoughts on revision and style are excellent. Like so many studies, however, the survey of the evolving writer suffers from hero worship. Many of the reexaminations called for in the last chapter of the dissertation—research based on the close examination of Rogers' original documents and on Rogers' own writings (rather than through anthologies put together for profit) lie ahead, as do psychological explorations of the great man. As director of the Will Rogers Memorial, Dr. Reba Collins is in a position to help others conduct the worthy investigations she has urged in her dissertation.

A more biographically oriented monograph is Samuel F. ("Fred") Roach, "Lariat in the Sun: The Story of Will Rogers" (1972), a study that carries Rogers from cradle to grave. Roach is really the first biographer to discuss openly some of the negative aspects of Rogers' upbringing, especially Rogers' ambivalent feelings for his father. Roach concludes that in childhood a "father-son antagonism" developed which gradually became "an established pattern of behavior within the Rogers family" (p. 23). Loss of a mother at the age of ten, friction with a father throughout childhood, and adjustment difficulties with peers, Roach concludes, produced a loner.

Roach finds that as a teen, Rogers enjoyed arguing, often in defense of his Indian blood. He was more comfortable teasing girls than flirting with them, for he was a shy boy. Poor performance in school only further raised "the wall of alienation and antagonism which was growing between Willie and his father" (p. 57). Rogers' flight from parental and school authority was the first important step in "a long and tortuous search for personal identity" (p. 60).

Roach correctly stresses that much of the Rogers mystique derived from the Oklahoman's careful storytelling—on stage, in print, to curious reporters. As a result, "Rogers created a romantic legend of success and adventure" (p. 128). This is quite a different evocation of Rogers than any yet described because it stresses the normal anxiety, despair, and construction of self which characterize human lives, not to mention the formation of public images. Unlike previous biographers, Roach attempts to probe beneath the surface. For example, here is a representative discussion—in this case of Rogers' famous energy:

> The exact motivation behind the cowboy-philosopher's energy defies precise definition. Nevertheless, some obvious elements seem apparent and bear mentioning. These include the desire of a wealthy man's son to repeat the family tradition of financial success, a possible natural instinct to excel, the necessity of achieving prominence as a way of compensating for feelings of racial inferiority, failure in the eyes of a respected parent (in this case, Will's father Clem), or a combination of all of these factors. Regardless of its origin, by the mid-1920s, Will had developed a driving ambition which dominated his person until his untimely death (p. 189).

No existing biography of Will Rogers—written either before or after Roach's study—has provided equally stimulating insights into the psychodynamics of the man. (An excellent study of Rogers' early conflicts and growth was published by Roach in 1980.)

The last seven chapters of "Lariat in the Sun" add nothing new to our knowledge of Rogers' mature career, although the conclusions chapter artfully integrates the psychological speculations of the early chapters with an analysis of themes in the writings of the mature Rogers. For reasons unexplained, Roach was not given access to all materials at the Will Rogers Memorial. He is not, therefore, entirely to blame for not contributing any new insights.

The most lavish biography of Will Rogers and the most fun to handle is Richard M. Ketchum's *Will Rogers: His Life and Times* (1973). At each subject point along the way, this biography (written for the American Heritage Company) attempts to relate the individual life to historical and cultural contexts. As a result, there are sallies into such areas as the history of the American Indian, the life of the American cowboy, the history of Ziegfeld's "glorification of the American girl," the growth of the motion picture industry, and many other interesting contextual explorations. For the general reader, such side trips help make sense of a life some long decades gone; however, the level of information supplied in the background discussions is rudimentary. In addition, the attention given to these peripheral matters leaves less space for Will Rogers. As a result, the Ketchum biography adds not a jot to our understanding of the man and his times, although the book — especially because of its photographs — is a delight to examine.

In 1972, *Publisher's Weekly* proclaimed that American Heritage would soon go to press with the first "authorized" biography of Will Rogers. Unfortunately, wisdom and insight cannot be manufactured as quickly as an article for *Sports Illustrated*; the special reconsideration which such a project should have inspired did not materialize. The book is dependent upon the existing biographies and did not profit from any of the special studies available. The president of American Heritage Publishing Company, Paul Gottlieb, perhaps succeeded too well in his promise to the public that "the book won't be pedantic" (p. 57). Certainly, the reviewer for *Time Magazine* found the book to be "short on analysis of the motivations of a man who was highly complicated and often contradictory" (p. 79). Considerable resources were wasted on a pretty picture book.

The ideal biographer of Will Rogers will need to have an understanding of frontier life and culture without being an advocate for its reintroduction; will have to study the true appeal of early Wild West, vaudeville, and motion picture shows to Americans at the turn of the century; and will need to tap the insights of psychology. The synthesis will show the daring of William Brown (1972), the detailed research of Peter Rollins (1976) and Franklin Lloyd (1975), the attention to original manuscripts of Reba Collins (1967), and the maturity and taste of Betty Rogers (1941) and Homer Croy (1943, 1953). With this bibliography and *The Writings of Will Rogers* available, there should be a number of young scholars who will rise to the challenge.

Hagiography: Teaching Moral Lessons through the Life of a Great Man

The memory of Will Rogers has been used to teach lessons about the good life: some have been aimed with high seriousness at an adult audience; other treatments have been for a juvenile readership. The most startling — perhaps even frightening—example is J. T. Mulligan, *Draft Will Rogers for President of the United States* (1931). The pamphlet promotes Will Rogers as a modern messiah ready to save Depression America from its economic, moral, and political woes. Rogers is compared with "Theodore Roosevelt . . . the 'Doer;' the man who DID things and talked about them afterwards" (p. 9). Mulligan espies a coordinated conspiracy of big business and big banking manipulating American society: "Either AMERICANISM, the hope of the race, will triumph or the MONEY BARRONS WILL CONQUER" (p. 45). The answer to America's troubles is simple: "Draft Will Rogers President of the United States. . . . He will turn the tears to smiles and make life worth living" (p. 47). Such hero worship is a sorry measure of the despair of the Depression.

Rogers was included among the model citizens in H. Hagedorn, *Americans: A Book of Lives* (1956), a work of hagiography written immediately after World War II. The author felt dutybound to present inspiring role-models "in the conviction that international anarchy can be overcome only by the growth of international understanding, and that great lives are international currency on the highest levels of trade" (p. vii). Unlike the hysteria of Mulligan's tract, Hagedorn's portrait of Rogers combines idealism with humanity, making it one of the most impressive efforts of the genre. In utter contrast is Ella Dixon Haggard, *Will Rogers and Thoughts* (1940), a handbook of poems—many of which relate to Will Rogers—which the author very aptly describes as "not being worthy of literary merit" (p. 3). Haggard's idolatry and jangled rhymes take hero worship into the realm of self-parody. Somewhere in between these two extremes is Leland Wilson, *The Will Rogers Touch* (1979), an attempt by a minister to show how much of the Oklahoman's philosophy paralleled Scripture. Quotations are supplied under such rubrics as Art, Analysis, Love, Morality, and Vanity. Much of the book is tastefully presented, although clearly Rogers would have been embarrassed by his being indiscriminately clustered with "David of the Old Testament, and Michelangelo, and Benjamin Franklin and Albert Schweitzer and Steve Allen, who can do many things well" (p. 13). A host of references in Chapter Five that are not discussed in this essay fall at various points along the spectrum between Mulligan's defiant nationalism and Haggard's tepid poetasting.

My search of the literature has led to at least ten volumes on Will Rogers written for children. All are exercises in hagiography, as one would expect; however, not all are totally useless to the serious student. Studies with pointed lessons to convey deal with Will Rogers as a success story (Cooper and Palmer, 1942; Garst, 1950), or a world traveler (Bennett, 1971), or an athletic lad who loved action (Van Riper, 1951), or in a tradition of great men (Musso, 1974). Others are pointless and so condescending as to be unattractive even to children (Montgomery, 1970).

A few of the children's biographies are to be praised. Although written for a juvenile audience, Kenneth Richards' *Will Rogers* (1968) is a solid overview that does not preach. For his *Boy's Life of Will Rogers* (1937), Harold Keith conducted original research, including interviews with relatives and neighbors who knew — or claimed to know — the hero when he was a boy. As a result, details of the early life appear in this study which are available nowhere else. The book ends with Will Rogers' marriage to Betty Blake in 1908. At first appearance, Beth Day's biography of Lucille Mulhall (1955) would seem irrelevant to the Will Rogers legacy, but her approach to Rogers as part of the Mulhall troupe lends new details of fact and interpretation concerning the developing personality of the cowboy who would become the cowboy philosopher. It seems hard to believe that Rogers was not influenced by the months he spent with a family which helped make the West a living myth for America's city dwellers. With the exception of Spi Trent, no other Rogers biographer gives the Mulhalls the consideration they deserve.

Most intriguing of the children's volumes for its psychological insights is Spencer Johnson, *The Value of Humor* (1976). The didactic objective of the book is to teach the virtue of laughter as a weapon for fighting stress. The selection of Rogers for such a story was extremely apt, and some of the insights about how a child's mind responds to loneliness and stress supplement the observations made by Roach (1972). Will Rogers is portrayed as a lonely boy who turns to roping to occupy his time. One day, he creates a fantasy companion, "Larry Ett" — his rope. Larry then follows Will through the remainder of his life, reminding the young man that laughter helps people to weather the major storms of existence: "It's the times when things aren't going so well that you need to have a sense of humor" (p. 14). Both Larry Ett and Will get seasick on their worldwide tours as they share the successes of rodeo and stage. When the Depression arrives, "Will's humor helped [Americans] get through some difficult times" (p. 53). The beauty of this study of Will Rogers is that it, like Roach's dissertation, stresses the emergence of an ironic point of view as a product of inner conflict and alienation; too many of the hagiographic studies for adults and children make the evolution toward greatness an easy and uncomplicated development. As Mark Twain once observed, humor more often springs from a sense of tragedy than from a simplistic buoyancy. As Roach has clearly shown, much of Rogers' humor was laced with anxiety, guilt, and aggression. Laughter was a way of transcending these feelings, a way of achieving acceptance and affirmation.

Miscellaneous Reminiscences

Many of the articles listed in Chapter 5 show by their titles that they are reminiscences of Will Rogers. The Rogers student will take an interest in the fragments which each adds to a full portrait of the man. Homer Croy's reminiscences are the most insightful, perhaps because he not only worked with

Rogers in Hollywood, but he later took pains to study Rogers as a phenomenon. In any case, the following observation by Croy still needs further thought and study, especially because Will Rogers is so often described as "playing himself."

> To say that he was an actor does not convey Will Rogers, as I came to understand him for Will Rogers built himself up as a certain kind of character, just as an actor might on the stage; but his building up went far deeper than that. He built himself up until he became, both on and off the stage, the Will Rogers the public knew. The older he grew, and the more successful he became, the more he played this character (*Country Cured,* p. 141).

Croy's shrewd observations raise rather than answer questions about identity formation and the relationship between private and public images.

Other show business figures have recalled their friend, Will Rogers. Irvin S. Cobb, *Exit Laughing* (1941), spends some time interpreting Rogers' famous observation about not meeting a man he didn't like. Cobb explains that the epigram was more an expression of a hope than an attempt at scientific accuracy. The Will Rogers student would have hoped for more information from Cobb; on the other hand, some of what Cobb had to say about Rogers may be part of the Betty Rogers biography—which Cobb helped to write. In *My Life Is in Your Hands* (1928), Eddie Cantor speaks of his relationship with Rogers as a case in which "the extreme East and Far West met and liked each other" (p. 134). Like *every* other *biographer,* Cantor in *As I Remember Them* (1963) claims that he was the first to urge Rogers to talk on stage. There are also a few personal incidents described which will interest those with a psychological bent. The memoirs of Cobb and Cantor provide useful insights into the tensions and struggles of a life in show business: it was demanding work which required endurance and grit as well as intelligence.

Chapter 2 of this bio-bibliography tries to block out the various characteristics imputed to Will Rogers. To many, he was the epitome of the rags-to-riches success story (Culver, 1925; Golden, 1928; Bell, 1935), but in actuality he came from a wealthy family, perhaps the wealthiest family in his region. Many others looked at Rogers as the quintessential family man (Rogers, 1941; Beatty, 1930), ignoring that he was often away from home for as long as six months at a stretch. Greatest in number are the observers who see Rogers as the perfect embodiment of the ideal American (Collins, 1935; Ferguson, 1935; Weeks, 1944; Cerf, 1947) at the expense of the man's individuality. An *omnium gatherum* of reminiscences—all positive because they were assembled as a memorial—is William Payne and Jake Lyons, *Folks Say of Will Rogers: A Memorial Anecdotage* (1936). The anthology is an excellent source of public perceptions of Rogers by his contemporaries;

while not necessarily reliable as factual accounts, they are fascinating as projections of cultural hopes and aspirations.

Anecdotes that add some salt to an often oversweet picture are hard to find, although a few exist. In "Will Rogers Was No Damned Good," H. Allen Smith relates a personal experience in which Rogers shrugged off the reporter at a rodeo. Smith claims that the hostility which Rogers displayed totally floored him and proved, at least to his satisfaction, that Rogers was an ambitious showman who only pretended to be a humanitarian. A less known article by Francis Poole (1969) relates a similar rude response by Rogers aboard ship en route to Japan. Neither article reveals anything other than that Will Rogers was human and may not always have been ready to be jostled by his adoring public. Irwin Hoover's report of his *Forty-two Years in the White House* (1934) as an expert on protocol gives a priggish perspective of Rogers. The excessively negative description of everything Rogers did during his visit to the White House in 1926 shows, if nothing else, that not everyone was overwhelmed by Rogers' folksiness. The most clever negative portrait of Will Rogers is an "open letter" by John Riddell (1929) in which Rogers' down-home style is parodied. Like the few existing anecdotes about Rogers and women or Rogers and booze, it seems that the exceptional cry of foul play highlights the rule of honesty.

Will Rogers As an American Humorist

Will Rogers was one of the first to describe his style of humor. "The Wit of Will Rogers: The Story of a Cowboy Who Became a Famous Comedian" (1919) is listed as an article by George Martin, but it is actually a series of extended quotations from Rogers on how to keep audiences laughing. In "The Extemporaneous Line," Rogers further identifies comic ploys: such techniques as adherence to factual material, use of the "topper" effect in storytelling, the importance of brevity, and the "roasting" technique are clearly and colorfully outlined. Fortunately, these essays have been collected with other reflections on humor in a volume entitled *"How to Be Funny" and Other Writings of Will Rogers* (1983), part of *The Writings of Will Rogers*.

A number of books, dissertations, and articles relate Rogers to a tradition of American humor. Jeannette Tandy's *Crackerbox Philosophers in American Humor and Satire* (1925) was the earliest academic study. It was superseded by Walter Blair's *Horse Sense in American Humor* (1942): seeing Rogers in a tradition from Benjamin Franklin's *Silas Dogood* to Ogden Nash helps account for the national appeal of the Oklahoman's humor. An M.A. thesis by Lois Walker, written in the same year that Blair's book was published, examines the writings of Will Rogers in the humorist tradition, identifying the elements characteristic of that tradition: exaggeration, juxtaposition, understatement, anticlimax, misquoting, puns, similes, metaphors, and cacography. Walker stresses Rogers' similarities to Peter Finley Dunne as an observer of the national scene, a likeness which Homer Croy (1953) explored in relation to manuscript materials. Probably enough has been written about the broad tradition of humor, but more study is needed to illuminate the immediate literary influences on Rogers.

A topical approach to the humor of Will Rogers is taken by E. Paul Alworth (1958 diss. published in 1974). In a succinct and clear series of chapters, Alworth examines how Rogers approached both national and international issues. While Alworth's "anatomy" of Rogers' humor adds nothing to the conclusions of Blair and Walker, he more clearly identifies the elements of Rogers' work which were *not* in the tradition, which made Rogers a special artist: the Rogers persona was not a mask that could be dropped; Rogers had no literary interests other than humor; Rogers dealt with short, pithy paragraphs, not with extended analyses; finally, the absence of bitterness set Rogers' work apart from others in the American humor tradition. Alworth concludes that Rogers

> fits no convenient category: he was not a rural New England comedian like Jack Downing and Sam Slick; he had no political axe to grind like James Russell Lowell; he had no talent for political vituperation like Petroleum V. Nasby; he did not often play the fool character like Artemus Ward and Bill Nye; he wrote no sustained literature like Mark Twain; and he had no zeal for political and social reform like Martin Dooley (p. 124).

Other surveys of humor introduce Rogers. In *The Enjoyment of Laughter* (1936), Max Eastman shows great admiration for Rogers as a comic artist. Rogers is introduced throughout the book to exemplify the following techniques: the pun, humor based on fact, allusion, and satire. James Fiebleman's *In Praise of Comedy* (1946) is an ambitious survey of the subject starting with the Greeks and working all the way up to the Marx Brothers. Given such eclecticism, it is a surprise to find that Fiebleman comes down so hard on Rogers as a toady to America's power elite. The premise of such criticism seems to be that no one could be so popular without selling out to the owners of the mass media. David Thomson (1981) echoes this sophomoric notion.

Stan Hoig's *The Humor of the American Cowboy* (1960) is a chauvinistic celebration of the horseman's way of life. Facets of cowboy life — such as loneliness, struggles with animals, food, newcomers, and "parlor sittin" — are seen from their comic perspective. The book helps identify the special coloration which the Southwest gave to the diction and metaphors of Will Rogers' writings, providing a perspective unavailable in studies of humor from a national perspective. According to Norris Yates (1964), Rogers succeeded with the large, national audiences because he mixed images and built contradictions into his humor. Rogers as a persona exhibited

> traits of the man idealized by the conservative who distrusts reformers and asks only to be left alone, and traits also of his counterpart in liberal mythology who participates in reform movements for the sake of getting the great corporations and militant unions to let him alone. Rogers tried to embody both images at once without sacrificing the approval of either faction (p. 119).

All of these categorizations have some truth.

Rhetorical analysis can be found in articles by William R. Brown (1972), Peter Rollins (1974, 1975, 1980), and Ivie Cadenhead (1963). All of these studies linger over specific works and yield the kind of detailed conclusions which the studies of broad traditions lack. Furthermore, detailed studies of speeches by Rogers can be found in the theses by William Gerk (1952) and Maurice McSpadden (1972). Helen Siegelin's thesis is particularly interesting because it critiques talks by Rogers which never appeared in book or article form; she looks at one convention address and two benefit speeches on the basis of the "morning after" reports by the *New York Times*. This area of analysis has been entirely ignored by researchers. Rogers was an indefatigable speaker, especially during years when he had money problems.

In his own time, there were two schools concerning the relevance and artistry of Will Rogers' humor. As early as 1922, the *New York Times* and the *Literary Digest* welcomed the Oklahoman as "Our Aristophanes"; he seemed to be a peculiar blend of the Greek satirist and Mr. Dooley. In 1933 and 1935, L. H. Robbins of the *New York Times* proclaimed that Will Rogers was indeed a philosopher whose humor derived from a coherent social vision. Other contemporaries of the Oklahoman—such as Henry S. Canby (1935)—were not as impressed by philosophical depth as by the service in realism which Rogers' writings supplied. When Rogers died in 1935, Canby was disappointed that "the chair is vacant" (p. 8). Another school of Rogers watchers developed in the 1930s. Granting the assertion that Rogers was a "wisecracker" and a "kidder," these observers felt that the delight which Americans took in making fun of big issues trivialized the problems and prevented the nation from addressing them intelligently. After Rogers came back from a trip to China, *The Christian Century* crystallized the objection rhetorically: "Must Americans Have Their Daily Joke?" (1932). The religious leaders felt that the virtues of the kidding strain were outweighed by "profound moral shortcomings" (p. 308). *The Christian Century* was not alone in its fear that Rogers might encourage the public to shrug off matters too quickly. In 1932, *America* expressed its impatience in an article which purported to describe when a "clown becomes a nuisance." Many serious-minded Americans feared that Rogers wielded too much power over the public. The *New Republic* in 1935 described "The Cowboy Philosopher" as "a truculent nationalist and an isolationist of the Hearst School" (August 28, p. 62). *Commonweal* said that Rogers could often be "complacent, limited, nationalistic" in an article sarcastically entitled "King Will" (1932). From the vantage point of hindsight, the historian wonders: could there have been some envy mixed in with all of this indignation?

Symbolic and Cultural Interpretations

Everyone who writes about Will Rogers must come to grips with the enormous appeal of the man; some articles, dissertations, and books have made such an issue the main focus of their investigations. Orrin Klapp (1954), a student of folklore, places Rogers in a tradition of clowns, fools, and other cultural figures who have attracted attention because of their physical or verbal "clever triumphs." According to Klapp, by always addressing his remarks at someone or something, by keeping the public on his side, by not attacking those in trouble, and by carefully and consistently playing the role of the "little man," Rogers tapped archetypal patterns. He was America's "clever hero" whose success was enormous: by 1931, Rogers was a "political seer and oracle rather than just a jester, a social force rather than a mere commodity of entertainment" (p. 34). William Savage (1979) asserts that Rogers blended the fool image with other popular American archetypes, including the sage, the Indian, and, most important, the cowboy.

The most ambitious attempt to interpret the appeal of Will Rogers is William R. Brown, *Imagemaker: Will Rogers and the American Dream* (1970). Brown begins with the assumption that Rogers' so-called philosophy was riddled with errors; therefore, the claim that he was a seer does not explain his profound impact. Brown is quick to concede, on the other hand, that Rogers countered public opinion sufficiently often to avoid any accusation that he merely reflected the lowest common denominator. In a "myth and symbol" approach to Will Rogers, Brown draws on such famous studies as R.W.B. Lewis, *The American Adam* (Chicago: University of Chicago Press, 1955), H. B. Parkes, *The American Experience* (New York: A. A. Knopf, 1955), and Marshall Fishwick, *American Heroes* (Washington, D.C.: Public Affairs Press, 1954). Against such a backdrop, he develops Will Rogers into a potent mythic figure, "a secular saint, an American talisman, the source of whose sainthood may not be understood" (p. 15).

The body of the book explores how Rogers appealed to the American public as an American Adam (Chapter 2), an American democrat (Chapter 3), a success story (Chapter 4), and an American Prometheus (Chapter 5). Rogers was popular because, unlike other prominent contemporaries, he partook of all four facets of the American Dream: "Clarence Darrow, champion of the underdog, perhaps symbolized the dreams of individualism, freedom, and equality; Ford was the personification of success; Lindbergh and Edison, of progress" (p. 269). Only Will Rogers could tie together all of the disparate strands. (An article by Brown [1979] brings the complex argument of the book into a short compass.)

Without doubt, Brown's book is an ambitious attempt to place Will Rogers into the colorful tapestry of American values. When Walter Blair reviewed the book, he found the study "vulnerable at several points." Anyone who becomes impatient after encountering three or more high-level abstractions in a sentence will find the style in which the ideas are presented to be irritatingly vague and unsettlingly strident — as if the author is unsure of his assertions. Blair's criticism may have been directed as much toward the turgid style of the book as to its content. Criticism notwithstanding, *Imagemaker* is still the most ambitious attempt to limn the complex pattern of national values which Will Rogers used as his aeolian harp.

Two American Studies scholars have attempted less grandiose approaches to the appeal of Will Rogers. In a 1975 dissertation entitled "Big Men and Regular Fellows," Franklin Lloyd presents a thorough, intelligent study of symbolic heroes of the 1920s: Babe Ruth, Henry Ford, and Will Rogers. Like his companion symbols, according to Lloyd, Rogers represented "traditional virtues like honesty, neighborliness, charity, and wholesomeness" in a complicated world too often concerned with "wealth, fame, or elaborate social conventions" (p. 219). Lloyd concludes that the American people made a smoother transition from the nineteenth to the twentieth century because they believed in such symbolic figures, heroes who reassured them that they could blend the best of the old with the new. My own study of Will Rogers as "symbolic man, journalist, and film image" (1976) uses original sources and documents available at the Will Rogers Memorial to demonstrate Rogers' symbolic importance for a society in transition. Lloyd and I have supplied a more detailed context for an interpretation than have Klapp or Brown, but all four studies taken together supply a stimulating analysis of the unique place Will Rogers occupied in the heart of his generation.

Cowboy Images and Cowboy Realities

No one can argue that Will Rogers did not love the cowboy image; the difficulty is in explaining what the cowboy image meant to him and to his contemporaries — including his cowboy contemporaries. We know that Rogers ran away from the Kemper Military Academy in 1898 and drifted to the Ewing Ranch in West Texas, where he lived the life of a *fin de siècle* ranch hand; at the same time, we know that he and other cowboy friends were avid readers of such pulp Westerns as Charles Siringo, *Fifteen Years on the Hurricane Deck of a Spanish Pony* (1886). Such evidence seems to point to an intertwining of myth and reality even for cowboys 'round the campfire. Not enough thought has been given to this paradox.

Certainly, Rogers loved the idea of the cowboy. He felt that Western paintings of Charles Russell captured the spirit of a special time and character. As Rogers explained in an introduction to a book by Russell in 1927, "We may have Cowboys just as good and we may occasionally round up a pretty good man, but us and the manicured tribe that is following us will never have the Real Cowboy, Painter and Man, combined that old Charley was" (p. xv). Such a statement shows a total commitment to a mythical view of the cowboy. It is the same kind of spirit exhibited in the 1980s by an entire nation dressed in jeans, cowboy boots, and Stetson hats.

Claims about Rogers' immersion in the cowboy myth must be counterbalanced by an acknowledgment that films such as *Doubling for Romeo* (1921) and *Two Wagons—Both Covered* (1924) graphically depict the unromantic and dusty aspects of cowboy and frontier life. Rogers seemed unwilling to accept the cowboy myth propagated by Hollywood; yet, he obviously revered a version of the myth found in the writings of Owen Wister and Theodore Roosevelt, or the paintings of the Western school.

What attracted Rogers most, of course, was trick roping. He entertained with the lariat at least twelve years before he aspired to be a "poet lariat." Evidently, the passion for roping can be as infectious as the disease affecting the hero of Rogers' short film, *The Roping Fool* (1922). According to Bobby Vincent, writing for *The Ranchman* (1941), "nothing can be more appealing to the imagination and to genuine human fancy than the gracefully floating rhythmic, endlessly floating on and on of a well-handled rope" (p. 14). Vincent explains that Rogers was not the first cowboy to make himself useless for practical work as a result of complete absorption in trick and fancy roping.

In *Will Rogers' Rope Tricks* (1969), Frank Dean starts with the simple "flat loop" exercises and progresses to the most difficult "mounted catches." Closeups of ropes, line drawings of tricks in various stages, and photographs of Will Rogers are supplemented by frame enlargements from *The Roping Fool*. Even the bookish will become fascinated by "the graceful floating of a well-handled rope" if they spend more than ten minutes with this fascinating volume. *Roping* by Chester Byers (1928) provides an interesting chapter on the history of the art. A tutor for many Hollywood stars, Byers ranks Will Rogers in the top three of roping history. As Will Rogers, Jr. notes in *Will Rogers' 1920s* (1976), his father made *The Roping Fool* because he realized that his skills would fade as he passed the age of forty-five. In the film, Rogers froze the cowboy image in time just at the moment he was moving on as a professional to become an artist of images and words.

Rogers of the Movies

The detailed production information in Chapter 6 of this book, together with the interpretive essay in Chapter 2, provides the most recent and reliable information concerning Will Rogers' movie experiences and images. The biography by Homer Croy (1953) should be consulted because Croy worked with Rogers in film. Otherwise, surveys of the silent era scarcely mention Rogers, or they do so with a lack of understanding. For reasons difficult to explain, film historians and film scholars — unlike Rogers' moviegoing contemporaries — have forgotten Hollywood's highest paid actor during the mid-Depression years. It is hoped that the factual and interpretive information brought together in this bio-bibliography will invite future efforts.

Rogers and Aviation

Will Rogers was a self-appointed ambassador for aviation, a form of transport that fascinated the world traveler. In his own day, Rogers' views on flight were recorded and discussed in an excellent article by Carl Clancy for the *Scientific American* (1929). Every biography gives a percentage of its space to the subject because of the quaint practices of the early days — such as Rogers being forced to weigh himself prior to trips because he flew as a piece of mail rather than as a passenger. In two specialized studies, the peculiar intensity of Rogers' attraction to flight is examined: Fred Roach (1979) characteristically looks at the impulse from a psychological perspective; Rollins (1984) tries to develop the notion in relation to a search for new frontiers in an era of increasing urbanization. Rogers' relationship with General William ("Billy") Mitchell and Charles Lindbergh deserves more detailed study.

The Will Rogers Memorial displays in a vertical glass case the rumpled business suit which Rogers wore the day Wiley Post's plane went down at Point Barrow; nearby, a Royal portable typewriter which Rogers carried with him is displayed with its keys frozen together — supposedly as a result of the fatal crash. There has been a continuing interest in details of the tragedy possibly because the accident which killed Rogers in 1935 was so traumatic. *Sourdough Sky* by Stephen Mills and James Phillips places the Wiley Post-Will Rogers flight within a context of exploratory aviation in a frontier state. The book was written by Alaskan aviators to commemorate the work of those who "did more than any other group to open Alaska to civilization" (p. 5) and shares Will Rogers' fascination with pilots as pioneers exploring a final area of open space. A special pamphlet written for the Smithsonian by Stanley Mohler and Bobby Johnson (1971) devotes a chapter to the crash. Narrative and technical information about the tragic Post-Rogers flight, including a discussion of the nose-heaviness of the plane, is provided. Evidently, Post knew the plane was dangerous but made the trip because Rogers was impatient to travel (p. 115). The symbolism of Rogers' death at the last point of land on the last American frontier was not missed by those who mourned.

Looking Ahead

The literature about Will Rogers should increase geometrically now that *The Writings of Will Rogers* is complete (twenty-three volumes). The availability of enormous amounts of factual information at the Will Rogers Memorial provides further incentive for such studies. In the coming years, America will begin to remember how important were the insights and the personal example of Will Rogers, chronicler of the foibles of his generation, but also its friend-in-need. His person, his written works, his radio and motion picture images all deserve serious reconsideration.

5

A CHECKLIST OF SOURCES CONCERNING WILL ROGERS

WORKS BY WILL ROGERS

Major Writings by Will Rogers

Convention Articles of Will Rogers. The Writings of Will Rogers. Ser. II, Vol. I. Eds. Joseph A. Stout, Jr. and Peter C. Rollins. Stillwater: Oklahoma State University Press, 1976.

Ether and Me or Just Relax. New York: G. P. Putnam's Sons, 1927. Reprinted as *The Writings of Will Rogers.* Ser. I, Vol. I. Ed. Joseph A. Stout, Jr. Stillwater: Oklahoma State University Press, 1973.

"He Chews to Run." Will Rogers' Life Magazine Articles, 1928. The Writings of Will Rogers, Ser. V, Vol. 1. Ed. Steven K. Gragert. Stillwater: Oklahoma State University Press, 1982.

"How to Be Funny" and Other Writings of Will Rogers. The Writings of Will Rogers. Ser. V, Vol. II. Ed. Steven K. Gragert. Stillwater: Oklahoma State University Press, 1983.

Illiterate Digest. New York: Albert and Charles Boni, 1924. Reprinted as *The Writings of Will Rogers.* Ser. I, Vol. III. Ed. Joseph A. Stout, Jr. Stillwater: Oklahoma State University Press, 1974.

Letters of a Self-Made Diplomat to His President. New York: Albert and Charles Boni, 1926. Reprinted as *The Writings of Will Rogers.* Ser. I, Vol. VI. Eds. Joseph A. Stout, Jr. and Peter C. Rollins. Stillwater: Oklahoma State University Press, 1977.

More Letters of a Self-Made Diplomat. The Writings of Will Rogers. Ser. V, Vol. II. Ed. Steven K. Gragert. Stillwater: Oklahoma State University Press, 1982.

Quotes. Los Angeles: Hessleim and McDerman, 1935.

Radio Broadcasts of Will Rogers. The Writings of Will Rogers. Ser. VI, Vol. I. Ed. Steven K. Gragert. Stillwater: Oklahoma State University Press, 1983.

Rogers-isms: The Cowboy Philosopher on the Peace Conference. New York: Harper and Brothers, Publishers, 1919. Reprinted as *The Writings of Will Rogers.* Ser. I, Vol. IV. Eds. Joseph A. Stout, Jr. and Peter C. Rollins. Stillwater: Oklahoma State University Press, 1975.

Rogers-isms: The Cowboy Philosopher on Prohibition. New York: Harper and Brothers, Publishers, 1919. Reprinted as *The Writings of Will Rogers.* Ser. I, Vol. V. Eds. Joseph A. Stout, Jr. and Peter C. Rollins. Stillwater: Oklahoma State University Press, 1975.

There's Not a Bathing Suit in Russia & Other Bare Facts. New York: Albert and Charles Boni, 1927. Reprinted as *The Writings of Will Rogers.* Ser. I, Vol. II. Ed. Joseph A. Stout, Jr. Stillwater: Oklahoma State University Press, 1973.

Twelve Radio Talks Delivered by Will Rogers During the Spring of 1930, Through the Courtesy of E. R. Squibb & Sons, 1930. (A pamphlet of transcriptions, Will Rogers Memorial, included in *Radio Broadcasts of Will Rogers, The Writings of Will Rogers.*)

Will Rogers' Daily Telegrams: The Roosevelt Years, 1933–1935. The Writings of Will Rogers. Ser. III, Vol. I. Eds. James M. Smallwood and Steven K. Gragert. Stillwater: Oklahoma State University Press, 1978.

Will Rogers' Daily Telegrams: The Hoover Years, 1929–1931. The Writings of Will Rogers. Ser. III, Vol. II. Eds. James M. Smallwood and Steven K. Gragert. Stillwater: Oklahoma State University Press, 1978.

Will Rogers' Daily Telegrams: The Hoover Years, 1931–1933. The Writings of Will Rogers. Ser. III, Vol. III. Eds. James M. Smallwood and Steven K. Gragert. Stillwater: Oklahoma State University Press, 1979.

Will Rogers' Daily Telegrams: The Roosevelt Years, 1933–1935. The Writings of Will Rogers. Ser. III, Vol. IV. Eds. James M. Smallwood and Steven K. Gragert. Stillwater: Oklahoma State University Press, 1979.

Will Rogers' Weekly Articles: The Coolidge Years, 1925–1927. The Writings of Will Rogers. Ser. IV, Vol. II. Eds. James M. Smallwood and Steven K. Gragert. Stillwater: Oklahoma State University Press, 1981.

Will Rogers' Weekly Articles: The Coolidge Years, 1927–1929. The Writings of Will Rogers. Ser. IV, Vol. III. Eds. James M. Smallwood and Steven K. Gragert. Stillwater: Oklahoma State University Press, 1981.

Will Rogers' Weekly Articles: The Harding/Coolidge Years, 1922–1925. The Writings of Will Rogers. Ser. IV, Vol. I. Eds. James M. Smallwood and Steven K. Gragert. Stillwater: Oklahoma State University Press, 1980.

Will Rogers' Weekly Articles: The Hoover Years, 1929–1931. The Writings of Will Rogers, Ser. IV, Vol. IV. Ed. Steven K. Gragert. Stillwater: Oklahoma State University Press, 1981.

Will Rogers' Weekly Articles: The Hoover Years, 1931–1933. The Writings of Will Rogers. Ser. IV, Vol. V. Ed. Steven K. Gragert. Stillwater: Oklahoma State University Press, 1982.

Will Rogers' Weekly Articles: The Roosevelt Years, 1933–1935. The Writings of Will Rogers. Ser. IV, Vol. VI. Ed. Steven K. Gragert. Stillwater: Oklahoma State University Press, 1982.

Wit and Philosophy from the Radio Talks of America's Humorist, Will Rogers. New York: The Squibb Company, 1930.

Book Introductions by Will Rogers

"A Few Words by Will Rogers." *Annie Oakley, Woman at Arms.* Courtney Ryley
Cooper. New York: Duffield and Company, 1927, pp. ii–iii.

"Foreword." *Roping: Trick and Fancy Rope Spinning.* Chester Byers. New York:
G. P. Putnam's Sons, 1928, pp. iii–x.

"Introduction." *Around the World in Eight Days.* Wiley Post and Harold Gatty.
Garden City, N.Y.: Garden City Publishing Company, 1931, pp. 9–16.

"Introduction." *Good Medicine, Memories of the Real West.* Charles M. Russell.
Garden City, N.Y.: Garden City Publishing Company, 1929, pp. 13–16.

"Introduction." *Pleasure — If Possible.* Karl K. Kitchen. New York: Rae D. Henkle
Company, 1928.

"Introduction." *Trails Plowed Under.* Charles M. Russell. New York: Doubleday
and Company, 1927, pp. xiii–xviii.

"Preface." *Fashions in Foods in Beverly Hills.* Ed. Beverly Hills Women's Club.
Beverly Hills, Calif.: Beverly Hills Citizen, 1926, pp. 53–55.

"Tribute and Recollections." *The Art of Charles Marion Russell, 1880-1926.* Ed. K.
Ross Roole. Helena: Historical Society of Montana, 1958.

"A Warning." *My Life Is in Your Hands.* Eddie Cantor as told to David Freedman.
New York: Blue Ribbon Books, 1928, pp. xi–xiv.

Newspaper Articles and Unpublished Items by Will Rogers

"An Open Letter to Will Durant." *New York Times,* July 5, 1931.

Articles for the *Detroit Journal,* December 14, 1917, and December 15, 1917. (On
file, Will Rogers Memorial.)

Article for the *Kansas City Star,* July 15, 1919. (On file, Will Rogers Memorial.)

Articles for the *New York American,* August 6, 1916, and August 9, 1916, August
10, 1916, n.p. (On file, Will Rogers Memorial.)

Convention articles for Newspaper Enterprises and The Goldwyn Clip Sheet, June-
July, 1920. (On file, Will Rogers Memorial.)

"Cowboy Ropes and Ties Our Critic: Will Rogers Avenges the Drama for All Ashton
Stevens Indignities of 25 Years." *Chicago Herald Examiner,* March 26, 1922.
(On file, Will Rogers Memorial.)

"Gag Book." Unpublished notebook. (On file, Will Rogers Memorial.)

"How I Broke into Show Business." Unpublished Mss., 30 pages. (On file, Will
Rogers Memorial.)

Letters to Betty Blake, 1900-1908. (On file, Will Rogers Memorial.)

Letters to family and friends, 1893-1903. (On file, Will Rogers Memorial.)

"Ye Town Gossip." *New York American,* May 7, 1917. (On file, Will Rogers
Memorial.)

THE ROGERS FAMILY FACTS

Books

Bell, George Morrison. *Genealogy of Old and New Cherokee Indian Families.*
Bartlesville, Okla.: n.p., 1972.

Collings, Ellsworth. *The Old Home Ranch, The Will Rogers Ranch in the Indian Territory.* Stillwater, Okla.: Redlands Press, 1964.

Collins, Reba. *Roping Will Rogers' Family Tree.* Vol. 1. Claremore, Okla.: Will Rogers Heritage Press, 1982.

Dale, Edward, and Morris Wardell. *History of Oklahoma.* New York: n.p., 1948.

Final Rolls of the Five Civilized Tribes. Washington, D.C.: U.S. Department of the Interior, 1906.

The History of Rogers County, Oklahoma. Claremore, Okla.: Claremore College Foundation, 1979.

Starr, Emmett. *History of the Cherokee Indians and the Legends and Folklore.* Oklahoma City, Okla.: Warden Company, 1921.

Thoburn, Joseph B., and Muriel H. Wright. *Oklahoma, A History of the State and Its People.* 4 vols. New York: Lewis Historical Publishing Company, 1929.

Articles

Bandy, B. J. "The Old Vann House in Georgia." *The Chronicles of Oklahoma* 32 (1954): 94–98.

Brown, John P. "Eastern Cherokee Chiefs." *The Chronicles of Oklahoma* 16 (1938): 3–35.

"Descendants of Noted Cherokees." *The Ranchman,* January 1942, pp. 34–36. (Magazine Article Scrapbook 3; Microfilm Reel 10.)

Foreman, Carolyn Thomas. "A Creek Pioneer: Mrs. William Penn Adair." *The Chronicles of Oklahoma* 21 (1943): 271–279.

Fullerton, Eula. "Necrology: Sallie Rogers McSpadden." *The Chronicles of Oklahoma* 22 (1944): 126–128.

Kaho, Noel. "Uncle Clem." *The Ranchman,* November 1941, pp. 12–14. (Magazine Article Scrapbook 3; Microfilm Reel 11.)

Keith, Harold. "Clem Rogers and His Influence on Oklahoma History." M.A. Thesis, University of Oklahoma, 1941.

Love, Paula McSpadden. "Clement Vann Rogers." *The Chronicles of Oklahoma* 48 (1970): 389–399.

McDavid, Mittie Owen. "The Irish-Indian Blood of Will Rogers." *Southern Literary Messenger* (May 1940): 18–26.

Meserve, John Bartlett. "Chief Thomas Mitchell Buffington and Chief William Charles Rogers." *The Chronicles of Oklahoma* 17 (1939): 135–148.

"Necrology: Clem Vann Rogers." *The Chronicles of Oklahoma* 8 (1930): 461.

Shadburn, Don L. "Cherokee Statesmen: The John Rogers Family." *The Chronicles of Oklahoma* 30 (1972): 12–40.

Smith, Micah Pearce. "The Latter Days of Dr. Emmett Starr." *The Chronicles of Oklahoma* 8 (1930): 339–340.

Miscellaneous Ancestral Documents

Authenticated Rolls of 1880 Cherokee Nation, Cooweescoowee District, Indian Archives, Oklahoma Historical Society.

Love, Paula M. Robert Rogers Genealogy, Clement V. Rogers Collection, Will Rogers Memorial, Claremore, Oklahoma.

Rogers, Clement Vann. Mss. Emmett M. Starr Collection, Library, Oklahoma Historical Society.

Sallie Rogers McSpadden Interview, Indian-Pioneer Papers, Indian Archives, Oklahoma Historical Society, Vol. 76, p. 158.

WRITTEN WORKS ABOUT WILL ROGERS

Books

Ainsworth, Edward M., ed. *The Cowboy in Art.* Cleveland: World Publishing Company, 1968.

Alworth, E. Paul. *Will Rogers.* New York: Twayne Publishers, 1974.

Armitage, Merle. *Accent on America.* New York: E. Weyhe, 1944.

_____. *Accent on Life.* Ames: Iowa State University Press, 1964.

Axtell, Margaret. *Will Rogers Rode the Range.* Phoenix: Allied Printing, 1972.

Beatty, Jerome. *The Story of Will Rogers.* New York: Saulfield Publishing Company, 1935.

Bennett, Cathereen L. *Will Rogers: The Cowboy Who Walked with Kings.* Minneapolis: Lerner Publications, 1971.

Bergman, Andrew. *We're in the Money: Depression America and Its Films.* New York: Harper Colophon Books, 1972.

Blair, Walter. *Horse Sense in American Humor: From Benjamin Franklin to Ogden Nash.* Chicago: University of Chicago Press, 1942.

Bolton, Sarah. *Lives of Poor Boys Who Became Famous.* 1st ed. New York: Thomas Y. Crowell Company, 1939; 2d ed. New York: Alfred A. Knopf, 1962.

Boren, Lyle H. *Who Is Who in Oklahoma.* Guthrie, Okla.: Cooperative Publishing Company, 1935.

Brady, William A. *Showman.* New York: E. P. Dutton and Company, 1937.

Bronner, Edwin, ed. *The Encyclopedia of the American Theatre, 1900–1975.* New York: A. S. Barnes and Company, 1980.

Brougher, James Whitcomb, Sr. *Life and Laughter.* Philadelphia: Judson Press, 1950.

Brower, Charles. *Fifty Years Below Zero.* New York and London: R. Hale, 1944.

Brown, John Mason. *The Worlds of Robert E. Sherwood.* New York: Harper and Row, 1965.

Brown, William Richard. *Imagemaker: Will Rogers and the American Dream.* Columbia: University of Missouri Press, 1970.

Byers, Chester. *Roping: Trick and Fancy Rope Spinning.* New York: G. P. Putnam's Sons, 1928.

Canby, Henry. *Seven Years' Harvest.* New York: Farrar and Rinehart, 1936.

Cantor, Eddie. *As I Remember Them.* New York: Duell, Sloan and Pearce, 1963.

_____, as told to David Friedman. *My Life Is in Your Hands.* New York: Harper and Brothers, 1928.

Carr, Henry. *Vaya con Dios, Will.* Los Angeles: Angelus Press, 1935.

Cobb, Irvin S. *Exit Laughing.* New York and Indianapolis: Bobbs-Merrill, 1941.

Collings, Ellsworth. *The Old Home Ranch: The Will Rogers Range in the Indian Territory.* Stillwater, Okla.: Redlands Press, 1964.

Collins, Reba. *Will Rogers*. Limited edition, 250 copies, graphic design by Paul LeFebvre, distributed to donors to the Will Rogers Memorial, Claremore, Oklahoma, 1969.

Cooke, Alistair. *One Man's America*. New York: Alfred A. Knopf, 1952.

Cooper, Alice, and Charles A. Palmer. *Twenty Modern Americans*. New York: Harcourt, Brace and Company, 1942.

Cottle, R. F. *Personal Philosophies, A Study of Happiness*. Vol. 2. Roy, Utah: n.p., 1956.

Croy, Homer. *Country Cured*. 1st ed. New York and London: Harper and Brothers, 1943; 2d ed. New York: Hurst and Blackett, Ltd., 1943; Armed Services Edition, 1943.

_____. *Our Will Rogers*. New York: Duell, Sloan and Pearce, 1953.

Daniels, Josephus. *Shirt-Sleeve Diplomat*. Chapel Hill, N.C.: University of North Carolina Press, 1947.

Davidson, Jo. *Between Sittings*. New York: Dial Press, 1951.

Day, Beth. *America's First Cow Girl, Lucille Mulhall*. New York: Julian Messner, 1955.

Day, Donald. *Will Rogers, A Biography*. New York: David McKay Company, 1962.

_____, ed. *The Autobiography of Will Rogers*. 1st ed. Boston: Houghton Mifflin Company, 1949; *The Reader's Digest Condensed Books*. Pleasantville, N.Y.: The Reader's Digest Association, Spring 1950; 2d ed. AMS Press, 1979.

_____, ed. *How We Elect Our Presidents*. Boston: Little, Brown and Company, 1952.

_____, ed. *Sanity Is Where You Find It*. Boston: Houghton Mifflin Company, 1950.

_____, and Beth Day. *Will Rogers, The Boy Roper*. Boston: Houghton Mifflin Company, 1952.

Dean, Frank E. *Will Rogers' Rope Tricks*. Colorado Springs, Colo.: The Western Horseman, 1969.

De Yong, Joe. *Friend Will*. Santa Barbara, Calif.: The Schnauer Printing Studio, 1936.

Director, Cyr Vita. *I Loved Him Too: An Interpretive Poem in Memory of Will Rogers*. Los Angeles: The Book Ranch, 1936.

Eastman, Max. *The Enjoyment of Laughter*. New York: Simon and Schuster, 1936.

Everson, William K. *American Silent Film*. New York: Oxford University Press, 1978.

Fiebleman, James. *In Praise of Comedy*. New York: Macmillan, 1946.

Garst, Doris Shannon. *Will Rogers, Immortal Cowboy*. New York: Julian Messner, 1950.

Gibson, Arrell Morgan, ed. *Will Rogers: A Centennial Tribute*. Vol. XII of the Oklahoma Series. Oklahoma City, Okla.: Oklahoma Historical Society, 1979.

Goldwyn, Samuel. *Behind the Screen*. New York: Doran, 1923.

Hagedorn, H. "Will Rogers." *Americans: A Book of Lives*. New York: John Day Company, 1956.

Haggard, Ella Dixon. *Will Rogers and Thoughts*. Knoxville, Tenn.: Archer Printing Company, 1940.

Hatch, Arthur Martin. *Will Rogers, Cadet: A Record of His Two Years as a Cadet at the Kemper Military School, Boonville, Missouri.* Boonville, Mo.: Kemper Military School, 1935.

Hays, Will. *The Memoirs of Will H. Hays.* New York: Doubleday and Company, 1955.

Hoig, Stan. *The Humor of the American Cowboy.* New York: Signet Books, 1960.

Hoover, Irwin Hood. *Forty-two Years in the White House.* Boston: Houghton Mifflin Company, 1934.

Hughes, Elenor. *Famous Stars of Filmdom: Men.* Boston: L. C. Page and Company, 1932.

Hunt, Rockwell D. *California's Stately Hall of Fame.* California Historical Foundation Publication No. 2. Stockton, Calif.: College of the Pacific, 1950.

Jacobs, Lewis. *The Rise of American Film;* 1939 Rpt. New York: New York Teachers College Press, 1969.

Johnson, Spencer. *The Value of Humor: The Story of Will Rogers.* Value Tales Series. San Diego: Value Communications, 1976.

Kaho, Noel. *The Will Rogers Country.* 1st ed. Norman: University of Oklahoma Press, 1941; 2d ed. Claremore, Okla.: Noel Kaho Company, 1950.

Karsner, David. *Sixteen Authors to One.* New York: Lewis Copeland Company, 1928.

Keith, Harold. *Boy's Life of Will Rogers.* New York: Thomas Y. Crowell Company, 1937.

Ketchum, Richard M. *Will Rogers: His Life and Times.* An American Heritage Biography. New York: Simon and Schuster, 1973.

Lahue, Kalton C. *World of Laughter.* Norman: University of Oklahoma Press, 1966.

Lait, Jack. *Our Will Rogers.* New York: Greenberg, 1935.

Laurie, Joe, Jr. *Vaudeville: From the Honky-Tonks to the Palace.* New York: Holt, 1953.

Lee, Josh. "Eulogy to Will Rogers." In *New Declamations by Boone.* Lester, comp. New York: Noble, 1943.

_____. "Eulogy to Will Rogers." In *One Hundred New Declamations by Boone.* Lester, comp. New York: Noble, 1936.

Lewin, Leonard C., ed. *A Treasury of American Political Humor.* New York: Dial Press, 1964.

Love, Paula McSpadden, comp. *The Will Rogers Book.* 1st ed. New York and Indianapolis: Bobbs-Merrill, 1961; 2d ed. Waco, Tex.: Texian Press, 1972.

Lyle, Guy R., and Kevin Guinagh, eds. *I Am Happy to Present.* New York: H. W. Wilson Company, 1953.

Milam, Irene McSpadden. *Will Rogers As I Knew Him.* Claremore, Okla.: n.p., 1935.

Mills, Stephen E., and James W. Phillips. *Sourdough Sky.* Seattle, Wash.: Superior Publishing Company, 1969.

Milsten, David Randolph. *An Appreciation of Will Rogers.* 1st ed. San Antonio, Tex.: Naylor Company, 1935; 2d ed. New York: Gordon Press, 1976.

_____. *The Cherokee Kid: Life of Will Rogers.* San Antonio, Tex.: Naylor Company, 1938.

Mohler, Stanley R., and Bobby H. Johnson. *Wiley Post, His Winnie Mae, and the World's First Pressure Suit.* Smithsonian Annals of Flight, No. 8. Washington, D.C.: Smithsonian Institution Press, 1971.

Montgomery, Elizabeth Rider. *Will Rogers, Cowboy Philosopher*. All American Series. Champaign, Ill.: Garrard Publishing Company, 1970.

Morris, Lerona Rosamond. *Oklahoma, Land of Opportunity*. Guthrie, Okla.: Cooperative Publishing Company, 1934.

Mulligan, John Thomas. *Draft Will Rogers for President of the United States*. Spokane, Wash.: American Age Publishing Company, 1931.

Musso, Louis. *Will Rogers, America's Cowboy Philosopher*. Outstanding Personalities Series. New York: Sam Har Press, 1974.

Nathan, Neil. *Will Rogers Speaks*. Los Angeles: Devores and Company, n.d.

O'Brien, P. J. *Will Rogers, Ambassador of Good Will, Prince of Wit and Wisdom*. Philadelphia: John C. Winston Company, 1935.

Payne, William Howard, and Jake G. Lyons, eds. *Folks Say of Will Rogers: A Memorial Anecdotage*. New York: G. P. Putnam's Sons, 1936.

Pickard, Roy. "Will Rogers." *Who Played Who in the Movies: An A-Z*. London: Frederick Muller Ltd., 1979.

Ragan, David. "Will Rogers." *Who's Who in Hollywood 1900-1976*. New Rochelle, N.Y.: Arlington House, 1976.

Reeves, Frank, Sr. *A Century of Texas Cattle Brands*. Fort Worth, Tex.: n.p., 1936.

Richards, Kenneth G. *Will Rogers*. People of Destiny Series. Chicago: Children's Press, 1968.

Robinson, W. W. *Beverly Hills*. Los Angeles: n.p., 1938.

Rogers, Betty. *Will Rogers: His Wife's Story*. 1st ed. Indianapolis: Bobbs-Merrill, 1941; 2d ed. Norman, Okla.: University of Oklahoma Press, 1979.

———. *Will Rogers: The Story of His Life Told by His Wife*. Garden City, N.Y.: Garden City Publishers, 1943.

Rowland, Lloyd. *Will Rogers*. Tulsa, Okla.: Paul E. Corrubia, 1940.

Russell, Charles M. *Trails Plowed Under*. New York: Doubleday and Company, 1927.

Staples, Betty. *Will Rogers, Cowboy Humorist*. When They Were Young Series. Ed. A. Howard White. Columbus, Ohio: Better Books Press, 1931.

Starr, Harris E., ed. *Dictionary of American Biography*. Vol. 2. New York: Scribners, 1944; Supplement I. New York: Scribners, 1946.

Sterling, Bryan B., ed. *The Best of Will Rogers*. New York: Crown Publishers, 1979.

———. *The Will Rogers Scrapbook*. New York: Grosset and Dunlap, 1976.

———, and Frances N. Sterling, eds. *A Will Rogers Treasury*. New York: Crown Publishers, 1982.

Tandy, Jeannette. *Crackerbox Philosophers in American Humor and Satire*. New York: Columbia University Press, 1925.

Thomas, Henry, and Dana Lee Thomas. *Fifty Great Americans*. Garden City, N.Y.: Doubleday and Company, 1948.

Thomson, David. "Will Rogers." *A Biographical Dictionary of Film*. 2d ed. revised. New York: William Morrow and Company, 1981.

Trent, Spi M. *My Cousin Will Rogers*. 1st ed. New York: G. P. Putnam's Sons, 1938; 2d ed. New York: G. P. Putnam's Sons, 1958.

Tully, Jim. "Tom Mix and Will Rogers: Oklahoma's Most Famous Cowboys." In *Oklahoma, Yesterday-Today-Tomorrow*. Ed. Lerona Rosamond Morris. Guthrie, Okla.: Cooperative Publishing Company, 1931.

Van Riper, Guernsey, Jr. *Will Rogers: Young Cowboy*. Indianapolis: Bobbs-Merrill Company, 1951.

Wagner, Charles. *Will Rogers Leans on a Piano.* New York: G. P. Putnam's Sons, 1940.
West, C. W. "Dub." *Will Rogers—Oklahoma's Gift to America.* Muskogee, Okla.: Muskogee Publishing Company, 1979.
Wilson, Leland. *The Will Rogers Touch.* Elgin, Ill.: Brethern Press, 1979.
Wortman, Art. *Will Rogers: Wise and Witty Sayings of a Great American Humorist.* Kansas City: Hallmark, 1969.
Yates, Norris W. *The American Humorist, Conscience of the Twentieth Century.* Ames, Iowa: Iowa State University Press, 1964.

Articles, Chapters, and Reviews

This list of articles, chapters, and reviews attempts to be as complete as possible, even though some entries can be rendered only partially. Some time around 1968, the scrapbooks and some manuscript files at the Will Rogers Memorial were microfilmed. A copy of the microfilm is at Oklahoma State University, Special Collections Division, Edmon Low Library. To help researchers, articles that appear on the microfilm are referenced by scrapbook and microfilm reel number. For example, the George Matthew Adams review of Betty Rogers' biography in Book Review Scrapbook 23 is on Microfilm Reel 12, and, at least in this case, full bibliographical data exist. On the other hand, the two additional entries by G. M. Adams are in Feature Article Scrapbook 2 and on Microfilm Reel 11, but little or no bibliographical data exist for these documents. Unfortunately, there are many articles in this checklist for which little bibliographical data exist other than that they are clippings at the Will Rogers Memorial—which is obviously a necessary stop for serious scholars of the life and times of Will Rogers.

Adams, F. P. "Book Review." *New York World,* October 31, 1926, p. 11.
Adams, George Matthew. "Will Rogers." Review of *Will Rogers, His Wife's Story,* by Betty Rogers. *Worcester (Mass.) Gazette,* December 2, 1941, n.p.; *Birmingham (Alabama) Age Herald,* December 2, 1941, n.p. (Book Review Scrapbook 23; Microfilm Reel 12.)
_____. "Will Rogers—Great American." Periodical unknown, August 8, 1952, n.p. (Feature Article Scrapbook 2; Microfilm Reel 11.)
_____. "Will Rogers—A Missed American." Periodical unknown, n.d., n.p. (Feature Article Scrapbook 2; Microfilm Reel 11.)
"American Heritage to Publish First Authorized Biography of Will Rogers." *Publisher's Weekly,* July 31, 1972, p. 57.
Amory, Cleveland. "America's Most Complete Human Document." *Saturday Review of Literature,* August 25, 1962, p. 14.
_____. Review of *Will Rogers* by Donald Day. *Saturday Review,* August 25, 1962, pp. 14-15.
Anderson, LaVere. "Under the Reading Lamp." Review of *The Autobiography of Will Rogers,* ed. by Donald Day. Periodical unknown, n.d., n.p. (Book Review Scrapbook 23; Microfilm Reel 12.)
Arnold, Oren. " . . . Only One Will Rogers." *Empire Magazine* 14 (July 1955): 6-7. (Magazine Article Scrapbook 3; Microfilm Reel 10.)
Bailey, Paul. "Rogers, Stone, and Bailey." *Long Island Forum,* May 1960, pp. 99-100, 116-117.

Barketter, K. "I'll Be at Doc Law's." *Photoplay,* January 2, 1934, p. 31.

Barnett, Victor F. "Claremore Days with Will Rogers." *Radio Digest,* August 1930, pp. 14–16, 89–90.

Beach, Rex. "Rogers' Visit to Alaska Pleased Old Sourdoughs." *The Denver Rocky Mountain News,* n.d., n.p. (Feature Article Scrapbook 2; Microfilm Reel 11.)

_____. "We Laughed at Will's Jokes; Today in Alaska We Mourn." (Fairbanks) Associated Press, 1935. (Feature Article Scrapbook 2; Microfilm Reel 11.)

Beatty, Jerome. "Betty Holds the Reins." *American Magazine,* October 1930, pp. 60–62, 113–114. (Magazine Article Scrapbook 3; Microfilm Reel 10.)

_____. "King Babbit's Court Jester." *Outlook,* April 8, 1931, pp. 496–498.

Bell, Brian. "Actor's Lack of Affectation and Tricks of Temperament Added to Esteem by Friends." (Los Angeles) Associated Press, August 16, 1935, n.p. (Feature Article Scrapbook 2; Microfilm Reel 11.)

_____. "Will Rogers Rises from Cowboy in Oklahoma to Become Famous Throughout World as Comedian." (Los Angeles) Associated Press, August 16, 1935. (Feature Article Scrapbook 2; Microfilm Reel 11.)

Bester, A. "Plain Old Will Rogers Jr." *Holiday,* December 20, 1956, pp. 143, 168–170, 172. (Magazine Article Scrapbook 1; Microfilm Reel 10.)

"A Biography to Enjoy." Review of *Our Will Rogers,* by Homer Croy. *New York Times Book Review,* October 11, 1953, sec. VII, p. 3. (Book Review Scrapbook 23; Microfilm Reel 12.)

Blair, Walter. Review of *Imagemaker: Will Rogers and the American Dream,* by William Richard Brown. *American Literature* 42 (1971): 470–471.

Blanchard, Edwin. "Book Review." *New York Sun,* May 28, 1927, n.p.

Blow, Joe. "Places I Go and Folks I Know." *The Ranchman,* November 1942, p. 22. (Magazine Article Scrapbook 3; Microfilm Reel 10.)

"The Bookshelf: Philosopher-Humorist." *Christian Science Monitor* 23, December 1941, p. 14.

Boone, Andrew R. "Southern Personalities." *Holland's Magazine,* June 1933, n.p. (Feature Article Scrapbook 2; Microfilm Reel 12.)

Branch, Douglas. "The First American Cowboys." *Oklahoma Yesterday-Today-Tomorrow.* Ed. Lerona Rosamond Morris. Guthrie, Okla.: Cooperative Publishing Company, 1930, pp. 659–664.

Brehm, H. M. "Will Rogers: 1879-1935." *Linn's Weekly Stamp News,* October 18, 1948, n.p. (Featured Article Scrapbook 2; Microfilm Reel 12.)

Bridges, S. Russell, and K. Singer. "I Managed Presidents." *South Atlantic Quarterly* 50 (1951): 313–314.

Brown, Edgar. "Bering Recalls Will Rogers' Kindness and Human Qualities." Periodical unknown, n.d., n.p. (Feature Article Scrapbook 2; Microfilm Reel 12.)

Brown, William R. "Will Rogers and His Magic Mirror." *The Chronicles of Oklahoma* 52 (1979): 300–325.

_____. "Will Rogers: Ironist as Persuader." *Speech Monographs* 39 (1972): 183–192.

Bruce, Horace V. "A Vote for Will Rogers." *Life,* June 28, 1928, p. 35.

Buford, C. C. "Bookworm Trail." Review of *Will Rogers, His Wife's Story,* by Betty Rogers. *Champaign* (Ill.) *News Gazette,* December 7, 1941, n.p. (Book Review Scrapbook 23; Microfilm Reel 12.)

Bush, T. Review of *Will Rogers: The Man and His Times,* by Richard M. Ketchum. *Retirement Living,* March 14, 1974, p. 55.

Butler, Bill. "The Bunkless Candidate." *Tulsa World Magazine,* July 12, 1959, pp. 20–21.

_____. "A Cowboy and His Castle." *Tulsa Sunday World Magazine,* November 4, 1956, p. 21.

Butterfield, Roger. "The Legend of Will Rogers." *Life,* July 18, 1949, pp. 78–94; *Readers' Digest,* November 1949, pp. 31–36.

Cadenhead, Ivie E., Jr. "Will Rogers: Forgotten Man." *Midcontinent American Studies Journal* 4 (1963): 51–57.

_____. "Will Rogers: Good Neighbor." *The Chronicles of Oklahoma* 38 (1960): 2–7.

Canby, Henry S. "Homespun Philosophers." *Saturday Review of Literature,* August 31, 1935, p. 8.

Cantor, Eddie. "Most Unforgettable Character I've Met." *Readers' Digest,* March 1960, pp. 179–184.

_____. "Now You Tell One." *Colliers,* December 24, 1927, pp. 13, 44.

Carter, John. "Will Rogers Takes His Lariat to Europe." *New York Times Book Review,* October 31, 1926, p. 2.

Cerf, Bennett. "He Made His Country Laugh." *Good Housekeeping,* November 1947, pp. 40–41, 215–218. (Feature Article Scrapbook 2; Microfilm Reel 12.)

"The Cherokee Kid." *The Indian Sign,* July-August 1955, pp. 1–4. (Magazine Article Scrapbook 3; Microfilm Reel 10.)

Christian, Mary Bazarth. "Will Rogers Spoke a Timely Word." *The Ranchman,* November 1942, pp. 13, 23–24. (Magazine Article Scrapbook 3; Microfilm Reel 10 and Feature Article Scrapbook 2; Microfilm Reel 12.)

"Chromosomes and Men." *Politics,* n.d., n.p. (Magazine Article Scrapbook 1; Microfilm Reel 10.)

Clancy, Carl Stearns. "Aviation's Patron Saint." *Scientific American,* October 1929, pp. 283–286.

Clark, Blue. "The Literary Will Rogers." *The Chronicles of Oklahoma* 57 (1979): 385–394.

_____. "The Literary Will Rogers." In *Will Rogers: A Centennial Tribute.* Ed. Arrell Morgan Gibson. Oklahoma Series 12. Oklahoma City: Oklahoma Historical Society, 1980, pp. 133–142.

Clark, C. Review of *Will Rogers,* by R. M. Ketchum. *Time,* December 24, 1973, p. 79.

Clark, Lois Carter. "The Will Rogers Memorial at Claremore, Oklahoma." *Antique Trader Weekly,* March 29, 1979, pp. 78–81.

"Clown Becomes a Nuisance." *America,* October 22, 1932, p. 55.

Clurman, H. "Theatre: J. Whitmore's One-Man Show." *The Nation* 25 (May 1974): 666–667.

Cobb, Irvin S. "Another Will Rogers." *Photoplay,* March 4, 1935, p. 34.

_____. "Cobb Praises Unselfish Character of Humorist." North American Newspaper Alliance, n.d. (Feature Article Scrapbook 2; Microfilm Reel 12.)

_____. "Observation." *Los Angeles Times,* August 26, 1936, n.p. (Feature Article Scrapbook 2; Microfilm Reel 12.)

_____. "One Who Being Dead Yet Lives." Periodical unknown, July 8, 1940, n.p. (Feature Article Scrapbook 2; Microfilm Reel 12.)

_____. "We May Not Git Together for Quite a Spell." North American Newspaper Alliance, 1935. (Feature Article Scrapbook 2; Microfilm Reel 12.)

Collins, Charles. "Will Rogers, the Cowboy Humorist—His Life Story." *Chicago Tribune,* August 18, 1935; August 21, 1935, n.p.

Collins, Reba. "A Will Rogers' Eye View of Oklahoma." *Oklahoma Today,* Autumn 1972, pp. 17-21.

_____. "Will Rogers: Part I." *Oklahoma Today,* Winter 1978-1979, pp. 6-9.

_____. "Will Took Pride in Oklahoma." *Oklahoma's Orbit,* November 1967, pp. 5-7.

Congressional Record. Vol. 69. Remarks in House concerning Will Rogers, pp. 1198, 1323.

_____. Vol. 74. "Will Rogers" (poem) by Ignatius Murphy, p. 6833.

Remarks in House relative to the radio appeal for contributions to the Red Cross made by Will Rogers, p. 2988.

Resolution passed by Voiture, p. 1082; Forty and Eight, Fort Smith, Arkansas, paying tribute to drought relief work of Will Rogers, p. 4712.

_____. Vol. 79. (Responses to death of Will Rogers.) Address over the radio delivered by Senator Gore on the death of Will Rogers, p. 14438.

Address delivered by Representative Lee of Oklahoma in memory of Will Rogers, p. 14779.

Address over the radio delivered by Rep. Nichols in Memory of Will Rogers, p. 13442.

Bill to authorize the interment in the Arlington National Cemetery of the remains of the late Will Rogers (see Bill S. 3436).

Editorials appearing in the *Wilmington (N.C.) Star-News* relative to the proposed erection of a memorial to—p. 13619.

Joint resolution for the coinage of a medal in commemoration of the achievements of—(see H. J. Res. 385).

Joint resolution authorizing the issuance of a special postage stamp in honor of—(see H. J. Res. 393).

Joint resolution designating United States Highway No. 66 the Will Rogers Highway (see H. J. Res. 395).

Joint resolution to erect a memorial in the District of Columbia to—(see H. J. Res. 397).

Joint resolution to create the Will Rogers student-aid fund (see H. J. Res. 404).

Poem by Waldo Wettengel relative to—p. 14574.

Remarks in House and Senate on the death of—pp. 13333, 13360, 13430, 13441, 14137, 14393.

Statement on the subject of the World Court submitted by—p. 686.

Statement in the *New York Times* relative to Senator Long and the Share-our-wealth movement written by—p. 9907.

Statement by Stanley R. Morgan relative to the airplane crash which resulted in the death of—p. 13943.

Telegram from Senator McAdoo to A. A. Cohn, Los Angeles, California on the death of—p. 14043.

_____, U.S. House of Representatives. "Acceptance of the Statue of Will Rogers. Presented by the State of Oklahoma. Proceedings in the Congress and in the Rotunda, U.S. Capitol." 16th Congress, 1st session, June 6, 1939.

Cooke, Alistair. "The Great Actor Myth." *The Listener,* September 25, 1935, p. 529.

_____. "Will Rogers." *Auslese,* August 1950, pp. 36–44. (Magazine Article Scrapbook 3; Microfilm Reel 10.)

Coolidge, Archibald D. "A Self-appointed Diplomat." *Saturday Review of Literature,* December 25, 1925, p. 465.

"Cowboy Clown." Review of *My Cousin Will Rogers,* by Spi M. Trent. Periodical unknown, n.d., n.p. (Book Review Scrapbook 23; Microfilm Reel 12.)

"The Cowboy Philosopher." *New Republic,* August 28, 1935, p. 62.

"A Cowboy Who Roped the Art of Being Funny." *Literary Digest,* November 15, 1919, pp. 60, 64. (Magazine Article Scrapbook 3; Microfilm Reel 11.)

Crawford, John. "Will Rogers Knows More Than He Pretends." Review of *The Illiterate Digest,* by Will Rogers. *New York Times Book Review,* December 14, 1924, p. 2. (Book Review Scrapbook 23; Microfilm Reel 12.)

Creel, George (The Gentleman at the Keyhole). "Will of the People." *Colliers,* July 4, 1931, p. 35.

Croy, Homer. "How Will Rogers Keeps Fit." *Physical Culture,* January 1934, pp. 14–15, 71–73. (Magazine Article Scrapbook 3; Microfilm Reel 10.)

_____. "I'll Always Remember the Words of Will Rogers." *Arkansas Gazette,* March 9, 1958, p. 2. (Magazine Article Scrapbook 3; Microfilm Reel 10.)

_____. "Will As I Knew Him." *Successful Farming,* January 1936, pp. 16, 24. (Magazine Article Scrapbook 3; Microfilm Reel 10.)

_____. "Will Rogers – Mystery Man of Radio." *Radioland,* February 1935, pp. 12–13, 94–95.

_____. "Will Rogers of the Movies." *Oklahoma Today,* Winter 1960, pp. 4–5, 32–33

Culver, D. J. "The Humor of Will Rogers." *The Dearborn Independent,* March 28, 1925, pp. 5, 15. (Magazine Article Scrapbook 3; Microfilm Reel 10.)

Davis, Herndon. "Claremore Remembers Will." Review of *The Autobiography of Will Rogers,* ed. by Donald Day. *Rocky Mountain Empire Magazine,* December 4, 1949, pp. 2–3. (Book Review Scrapbook 23; Microfilm Reel 12.)

Day, Donald. "Will Rogers." In *This I Believe,* by Edward R. Murrow. Vol. 2. New York: Simon and Schuster, 1954, pp. 219–221.

Deason, J. D. "From Me to You." Review of *Will Rogers, His Wife's Story,* by Betty Rogers. *Seminole* (Okla.) *Producer,* November 12, 1941, n.p. (Book Review Scrapbook 23; Microfilm Reel 12.)

"Death in the Arctic." *Time,* August 26, 1935, pp. 32–35.

Debus, Allen G. "The Recordings of Will Rogers." *Hobbies,* January 11, 1956, pp. 30, 35.

DeYong, Joe. "Bootlegger – One of the Best." *Western Horseman,* January 1949, pp. 42–46.

Dix, Dorothy. "New Orleans Greeting to Will Rogers." *The Southern Plumber,* June 20, 1927, n.p.

"Dorothy Stone Recalls Rogers' Cowboy Days." International News Service, 1935, n.p. (Feature Article Scrapbook 2; Microfilm Reel 12.)

Doyle, Thomas H. "Address." *The Chronicles of Oklahoma* 16 (1938): 52–57.

Eitner, Walter. "Will Rogers: Another Look at His Act." *Kansas Quarterly* 2 (1970): 46–52.

"Etiquette, As Lassoed by Will Rogers." *Literary Digest,* October 6, 1923, pp. 46–50.

Evans, Charles. "Two Oklahomans Honored." *The Chronicles of Oklahoma* 29 (1951): 4–23.

Evans, Harry. "Reminiscences About Will Rogers." *Family Circle,* October 1935, pp. 20–21. (In Box 3-D at Memorial, Claremore, Oklahoma; also Magazine Article Scrapbook 3; Microfilm Reel 10.)

"Fame's Favorite A&M." *Oklahoma A&M College Magazine,* October 1951, pp. 22–23. (Magazine Article Scrapbook 3; Microfilm Reel 10.)

Ferguson, Otis. "Two Show Figures." *New Republic,* September 4, 1935, p. 104.

Flaherty, D. C. "The Will Rogers Story." *The Blue Book,* October n.d., pp. 34–41. (Magazine Article Scrapbook 3; Microfilm Reel 10.)

Ford, Daniel S. "Remembering Will Rogers: Outtakes from the Life of an Actor." *Mankind: The Magazine of Popular History,* February 1978, pp. 14–18.

"Fort Worth Unveils Will Rogers Statue." *American City,* December 1947, p. 62.

Franks, Kenny A. Review of *There's Not a Bathing Suit in Russia and Other Bare Facts,* by Will Rogers. Ed. Joseph A. Stout, Jr. *The Chronicles of Oklahoma* 52 (1974): 383–384.

Freeman, Irene Felker. "The Marriage of Betty Blake and Will Rogers." *The Ranchman,* November 1941, p. 10. (Magazine Article Scrapbook 3; Microfilm Reels 11 and 12.)

Fry, Culver Maggie. "Will Rogers Country." *Oklahoma Today,* Spring 1964, pp. 30–33.

Gibson, Arrell Morgan. "Will Rogers: An Introduction." *The Chronicles of Oklahoma* 57 (1979): 255–258.

Gill, B. "Theatre: J. Whitmore's One-Man Show." *The New Yorker,* May 20, 1974, p. 50.

Golden, Sylvia A. "Will Rogers — Business." *Forbes,* February 15, 1928, n.p. (Feature Article Scrapbook 2; Microfilm Reel 12.)

Goodwin, Vergie. "Lover of Life — Will Rogers." Periodical unknown, 1951, n.p. (Feature Article Scrapbook 2; Microfilm Reel 12.)

"The Gossip Shop." *Bookman,* November–December 1919, pp. 3–4.

Guiterman, Arthur. "Will Rogers" (poem). *Life,* November 2, 1928, p. 23. (Magazine Article Scrapbook 3; Microfilm Reel 10.)

Harrison, Walter M. "Barnstorming with Will Rogers." *Me and My Big Mouth.* Oklahoma City: Britton Printing Company, 1954, pp. 167–170.

Hart, William S. "As One Cowpuncher to Another." *Life,* June 28, 1928, p. 38. (Magazine Article Scrapbook 3; Microfilm Reel 10.)

Hartt, Rollin Lynde. "Roping Will Rogers." *Everybody's,* June 1925, pp. 34–35, 164–168.

Herald, Don. "Review of *Illiterate Digest.*" *New York Herald Tribune.* March 1, 1925, n.p.

Hewes, H. "Theater: Re-Creation of a Chautauqua Performance by J. Whitmore." *Saturday Review,* October 10, 1970, p. 19.

Hildreth, Reed C. "U.S.S. Will Rogers." *Oklahoma Today,* Autumn 1968, pp. 14–16.

"Homespun Philosophers." *Saturday Review of Literature,* August 31, 1935, p. 8.

Hout, A. P. "Little Human Happiness." Excerpt from *The Lion. Readers' Digest,* October 2, year unknown, pp. 121–122.

Howden, Benjamin. "Will Rogers' Philosophy Told in Book by Wife." Review of *Will Rogers, His Wife's Story,* by Betty Rogers. *Los Angeles Times,* December 7, 1941, n.p. (Book Review Scrapbook 23; Microfilm Reel 12.)

Hughes, Elizabeth. "Let's Talk About Books." Review of *My Cousin Will Rogers,* by Spi M. Trent. Periodical unknown, n.d., n.p. (Book Review Scrapbook 23; Microfilm Reel 12.)

Hurd, Myron A. "Old Timers of the Will Rogers Country." *The Ranchman,* November 1959, pp. 38–41. (Magazine Article Scrapbook 3; Microfilm Reel 10.)

———. "Will Rogers' Brand of Citizenship." *The Ranchman,* November 1953, pp. 32–34. (Magazine Article Scrapbook 3; Microfilm Reel 10.)

"I Never Met A Man I Didn't Like." *Senior Scholastic,* November 4, 1966, p. 3.

"The Incomparable Will Rogers." *The Indiana Freemason,* October 1958, pp. 4–7, 20–32. (Magazine Article Scrapbook 3; Microfilm Reel 11.)

Jackson, James G. "More on Will Rogers." *The Western Horseman,* January 1980, pp. 6–8.

Jacobs, Mary. "Hidden Sacrifices of Will Rogers." *The Oklahoma Meter,* n.d., pp. 22–23, 82. (Magazine Article Scrapbook 3; Microfilm Reel 10.)

James, Robert. "The Most Popular Man in the United States." Periodical unknown, n.d., n.p. (Feature Article Scrapbook 2; Microfilm Reel 12.)

Janis, Elsie. "What I Know About Will Rogers." *Liberty,* March 11, 1933, pp. 32–34. (In Box 3-D at Memorial, Claremore, Oklahoma.)

Jaspersen, Ronald. "I Never Met a Man I Didn't Like." Periodical unknown, July 3, 1953, pp. 23–25. (Magazine Article Scrapbook 3; Microfilm Reel 10.)

"Joel McCrea Visits Oklahoma; Recalls Friendship with Beloved Will Rogers." *Boxoffice,* September 25, 1978, pp. 1–3.

Johnson, B. H. Review of *Will Rogers, His Wife's Story,* by Betty Blake Rogers. *Arizona and the West—A Journal of History* 23 (1981): 69–70.

Jones, Alfred Haworth. "The Year Will Rogers Ran for President." *The Chronicles of Oklahoma* 50 (1972): 2–11.

"Kaho's *Will Rogers Country* Is Released." Periodical unknown, n.d., n.p. (Book Review Scrapbook 23; Microfilm Reel 12.)

Karsner, David. "A Writer Who Knows the Ropes." *The Tulsa Daily World Sunday Magazine,* November 27, 1927, p. 7. (Scrapbook 2; Microfilm Reels 11–12.)

Kent, G. "The Mammy and Daddy of Us All." *Photoplay,* May 6, 1934, p. 32.

Ketcham, George. "Oklahoma Needs a Will Rogers Day." *The Oklahoma Roundup,* June 1946, pp. 2–3. (Magazine Article Scrapbook 3; Microfilm Reel 10.)

Ketchum, Richard M. "Will Rogers." *The Atlantic Monthly,* November 1973, p. 122.

———. "Will Rogers: The Man and His Times." *Retirement Living,* March 1974, p. 55.

"The Kindly Philosopher." *Everybody's,* February 10, 1945, p. 6. (Magazine Article Scrapbook 3; Microfilm Reel 10.)

King, Ferne E. "A Message to Will Rogers." Periodical unknown, November 1953, p. 4. (Magazine Article Scrapbook 3; Microfilm Reel 10.)

"King Will." *Commonweal,* December 14, 1932, p. 173.

Klapp, Orrin Edgar. "The Clever Hero." *Journal of American Folklore* 67 (1954): 21–34.

Kraemer, Sandy F. "Will Rogers—The Legal Profession's Best Critic." *American Bar Association Journal* 59 (1973): 1431–1433.

Lait, Jack. "The Will Rogers Book." Review of *Will Rogers, His Wife's Story,* by Betty Rogers. *Sunday Mirror Magazine,* November 23, 1941, pp. 16–17. (Book Review Scrapbook 23; Microfilm Reel 12.)

Landry, R. "Will Rogers: Folk Hero." *Variety,* January 16, 1974, p. 20.

Lang, Harry. "Money Is No Joke." Periodical unknown, n.d., pp. 54–84. (Feature Article Scrapbook 2; Microfilm Reel 12.)

Lardner, Ring. "With Hope and Gum; or, Up from the Ranch." *Colliers,* February 2, 1929, pp. 13, 43.

"Last Film Role As Trainer in *In Old Kentucky.*" *Literary Digest,* August 24, 1935, p. 8; November 30, 1935, p. 24.

Laughlin, E. O. "A Knight of Today." *Literary Digest,* July 9, 1932, p. 38.

"Laughter Never Dies." *Coronet,* February 1942, n.p. (Magazine Article Scrapbook 3; Microfilm Reel 10.)

Lee, Josh. "Eulogy to Will Rogers." *Southern Magazine,* August–September 1935, pp. 30 + .

Lester, Patricia. Review of *Ether and Me or Just Relax,* by Will Rogers. Ed. Joseph A. Stout, Jr. *The Chronicles of Oklahoma* 51 (1973): 365.

_____. Review of *Wiley Post, His Winnie Mae, and The World's First Pressure Suit,* by Stanley R. Mohler and Bobby H. Johnson. *The Chronicles of Oklahoma* 50 (1972): 237–239.

Lewis, R. J., Jr. "Speaking of Books." Review of *Will Rogers, His Wife's Story,* by Betty Rogers. *Albany* (New York) *Times Union,* November 26, 1941, n.p.; *New York American,* December 3, 1941, n.p. (Book Review Scrapbook 23; Microfilm Reel 12.)

"The Life of Will Rogers." *Oklahoma State Alumnus,* February 1968, pp. 5–11.

"Like Father, Like Son." *Coronet,* February 1951, p. 117.

"Lindbergh's Embassy of Good Will to Mexico." *Literary Digest,* December 1927, pp. 1, 4. (Magazine Article Scrapbook 3; Microfilm Reel 10.)

Lindsey, Ben. "Will Rogers for President: A Keynote Speech." *Life,* May 24, 1928, p. 4.

Lipman, Jerry. "The Printer Learned from Will." *Oklahoma's Orbit,* August 5, 1975, p. 2.

Little, Walter. "Glimpses of Interesting Americans: Will Rogers." *Century Magazine,* June 1925, pp. 305–320.

Lobdell, Charles W. "Will Rogers, the World Laughs with Him." *Liberty,* Winter 1972, pp. 50–52; reprinted from *Liberty,* November 29, 1924. (Magazine Article Scrapbook 3; Microfilm Reel 10.)

Love, Paula McSpadden. "The Best of Will Rogers." *Oklahoma Today,* Fall 1959, pp. 26–27.

_____. "The Statue of Will Rogers." *The Chronicles of Oklahoma* 17 (1939): 336–340.

_____. "The Will Rogers Memorial." *The Chronicles of Oklahoma* 20 (1942): 404–406.

_____. "The Will Rogers Memorial." *The Ranchman,* November 1941, pp. 21–22. (Magazine Article Scrapbook 3; Microfilm Reel 11.)

_____. "Will Rogers' Saddles." *The Western Horseman,* May 5, 1953, pp. 65–69. (Magazine Article Scrapbook 3; Microfilm Reel 10.)

Lyttleton, Edith. "Letter to the Editor." *Spectator,* August 23, 1935, p. 293.

McAllister, Sue. "Will Rogers: His Impact! His Philosophy! His Life!" *Oklahoma State Alumnus,* January 1971, pp. 4–9.

McCleneghan, Lew. "Will Rogers Tried—But Echo Lost." Review of *Our Will Rogers,* by Homer Croy. *Tucson (Ariz.) Citizen,* December 5, 1953, n.p. (Book Review Scrapbook 23; Microfilm Reel 12.)

McClusky, Thorp. "Will Rogers, Showman." *Sir,* October 25, 1949, pp. 21-23, 60-61. (Feature Article Scrapbook 2; Microfilm Reel 12.)

McCord, David. "Review of *Illiterate Digest.*" *Saturday Review of Literature,* February 21, 1925, p. 540.

McCrea, Joel. "My Friend Will Rogers." *Persimmon Hill,* Fall 1970, pp. 3-7.

McDavid, Mittie Owen. "The Indian in That Irish-Cherokee Will Rogers." *Southern Literary Messenger* 2 (1940): 291-295.

McIntyre, O. O. "Fly On, Will Rogers." McNaught Syndicate, 1935. (Feature Article Scrapbook 2; Microfilm Reel 12.)

_____. "Our Will." *Cosmopolitan Magazine,* October 1931, pp. 82-83. (Magazine Article Scrapbook 3; Microfilm Reel 10.)

MacNeil, N. "Old Cowhand: Will Rogers' U.S.A. at Washington's Ford Theatre." *Time,* September 28, 1970, p. 76.

McSpadden, Herb. "Horses and Horse Collars." *The Ranchman,* November 1942, pp. 11-12. (Magazine Article Scrapbook 3; Microfilm Reel 11 and Feature Article Scrapbook 2; Microfilm Reel 12.)

_____. "Just Restin' Awhile." *The Ranchman,* November 1941, pp. 3-5. (Magazine Article Scrapbook 3; Microfilm Reel 11.)

McSpadden, Sallie Rogers. "Sketch of the Early Life of Will Rogers." *The Ranchman,* November 1941, p. 7. (Magazine Article Scrapbook 3; Microfilm Reel 11.)

Mahaffey, J. Q. "How Will Rogers Changed My Life." *Readers' Digest,* August 1956, p. 143.

Maltz, Lawrence. "That Man: Will Rogers." *Progressive Life,* September 1973, pp. 9-17.

Marquis, Arnold. "What This Country Needs Is Another Will Rogers." *Tulsa,* April 1970, pp. 22-34.

Martin, George. "Wit of Will Rogers: The Story of a Cowboy Who Has Become a Famous Comedian." *American Magazine,* November 1919, pp. 34-35, 106-110; also in *Literary Digest,* November 15, 1919, pp. 60-64.

Mayer, Arthur L. "Country Boy, With Rope, Who Got Along in the World." Review of *Our Will Rogers,* by Homer Croy. *New York Herald Tribune,* October 18, 1953, n.p. (Book Review Scrapbook 23; Microfilm Reel 12.)

Mayer, Edwin Justus. "Will Rogers." Periodical unknown, n.d., n.p. (Feature Article Scrapbook 2; Microfilm Reel 12.)

Meredith, H. L. "Beyond Humor: Will Rogers and Calvin Coolidge." *Vermont History* 60 (1972): 178-184.

_____. "Will Rogers' Roots." *The Chronicles of Oklahoma* 57 (1979): 259-265.

Metchalfe, L. "All Sweet and Pretty." *Photoplay,* July 2, 1919, p. 59.

"Miami? — Never Heard of It!" *The Miami Gondolier,* January 17, 1926. (On file at Will Rogers Memorial.)

Milsten, David. "Will Rogers." (2 articles.) *The Oklahoma Roundup,* June 1946, n.p. (Magazine Article Scrapbook 3; Microfilm Reel 10.)

"Minutes of Special Meeting of the Oklahoma Historical Society, at 2:15 PM February 13, 1938." *The Chronicles of Oklahoma* 16 (1938): 128-129.

"Miss Mary Rogers." *Beverly Hills Script,* June 15, 1929, pp. 25-26. (Magazine Article Scrapbook 3; Microfilm Reel 10.)

Mitchell, Ruth. "Saga of Billy Mitchell." *Reader's Digest Condensed Books.* Pleasantville, N.Y.: The Reader's Digest Association, May 1954, pp. 163–180. (Magazine Article Scrapbook 3; Microfilm Reel 10.)

Mok, Michael. "The Cowboy Ambassador." *New York Post,* August 17, 1935, n.p. (Feature Article Scrapbook 2; Microfilm Reel 12.)

Morse, Wilbur, Jr. "Will Rogers." *Nominating,* n.d., n.p. (Feature Article Scrapbook 2; Microfilm Reel 12.)

Moseley, Seth H. "The Will of the People; He Also Ran." *Oklahoma's Orbit,* April 6, 1978, pp. 3–4.

Myers, Debs. "Will Rogers' Home Town." *Holiday,* April 1951, pp. 72–90. (Magazine Article Scrapbook 3; Microfilm Reel 10.)

Nash, Ogden. "The Story of Will Rogers." Review of *Will Rogers, His Wife's Story,* by Betty Rogers. *New York Journal American,* November 30, 1941, n.p. (Book Review Scrapbook 23; Microfilm Reel 12.)

"Necrology." *The Biographical Encyclopedia & Who's Who of the American Theatre.* Ed. Walter Rigdon. New York: James H. Heinman, 1966.

Neill, Wilfred. "Will Rogers' Cherokee Nation." *Golden West,* July 1970, pp. 24–29.

"New *Ah Wilderness* Cast Headed by Will Rogers." *Newsweek,* May 12, 1934, p. 23.

Nicholson, Meredith. "Let's All Be Ourselves." *Rotarian,* November 1933, pp. 6–7.

"Obituary." *Illustration,* August 24, 1935, p. 555.

"Obituary." *Newsweek,* July 3, 1944, p. 58.

"Obituary." *Publisher's Weekly,* August 24, 1935, p. 514.

"On the Current Screen." *Literary Digest,* April 20, 1935, p. 34.

"One Spouse's Appraisal." Review of *Will Rogers, His Wife's Story,* by Betty Rogers. *Jacksonville* (Fla.) *Times Union,* November 23, 1941, n.p. (Book Review Scrapbook 23; Microfilm Reel 12.)

"An Optimist Tribute to Will Rogers." *The Optimist,* December 1953, pp. 6–8. (Magazine Article Scrapbook 3; Microfilm Reel 10.)

"Our Country Is Richer Because of Their Lives." *Instructor,* May 1950, p. 23.

"Our Cover Page." *The Ranchman,* November 1942, p. 2. (Magazine Article Scrapbook 3; Microfilm Reel 10.)

"Our Favorite Actor, No. 5." *Beverly Hills Script,* June 8, 1929, p. 4. (Magazine Article Scrapbook 3; Microfilm Reel 10.)

"Outstanding American Indian of 1960, Will Rogers, Jr." *American Indian Exposition,* Anadarko, Oklahoma, August 15-20, 1960, p. 5. (Magazine Article Scrapbook 1; Microfilm Reel 10.)

Parsons, Louella. "Like Son, Like Father." *Movie Citation,* n.d., pp. 15–16. (Magazine Article Scrapbook 1; Microfilm Reel 10.)

Patterson, Ada. "Via Long Distance." *Photoplay,* September 1921, pp. 35, 114. (In Box 3-D at Memorial, Claremore, Oklahoma. Magazine Article Scrapbook 3; Microfilm Reel 10.)

Peterson, Elmer T. "Will Rogers in His Garden." *Better Homes and Gardens,* June 1928, pp. 22–23. (In Box 3-D at Memorial, Claremore, Oklahoma. Feature Article Scrapbook 2; Microfilm Reel 12 and Magazine Article Scrapbook 3; Microfilm Reel 10.)

Pierce, Earl Boyd. Review of *Will Rogers—Oklahoma's Gift to America,* by C. W. "Dub" West. *The Chronicles of Oklahoma* 58 (1980): 115–117.

Pollock, Channing. "Our Follies—and Mr. Ziegfeld's." *The Green Book.* Ed. Ray Long. September 1918, n.p.

Poole, Francis. "Reminiscences of Will Rogers." *Oklahoma Today,* Autumn 1969, pp. 20–21.

Pope, Edwin. "For Meeshegan, y'know." *The Michigan Alumnus,* October 20, 1956, p. 27. (Magazine Article Scrapbook 3; Microfilm Reel 10.)

"Portrait." *Colliers,* June 5, 1926, p. 17; December 24, 1927, p. 13; April 7, 1928; and June 29, 1935.

"Portrait." *Current Opinion,* January 1925, p. 39.

"Portrait." *Ladies Home Journal,* October 1937, p. 53.

"Portrait." *Literary Digest,* April 11, 1925, p. 23; December 24, 1927; and May 4, 1929.

"Portrait." *National Education Association,* March 14, 1925, p. 101.

"Portrait." *Newsweek,* October 7, 1933, p. 9; and November 4, 1933, p. 6.

"Portrait." *Outlook,* June 3, 1931, p. 132.

"Portrait." *Radio Broadcast,* November 6, 1924, p. 39.

"Portrait." *Saturday Evening Post,* January 8, 1927, p. 14.

"Portrait." *Sunset,* January 1928, p. 41.

"Portrait." *Time,* November 4, 1935, p. 46.

"Prairie Pantaloon." *Time,* July 19, 1926, pp. 20–22. (Magazine Article Scrapbook 3; Microfilm Reel 10.)

Pringle, H. F. "King Babbit's Court Jester." *Outlook and Independent,* April 8, 1931, pp. 494–498.

Ratliffe, S. K. "Will Rogers – Philosopher-Humorist." *The Spectator,* August 23, 1935, pp. 287–288.

Raviner, R. "On the Set with Will Rogers." *Photoplay,* August 3, 1935, p. 36.

Ray, Ed. "Peddling Will Rogers' Body." *New Masses,* September 17, 1935, pp. 29–30. (In Box 3-D at Will Rogers Memorial.)

Rayburn, H. "Poet Lariat, Twenty Years After His Death." *The Gasser,* August 1955, pp. 16–21. (Magazine Article Scrapbook 3; Microfilm Reel 10.)

"Rebuke from Will Rogers." *Outlook and Independent,* June 3, 1931, p. 132.

Reese, James R. "The Low-down on Will Rogers." *Life,* June 12, 1928, n.p. ("Roses and Raspberries" Sect.)

Reid, Dorothy C. "In Miniature – Mrs. Will Rogers." *McCall's,* February 1929, pp. 8, 66.

_____. "Mrs. Will Rogers Talks About Her Husband." *Home Magazine,* September 1930, pp. 22–23, 128.

Reston, James B. "Broadway Loses a Friend." *Chattanooga Sunday Times,* August 25, 1935, n.p. (Feature Article Scrapbook 2; Microfilm Reel 12.)

Reynolds, Ruth. "How a Cowboy Talked His Way into History." *The Ranchman,* June 1958, n.p. (Magazine Article Scrapbook 3; Microfilm Reel 10.)

Riddell, John. "An Open Letter to Will Rogers." *Vanity Fair,* October 1929, p. 90.

Roach, Fred, Jr. "Vision of the Future: Will Rogers' Support of Commercial Aviation." *The Chronicles of Oklahoma* 57 (1979): 340–364.

_____. "Will Rogers' Youthful Relationship with His Father, Clem Rogers: A Story of Love and Tension." *The Chronicles of Oklahoma* 58 (1980): 325–342.

Robbins, L. H. "American Humorists." *New York Times Magazine,* September 8, 1933, pp. 8–9, 14.

_____. "Portrait of an American Philosopher." *New York Times Magazine,* November 3, 1935, pp. 4, 21.

Robbins, Peggy. "Will Rogers: The Immortal Cherokee Kid." *American History Illustrated,* July 1974, pp. 4–11.

Rogers, Betty Blake. "Uncle Clem's Boy." *Saturday Evening Post,* October 5, 1940, pp. 9–11, 118–120; October 12, 1940, pp. 28–29, 110–117; October 19, 1940, pp. 24–25, 62–70; October 26, 1940, pp. 26–27, 109–114; November 2, 1940, pp. 22–23, 74–78; November 9, 1940, pp. 24–25, 83–88; November 16, 1940, pp. 34–36, 82–88; November 30, 1940, pp. 24–25, 59–60.

"Rogers Conquered the World with Humor." *Literary Digest,* August 24, 1935, p. 8.

"Rogers' Fans Want Their Idol Kept Immortal on the Screen." *Newsweek,* September 14, 1935, p. 28.

"Rogers and Post." *Commonweal,* August 30, 1935, p. 416.

"Rogers' Thesaurus." *Saturday Review,* August 25, 1962, pp. 14–15.

"Rogers, Will." *Who Was Who in America: A Companion Volume to Who's Who in America.* Vol. 1. Chicago: A. N. Marquis Company, 1943.

Rogers, Will, Jr. "How I Discovered Dad." *Family Circle,* October 1956, pp. 44–45, 101.

_____. "How I Discovered Will Rogers." *This Week Magazine,* May 1956, pp. 7, 26, 42–43.

_____. "I Remember Dad." *Oklahoma Today,* July 1956, pp. 1–2.

_____. "Last Chance in Asia." *McClean's,* June 15, 1944, pp. 13, 22, 24, 26.

_____. "Starvation Without Representation." *Look,* March 10, 1948, pp. 36, 38, 40–41.

_____. "Will Rogers, Past, Present, and Future." *Guideposts,* July 1957, pp. cover, 2–5. (Magazine Article Scrapbook 1; Microfilm Reel 10.)

Rollins, Peter C. "The Context and Rhetorical Strategy of Will Rogers' *Letters from a Self-Made Diplomat to His President." Journal of American Culture* 3 (1980): 70–79.

_____. "The Evolving Career of Will Rogers." In *Rogersisms: The Cowboy Philosopher on Prohibition, The Writings of Will Rogers.* Ser. I, Vol. V. Eds. Joseph A. Stout, Jr. and Peter C. Rollins. Stillwater: Oklahoma State University Press, 1975, pp. 47–52.

_____. "From Hemp to Verbal Lariat." In *Rogersisms: The Cowboy Philosopher on the Peace Conference. The Writings of Will Rogers.* Ser. I, Vol. IV. Eds. Joseph A. Stout, Jr. and Peter C. Rollins. Stillwater: Oklahoma State University Press, 1975, pp. 41–47.

_____. "Innocence Protected: Will Rogers and *Steamboat 'Round the Bend." American Classic Screen,* May-June 1979, pp. 8–12.

_____. "The Making of *Will Rogers' 1920s:* One Participant's Narrative Report." *Film and History* 7 (1977): 1–5.

_____. "Will Rogers, Ambassador Sans Portfolio: *Letters from a Self-Made Diplomat to His President." The Chronicles of Oklahoma* 57 (1979): 326–339.

_____. "Will Rogers on Aviation: A Means of Fostering Frontier Values in an Age of Machines and Bunk?" *Journal of American Culture.* Forthcoming, 1984.

_____. "Will Rogers: Symbolic Man and Film Image." *Journal of Popular Film* 2 (1973): 323–352.

_____. "Will Rogers: Symbolic Man, Journalist, and Film Image." *Journal of Popular Culture* 9 (1976): 851–877.

_____, and Harry W. Menig. "Regional Literature and Will Rogers: Film Redeems a Literary Form." *Literature Film Quarterly* 3 (1974): 70–83.

_____, R. C. Raack, and Marilyn L. Raack, eds. *Will Rogers' 1920s: A Cowboy's Guide to the Times.* (Workbook to accompany film.) San Francisco: Film Resource Materials, 1976.

Rubin, M. "Mr. [John] Ford and Mr. Rogers: The Will Rogers Trilogy." *Film Comment,* January-February 1974, pp. 54-57.

St. Johns, Adela Rogers. "Love, Laughter and Tears—Symbol of Old West." *The American Weekly,* December 31, 1950, pp. 12-13. (Magazine Article Scrapbook 3; Microfilm Reel 10.)

Sargent, Thornton. "What Can You Do with Will Rogers?" *Movie Mirror,* March 1935, pp. 44-45, 107-109. (In Box 3-D at Will Rogers Memorial.)

_____. "Will Outwits the Sexy Fellas." *Photoplay,* September 1934, n.p. (Feature Article Scrapbook 2; Microfilm Reel 12.)

Savage, William W., Jr. "Top Hand: Will Rogers and the Cowboy Image in America." *The Chronicles of Oklahoma* 57 (1979): 376-384.

Scanlon, Robert. "Ride 'Em Author" (Interview). *Colliers,* December 13, 1924, pp. 8, 48-49.

Schmidt, Karl. "The Philosopher with the Lariat." *Everybody's,* October 1917, pp. 494-495. (Feature Article Scrapbook 2; Microfilm Reel 12.)

Seldes, Gilbert. "The Death of Satire." *New Republic,* January 5, 1927, p. 193.

_____. "Will Rogers Solitary." *Literary Digest,* January 15, 1927, p. 29.

Shelley, Hazel. "You Know What I Mean." *Motion Picture Classic,* n.d., n.p. (In Box 3-D at Memorial, Claremore, Oklahoma.)

Shirk, George. "Oklahoma's Two Commemorative Stamps." *The Chronicles of Oklahoma* 27 (1949): 16, 89-94.

Slide, A. "Films on 8 & 16." *Film in Review,* November 30, 1979, pp. 554-556.

Smallwood, James. "Will Rogers: A Centennial Review of His Career." *The Chronicles of Oklahoma* 57 (1979): 269-298.

Smith, Charlotte Anne. "Will Rogers' Birthplace Restored." *Oklahoma's Orbit,* April 16, 1978, pp. 3-4.

Smith, H. Allen. "Will Rogers Was No Damned Good." *Esquire,* May 1974, pp. 122-124, 155.

Smith, Norman D. "A Loop Over the 20s." Review of *Will Rogers' 1920s: A Cowboy's Guide to the Times. Literature/Film Quarterly* 6 (1977): 91-92.

Smith, Priscilla. "Will Rogers: The Thinking Man's Cowboy." *Humanities* 8 (1978): 7.

Southard, Bruce. "Will Rogers and the Language of the Southwest: A Centennial Perspective." *The Chronicles of Oklahoma* 57 (1979): 365-376. Reprinted in *Will Rogers: A Centennial Tribute.* Ed. Arrell Morgan Gibson. Oklahoma Ser. 12. Oklahoma City: Oklahoma Historical Society, 1980, pp. 113-123.

Speer, Lou. "Will Rogers Just Visiting." *Oklahoma's Orbit,* March 7, 1971, pp. 12-14.

Starr, Dr. Orange. "Cherokee Medicine Man." *The Ranchman,* June 1958, pp. 39-40. (Magazine Article Scrapbook 3; Microfilm Reel 10.)

Steele, Harry. "Will Rogers." *Radio Guide,* November 24, 1934, n.p. (Feature Article Scrapbook 2; Microfilm Reel 12.)

_____. "Will Rogers—Prairie Plato." *Radio Guide,* December 1, 1934, n.p. (Feature Article Scrapbook 2; Microfilm Reel 12.)

————. "Will Rogers—Prairie Plato." *Radio Guide,* December 8, 1934, n.p. (Feature Article Scrapbook 2; Microfilm Reel 12.)

————. "Will Rogers—Prairie Plato." *Radio Guide,* December 15, 1934, n.p. (Feature Article Scrapbook 2; Microfilm Reel 12.)

Sterling, Bryan. "An Interview with Will Rogers." (Imaginary conversation). *Oklahoma Today,* Spring 1971, pp. 12-16.

Stone, Fred. "The Will Rogers I Knew." Periodical unknown, n.d., pp. 33, 80. (Magazine Article Scrapbook 3; Microfilm Reel 10.)

Stone, Mrs. Fred. "Will Rogers—A Home Man." Periodical unknown, n.d., n.p. (Feature Article Scrapbook 2; Microfilm Reel 12.)

Stone, Irvin. "Beverly Hills." *Holiday,* October 1952, pp. 31, 36-38, 40, 42, 141-142, 144, 146-148.

Stout, Joseph A., Jr. "The Will Rogers Project." *The Chronicles of Oklahoma* 51 (1973): 356-358.

————. "Will Rogers as Social Critic." *The Chronicles of Oklahoma* 57 (1979): 289-299.

Stovall, J. "The Films of Will Rogers." *Classic Film Collector,* Spring 1978, p. 48.

Sunday, Uncle Ed. "Willie Rogers of Oologah." Periodical unknown, November 1942, pp. 11, 19-20. (Feature Article Scrapbook 2; Microfilm Reel 12.)

Thomas, K. C. "Why Will Rogers Is the Greatest Film Star." *Screenland,* March 1935, pp. 51, 96. (Feature Article Scrapbook 2; Microfilm Reel 12.)

"Time's Up, Folks, S'long." *Musician,* August 1935, p. 11.

Tittle, Walter. "Glimpses of Interesting Americans." *Century Magazine,* July 1926, pp. 305-320.

"Tragedy: Two Great Men Die, Proving Pilot's Maxim." *Newsweek,* August 24, 1935, pp. 18-19.

Tully, Jim. "Tom Mix and Will Rogers." *College Humor,* November 1928, pp. 42-46, 118; reprinted in *Oklahoma Yesterday-Today-Tomorrow.* Ed. Lerona Rosamond Morris. Guthrie, Okla.: Cooperative Publishing Company, 1930, pp. 709-713. (In Box 3-D at Will Rogers Memorial.)

"20,000 Dedicate Memorial to America's Favorite Son." *Newsweek,* November 14, 1938, p. 15.

"Two Great Oklahomans." *The Oklahoma Meter,* n.d., p. 2. (Magazine Article Scrapbook 3; Microfilm Reel 10.)

Tyson, Carl. "I'm Off to Coolidge's Follies: Will Rogers and the Presidential Nominations, 1924-1932." *The Chronicles of Oklahoma* 54 (1976): 192-198.

Ueland, A. "Will Rogers, the Cowboy Philosopher." Program published by the Moslah Temple, 1953. (Magazine Article Scrapbook 3; Microfilm Reel 10.)

Van de Water, Frederick. "Books and So Forth." *New York Herald Tribune,* January 5, 1925, n.p. (Book Review Scrapbook 23; Microfilm Reel 12.)

Van Doren, Dorothy. "Will Rogers, the Bunkless Candidate." *Nation,* October 3, 1928, pp. 314-315.

Vaughan, Bill. "Unique Hold of Will Rogers on People over World Is Clear in New Biography." Review of *Our Will Rogers,* by Homer Croy, *Kansas City Times,* October 16, 1953, n.p. (Book Review Scrapbook 23; Microfilm Reel 12.)

Vincent, Bobby. "In the Ring." *The Ranchman,* September 1954, pp. 30-32. (Magazine Article Scrapbook 3; Microfilm Reel 10.)

————. "They Gave Will Rogers Enough Rope and He Knew What to Do with It." *The Ranchman,* November 1941, pp. 14-16, 18, 21. Reprinted in November

1953, n.p. (Magazine Article Scrapbook 3; Microfilm Reel [1941] p. 11.)

_____. "Will Rogers." *The Ranchman,* February 1957, p. 18. (Magazine Article Scrapbook 3; Microfilm Reel 10.)

Waddy, Ol'. "Will Rogers World Championship Rodeo." *The Western Horseman,* December 1960, pp. 22-23, 69. (Magazine Article Scrapbook 3; Microfilm Reel 10.)

Wagner, Robert. "In Memoriam." *Rob Wagner's Script,* September 7, 1936, p. 2. (Magazine Article Scrapbook 3; Microfilm Reel 10.)

_____. "Will Rogers, Artist." *Rob Wagner's Script,* August 24, 1935, pp. 1-2. (Magazine Article Scrapbook 3; Microfilm Reel 10.)

Walker, Paula. "Address in Commemoration of Wiley Post Before the Oklahoma State Society of Washington, D.C.: Resolutions of the Oklahoma State Society of Washington, D.C. on the Death of Will Rogers and Wiley Post." *The Chronicles of Oklahoma* 13 (1935): 375-380.

Walker, S. "Examination of the Theory That All People, Once You Get to Know Them, Are Lovable." *New Yorker,* June 7, 1941, p. 17.

Walker, Stanley. "Home Story of a Hero." *New York Herald Tribune,* November 16, 1941, p. 24.

Wallace, Debbie. "Remembering Will Rogers." *LaVerne Magazine,* June 1977, pp. 8-11.

Weadick, Guy. "Cowboys I Have Known." *West Magazine,* August 1935, n.p. (Magazine Article Scrapbook 3; Microfilm Reel 10.)

Wecter, Dixon. "Will Rogers." *Dictionary of American Biography,* Vol. 21, Supp. 1. Ed. Harris E. Starr. New York: Charles Scribner's Sons, 1944.

"Weekly May Become a Daily Under Bill, Son of Will." *Newsweek,* November 1935, p. 20.

Weeks, Edward. "The Peripatetic Reviewer." *Atlantic Monthly,* December 1944, pp. 88-90.

Wheeler, Edgar C. "The Science of Laughter: An Interview with Will Rogers." *Popular Science,* May 1923, p. 31. (In Box 3-D at Will Rogers Memorial.)

"Where the Loss of Will Rogers May Be Most Deeply Felt." *Christian Century,* August 28, 1935, p. 1075.

Williams, Guinn (Big Boy), as told to Ed Churchill. "The Will Rogers Nobody Knows!" *Hollywood,* May 1935, pp. 28-29, 68-69. (In Box 3-D at Will Rogers Memorial; Magazine Article Scrapbook 3; Microfilm Reel 10.)

"Will Rogers." *Literary Digest,* February 22, 1936, p. 17.

"Will Rogers." *National Encyclopedia of American Biography.* New York: James and White, 1947, p. 33.

"Will Rogers." *Survey,* September 1935, p. 274.

"Will Rogers." *Telegraph World,* January 1953, p. 11. (Magazine Article Scrapbook 3; Microfilm Reel 10.)

"Will Rogers." *Variety,* August 21, 1935, pp. 2-4.

"Will Rogers: American Legend." *Coronet,* January 27, 1950, pp. 133-140. (Magazine Article Scrapbook 3; Microfilm Reel 11.)

"Will Rogers—Beloved American Wit." Review of *Will Rogers, His Wife's Story,* by Betty Rogers. *Greensboro* (N.C.) *News,* November 16, 1941, n.p. (Book Review Scrapbook 23; Microfilm Reel 12.)

"Will Rogers Comes Home." *Beverly Hills Script,* June 8, 1929, pp. 3-41. (Magazine Article Scrapbook 3; Microfilm Reel 10.)

"Will Rogers, Cowboy Comedian." *Current Opinion,* January 1923, pp. 103–104.

"Will Rogers—Fool." *Beverly Hills Script,* June 8, 1929, pp. 1–3. (In Box 3-D at Will Rogers Memorial.)

"Will Rogers Greets ANPA Members." *Editor and Publisher,* September 25, 1931, p. 14.

"Will Rogers in His Garden." *Better Homes and Gardens,* June 1928, pp. 22–23, 103–105. (Magazine Article Scrapbook 3; Microfilm Reel 10.)

"Will Rogers: The Immortal Cherokee Kid." *Ideals,* January 1977, pp. 52–59; reprint from *American History Illustrated,* July 1974, pp. 4–11.

"Will Rogers Jr.: Portrait." *Newsweek,* February 7, 1938, p. 26.

"Will Rogers Library, Claremore, Oklahoma." *Library Journal* 62 (1937): 310.

"Will Rogers Life Assayed." Review of *Our Will Rogers,* by Homer Croy. *The Commercial Appeal* (Memphis), November 8, 1955, n.p. (Book Review Scrapbook 23; Microfilm Reel 12.)

"Will Rogers' Literary Roundup." *Current Opinion,* January 1925, pp. 39–40.

"Will Rogers in London." *Literary Digest,* August 28, 1926, pp. 22–23.

"Will Rogers Memorial." *Link,* October 1944, pp. 6–7, 16–19. (Magazine Article Scrapbook 3; Microfilm Reel 11.)

"Will Rogers at the Microphone." *World's Work,* June 1930, pp. 17–18.

"Will Rogers, the Most Brilliant Humorist Since Mark Twain." Lecture Program. (Magazine Article Scrapbook 3; Microfilm Reel 10.)

"Will Rogers at Oologah." *The Ranchman,* November 1942, pp. 11, 19. (Magazine Article Scrapbook 3; Microfilm Reel 10.)

"Will Rogers As Our Aristophanes." *Literary Digest,* December 16, 1922, p. 29.

"Will Rogers—Plain American." *World Digest,* October 1935, pp. 869–872. (Magazine Article Scrapbook 3; Microfilm Reel 11.)

"Will Rogers' Ranch." *Los Angeles Times Home Magazine,* June 22, 1952, pp. 4, 28, 29, 31. (Magazine Article Scrapbook 3; Microfilm Reel 10.)

"Will Rogers Recycled." *Time,* October 7, 1974, pp. 90–91.

"Will Rogers Ropes the Digest Poll." *Literary Digest,* November 15, 1924, pp. 42–44.

"Will Rogers Shrine in California: Ranch Home in Santa Monica." *Hobbies,* April 1941, p. 32.

"Will Rogers: Solitary." *Literary Digest,* January 15, 1927, p. 29.

"Will Rogers Sparkles at Banquet." *Beverly Hills Script,* June 15, 1929, n.p. (Magazine Article Scrapbook 3; Microfilm Reel 10.)

"Will Rogers Stamp." *Scholastic,* October 27, 1948, p. 28.

"Will Rogers' Thoughts on Hereafter." *Public Opinion,* March 1936, p. 13. (Magazine Article Scrapbook 3; Microfilm Reel 10.)

"Will Rogers Weighs Up the New Ford." *Literary Digest,* November 7, 1925, pp. 78–81.

"Will Rogers: Wise Words and (Wise) Cracks." *New York Times Magazine,* August 7, 1960, p. 35.

"Will's Playmates." *Life,* January 23, 1950, p. 25. (Magazine Article Scrapbook 3; Microfilm Reel 10.)

Wilson, Charles Banks. "Hold Before the Young." *Oklahoma Today,* Winter 1968–1969, pp. 14–15.

Winterich, John T. "Simon-Pure Rogersana." *Saturday Review,* October 15, 1949, p. 19. (Book Review Scrapbook 23; Microfilm Reel 12.)

_____. "Wit on a Lariat." Review of *Our Will Rogers,* by Homer Croy. *Saturday*

Review, December 5, 1953, p. 37. (Book Review Scrapbook 23; Microfilm Reel 12.)

"The Wisdom of a Modest Humorist." *Christian Century,* June 10, 1931, p. 764.

"Wit and Wisdom of Will Rogers." *World Digest,* October 1935, p. 872. (Magazine Article Scrapbook 3; Microfilm Reel 11.)

Wood, Thomas. "Will Rogers, Jr. 'Double for Dad.' " *Colliers,* June 7, 1952, pp. 21, 45.

Woodward, W. E. "Humor Dead or Alive." *The Nation,* February 11, 1925, p. 160.

Yates, Norris W. "The Crackerbarrel Saga in the West and South: Will Rogers and Irvin S. Cobb." In *The American Humorist; Conscience of the Twentieth Century.* Ames: Iowa State University Press, 1964, pp. 113–136.

Young, Roger. "Lassoing." Periodical unknown, n.d., n.p. (In Box 3-D at Will Rogers Memorial.)

"Yours, Betty Rogers." Review of *Will Rogers, His Wife's Story,* by Betty Rogers. *Beverly Hills Citizen,* November 28, 1941, n.p. (Book Review Scrapbook 23; Microfilm Reel 12.)

Theses, Dissertations, and Other Unpublished Studies

Alworth, E. Paul. "The Humor of Will Rogers." Ph.D. Diss., University of Missouri, 1958. (See also volume published by Twayne, 1974.)

Brown, William Richard. "The Rhetorical Techniques of Will Rogers." Ph.D. Diss., University of Oklahoma, 1964. (See also volume published by University of Missouri, 1970.)

Collins, Reba. "Will Rogers: Writer and Journalist." Ed.D. Diss., Oklahoma State University, 1967.

Gerk, William. "An Analysis of the Use of Humor in Three Representative Speeches of Will Rogers." M.A. Thesis, University of Iowa, 1952.

Jones, Dean Crawford. "Will Rogers: Depression Humorist, 1928–1935." M.A. Thesis, University of South Carolina, 1961.

Lloyd, Franklin Robert. "Big Men and Regular Fellows: Popular Heroes of the 1920s." Ph.D. Diss., University of Iowa, 1975.

McSpadden, Maurice. "The Public Speaking of Will Rogers." M.A. Thesis, University of Arizona, 1972.

Nelson, Linda Hodges. "An Analysis of Will Rogers' 1933 Radio Broadcasts: A Study in Ethos." M.A. Thesis, University of South Dakota, 1970.

Peak, Mayme Obet. "Will Rogers: America's Court Jester." A manuscript sent to Betty Rogers by Mayme Peak, Hollywood correspondent for the *Boston Globe.*

Roach, Samuel Frederick ("Fred"), Jr. "Lariat in the Sun: The Story of Will Rogers." Ph.D. Diss., University of Oklahoma, 1972.

Siegelin, Helen. "A Rhetorical Analysis of the Use of Humor by Will Rogers Senior in Selected Performances." M.A. Thesis, Miami University (of Ohio), 1964.

Spafford, Mary Nell. "Will Rogers: Cowboy Commentator." M.A. Thesis, University of Georgia, 1975.

Walker, Lois Howell. "Traditional American Humor and Will Rogers." M.A. Thesis, The Stephen F. Austin State University Teachers's College, Nacogdoches, Texas, 1942.

FILMS ABOUT WILL ROGERS

Grinberg, Sherman, prod. *Will Rogers Lost.* Narrator, Tom Hudson. 3 min., sound, B&W, 16 mm. Greatest Headlines of the Century Series, Filmrite Associates, released by Official Films, 1960.

Grogan, Dennis, prod. *Will Rogers.* 3 min., silent, B&W, 8 mm. Documents Project, No. 351, Thorne Films, 1971.

Hyatt, Donald B., dir. and prod. *The Story of Will Rogers.* Narrator, Bob Hope. 56 min., sound, B&W, 16 mm. Project 20 Series, NBC-TV, 1961.

Landsburg, Alan, dir. and prod. *Will Rogers.* Narrator, Mike Wallace. 27 min., sound, B&W, 16 mm. Wolper Productions, released by Official Films, 1962.

Rollins, Peter C., dir. and prod. *Will Rogers' 1920s: A Cowboy's Guide to the Times.* 41 min., sound, color, 16 mm. Churchill Films, 1976.

Sklar, Mike. *The Cowboy Humorist.* Producer, Jack Kuhne. 13 min., sound, B&W, 16 mm. Greatest Drama Series, Movietone News, 1954.

The Story of Will Rogers. 109 min., sound, color, 35 mm. Warner Bros., 1952.

Will Rogers' California Ranch. 41 min., color, 16 mm. Churchill Films, 1976.

Will Rogers Memorial. 41 min., B&W, 16 mm.

AUDIOVISUAL PROFILES OF WILL ROGERS

Ballard, Louis. "Portrait of Will Rogers." Music and voice composition. Excerpts from the writings of Will Rogers. Melville, N.Y.: Belwin-Mill Publishing, 1975.

"Biography in Sound: Will Rogers." NBC News, May 22, 1935. (Available at the Will Rogers Memorial.)

"Evening with Will Rogers." WKY-TV News, November 28, 1961.

Whitmore, James. *James Whitmore, Will Rogers' U.S.A.* Paul Shyre, adpt. and dir. Two-record set. Columbia SG30546, 1972.

Act I—Side 1
Opening
Hollywood
Cherokees—Grass and Water
Fourth Grade McGuffy's
Republican Party Convention
Democratic Party Convention
Dollar Diplomacy

Act I—Side 2
A Man of Peace
Passport to Europe
The Prince of Wales
Rope Tricks Is All Little
All I Know Is What I Read in the Newspapers
Doctoring Is a Funny Thing

Act II—Side 3
The Ziegfeld *Follies*

We Sure Love Slogans in This Country
Charlie Russell—Artist
Women and Money
The Congressional Record
Dopey—the Pot-bellied Pony
Newspapers Is a Joke Book
Free Rent at the White House

Act II—Side 4
Calvin Coolidge Done Nothing, but He Done It Better
Pilgrims, Plymouth and Praying
News of the Day
Women's Corsets
Liberty
Wiley Post and Me

Slides and program. Oklahoma Humanities Committee financed. Available from the Will Rogers Memorial, P.O. Box 157, Claremore, Oklahoma 73017.

RECORDINGS OF WILL ROGERS

Victor released three recordings of Rogers' talks in 1923-1924—45347, 45369, 45374. Four of these sides were reissued after his death, and one, "Timely Topics," is available on *The Old Curiosity Shop* (LCT1112).

The Voice of Will Rogers. American Heritage Record P11794, 1973.
   "Timely Topics"—1920s *Follies* act recreated.
   "Address to Traffic Chiefs"—1922. Recorded on lecture circuit.
   "Unemployment Speech"—October 18, 1930. Same as "Bacons and Beans and Limousines."
   "Democratic Convention"—1932. Rogers speaks to convention.
   "President's Day"—April 30, 1933. "Good Gulf Show."
   "Badwill Tour"—July 8, 1934. "Good Gulf Show."
   "Treaties"—March 31, 1935. "Good Gulf Show."
   "Government Spending"—April 7, 1935. "Good Gulf Show."
   "Pilgrims and Pioneers"—April 14, 1935. "Good Gulf Show."
   "Inheritance Taxes"—April 28, 1935. "Good Gulf Show."
   "Mother's Day"—May 12, 1935. "Good Gulf Show."
   "Congressional Record"—May 12, 1935. "Good Gulf Show."
   "Supreme Court"—June 2, 1935. "Good Gulf Show."
   "Last Broadcast"—June 9, 1935. "Good Gulf Show."

Will Rogers. Bryan B. Sterling, prod. and ed. Distinguished Records DR3001, distributed by Sumark Enterprises, 1960.

Side 1
"The Dust Bowl"—April 14, 1935*
"President's Day"—April 30, 1935

*Dates refer to broadcasts of the "Good Gulf Show," sponsored by the Gulf Oil Company.

"Economics"—April 7, 1935
"The Pilgrims"—April 14, 1935

Side 2
"Mother's Day"—May 12, 1935
"Plan Day"—April 21, 1935
"Inheritance Tax"—April 28, 1935
"The Congressional Record"—May 12, 1935

Will Rogers Says. Columbia ML4604, n.d. A collection of excerpts from speeches and broadcasts, narrated by Will Rogers, Jr.

The Wit and Wisdom of Will Rogers in His Own Voice. 2-record set. Caedmon TC2046, 1970.

Side 1
"Roosevelt and Taxes"—April 7, 1935.*
"Rogers' Plan (Phase I)"—"The Pilgrim Fathers"—"The Great Dust Storms of History"—"Conservation," April 14, 1935.

Side 2
"Social Security Plan"—"The Townsend Plan"—"Rogers' Plan (Phase II)"—"The Agricultural Plan"—"Other Plans"—"Big Business Plan," April 21, 1935.

Side 3
"Rogers' Plan (Phase III)"—"The Inheritance Tax"—"The Morgenthau Plan"—"Franklin D. Roosevelt," April 28, 1935.

Side 4
"Chain Letters"—"Lotteries"—"Rogers' Plan (Phase IV)," May 5, 1935.
"Mother's Day"—"Rogers' Plan (Phase V)"—"Congressional Record," May 12, 1935.

*All dates refer to broadcasts of the "Good Gulf Show," sponsored by Gulf Oil Company.

6

CHRONOLOGY AND SYNOPSES

THE WORLD AND WILL ROGERS: A SELECTIVE CHRONOLOGY

Much of the thought and humor of Will Rogers lacks resonance without an awareness of contemporary events and trends. The purpose of this chronology is to show the flow of history and society in relation to the evolving career of social commentator Will Rogers.

The World: 1879-1935

1879, October 21
Thomas Edison perfects the incandescent lamp.

1883, September 8
The Northern Pacific Railroad completed; it is the second transcontinental line.

1885, March 4-1889, March 3
Grover Cleveland, twenty-second president.

1886
Period of labor unrest.

1887, February 8
The Dawes Act allows the president to put a stop to tribal government and communal ownership of land among the Indians. It allocates a quarter section of the land to each head of a family.

Will Rogers: 1879-1935

1879, November 4
Will Rogers is born on his father's ranch near Oologah, Oklahoma. (Full name: William Penn Adair Rogers.)

1887-1892 — Schooling:
Drumgoole School near Chelsea Presbyterian Mission School, Tahlequah Harrell Institute, Muskogee Willie Halsell College, Vinita (All in Indian Territory)

The World: 1879–1935

Will Rogers: 1879–1935

1889
First movie film developed in America by Thomas A. Edison.

1889, April 22
Official opening of Oklahoma lands, involving the famous "run."

1889, March 4–1893, March 3
Benjamin Harrison, twenty-third president.

1890, May 2
Oklahoma Territory created by an Act of Congress.

1890, May 28
Mary America Rogers, mother of Will Rogers, dies. Will Rogers is ten years old.

1891, August 24
First patent in America for a motion picture filed by Thomas Edison.

1892, December 29
First important radio patent awarded to Thomas Edison.

1892–1896 — *Schooling:*
Scarritt Collegiate Institute, Neosho, Missouri
Kemper Military School, Boonville, Missouri

1893, March 4–1897, March 3
Grover Cleveland, president for second time.

1893
Frederick Jackson Turner, president of the American Historical Association, announces the closing of the frontier and ponders the implications for American society and character.

1894
Rising U.S. unemployment, "Coxey's Army." (Coxey marches from Ohio to Washington, D.C., to demonstrate in favor of projects to relieve unemployment.)

1896, September 2
Marconi invents wireless telegraphy.

W.K.L. Dickson forms American Mutoscope and Biograph Company.

1897, March 4–1901, September 14
William McKinley, twenty-fifth president.

The World: 1879–1935	*Will Rogers: 1879–1935*

1898, April 24–1898, December 10
The Spanish-American War.

1898
The Curtis Act ends free range.
Clem Rogers, Will's father, moves to Claremore, Oklahoma — about twelve miles from the Oologah ranch.

1898–1902
Ranching activities: After running away from Kemper Military School, Rogers works on Ewing Ranch near Higgins, Texas; later manages Rogers Ranch in Oologah, Indian Territory. Spends much of his time with cousin Spi Trent.

1899
Will Rogers meets Betty Blake for the first time at Oologah. She is visiting relatives and arrives by train from Rogers, Arkansas.

1899
Rogers meets Colonel Zack Mulhall at the St. Louis fair.

1900
Less than 8,000 automobiles in the United States. The first automobile factory established by Olds Company in Detroit.

1900, July 4
Rogers' first time to win a roping contest in Claremore.

1901, September 6
Assassination of President McKinley.

1901, September 14–1909, March 3
Theodore Roosevelt, twenty-sixth president.

1901
Marconi's first transatlantic wireless transmission from England to Newfoundland.

Queen Victoria's funeral filmed.

Experiments on voice transmission begun by Reginald Fessenden.

1902
First great oil strike in Texas.

1902
Rogers leaves for South America via England. He works for about five months with gauchos, then leaves for South Africa.

He is a young man in search of himself.

The World: 1879–1935

1902, May 10
Cuban Independence.

1903
The Passion Play, which ran for thirty-six minutes, was one of the longest motion pictures shown in the United States at that time.

1903
America's first attempt at narrative filmmaking: *The Life of an American Fireman.*

Henry Ford becomes president of the Ford Motor Company.

1903, December 17
Wilbur and Orville Wright demonstrate the first motor-driven airplane at Kitty Hawk, North Carolina.

1906
Lee De Forest invents Audion Vacuum tube.

Biograph Film Company's 14th Street Studio opens in Manhattan.

1907, November 14–December 20
Central American Peace Conference.

Will Rogers: 1879–1935

1902–1903
Will Rogers begins his show business career in South Africa with Texas Jack's Wild West Show as "The Cherokee Kid." Then he tours Australia and New Zealand in the Wirth Brothers Circus. Finally, he returns to Claremore.

1904
Rogers performs in Colonel Zack Mulhall's Wild West Show at St. Louis, Missouri. He tries a few vaudeville engagements in Chicago after the St. Louis gig.

1905
Rogers is again with the Mulhall show, this time in New York's Madison Square Garden. When a bull escapes into the stands, Rogers shows his aplomb by roping and restraining the beast. For this act he is celebrated by New York City newspapers.

He remains in New York to exploit the publicity.

1907, Spring
Rogers sails with Buck McKee and two other cowboys to England. The act involves roping Buck and a horse on stage; it is a silent act emphasizing trick roping.

The World: 1879–1935

1908, December 25
Early film censorship established in New York City by the Society for the Prevention of Crime.

1909, March 4–1913, March 3
William Howard Taft, twenty-seventh president.

1910
D. W. Griffith and his company spend the winter in Los Angeles. Within the next few years, film activity shifts from New York to Los Angeles.

1912, August 14
U.S. intervention in Nicaragua.

1912
Mack Sennett's first Keystone Comedy produced.

1912
Height of the progressive movement, bringing a multitude of laws related to wages and hours, the employment of women and children, and safety conditions in factories.

1913, March 4–1921, March 3
Woodrow Wilson, twenty-eighth president.

1913, March 4–1921, March 4
Relations with Mexico: the U.S. Marines occupy Vera Cruz; Wilson refuses to recognize the Huerta regime.

Will Rogers: 1879–1935

1908, November 25
Rogers marries Betty Blake.

1911, October 28
Rogers' father, Clem Vann Rogers, dies. The stern father and the recalcitrant son are reconciled prior to "Uncle Clem's" death.

1911, October 29
Birth of Will Rogers, Jr. in New York.

1912–1913
Rogers appears in the Broadway show *The Wall Street Girl,* starring Blanche Ring.

1913, May 18
Birth of Mary Amelia Rogers in Rogers, Arkansas.

1914, Spring
Rogers leaves for his third European tour with Betty. In London, he appears in the show *Merry-Go-Round.*

The World: 1879–1935	*Will Rogers: 1879–1935*

1915, March 9
Francisco Villa raids Columbus, New Mexico. The United States sends punitive expeditions into Mexico on March 15 under John J. Pershing. These troops are withdrawn on February 5, 1917, after an ignominious failure to find Villa.

1915
D. W. Griffith's *The Birth of a Nation* marks the beginning of a new period in film history: motion pictures show their artistic potential.

1915, January 25
First transcontinental telephone call.

1916, June 3
National Defense Act, first important result of the "preparedness program."

1917
Bolshevik Revolution. Russia becomes the Union of Soviet Socialist Republics.

1917, April 6
The United States declares war on Germany.

1917, June 13
The First Division embarks for France.

1917, October 28
The National Prohibition Act, also known as the Volstead Act, passes over President Wilson's veto. All beverages containing more than one-half of 1 percent alcohol are considered intoxicating and prohibited.

1915
Rogers ventures his first airplane flight at Atlantic City, New Jersey.

He appears in the musical *Hands Up*, Ned Wayburn's *Town Topics*, and Ziegfeld's *Midnight Frolic*.

Birth of second son, James Blake Rogers, July 25, 1915, on Long Island.

1916
Ziegfeld asks Rogers to join the cast of the *Follies* permanently. Later in the year in a pivotal moment for his career, Rogers performs before President Woodrow Wilson. He stays with the *Follies* until 1925.

1918, July 15
His third son, Fred Stone Rogers, is born.

1918, Summer
Rogers makes his first motion picture, *Laughing Bill Hyde,* at Goldwyn's Fort Lee Studio in New Jersey.

The World: 1879–1935	Will Rogers: 1879–1935
	1918 Samuel Goldwyn offers Rogers a two-year contract to make motion pictures in Hollywood.
1919, January 6 Theodore Roosevelt dies.	**1919** Rogers publishes his first two books, collections of his jokes: *Rogersisms: The Cowboy Philosopher on the Peace Conference;* and *Rogersisms: The Cowboy Philosopher on Prohibition.* Both are published by Harper Bros.
1919, January 18 Peace Conference concluding World War I convenes in Paris in the Versailles Palace.	
1919, February President Wilson returns to the United States to campaign for the League of Nations.	**1919** Rogers moves to California after signing a two-year contract with the Goldwyn Studio.
1919, June 28 The Versailles Treaty is signed.	**1919** Rogers announces his fourteen points on the moving picture business in Wid's Yearbook, published by the *Film Daily.* The points parody panaceas but focus on show business rather than politics.
1919, October 2 President Wilson suffers a stroke.	
1920 American domination of world film industry is established. Radio station KDKA begins broadcasting in Pittsburgh.	**1920, June 17** Death of Fred Stone Rogers—diphtheria.
1920, June 8 The Republican National Convention begins in Chicago; Warren G. Harding is nominated.	**1920** Will Rogers starts writing for the McNaught Syndicate, beginning with an assignment to cover the presidential conventions. The work continues through 1932.
1920, June 28 The Democratic Convention begins in San Francisco. James M. Cox of Ohio is nominated for the presidency during the convention.	
1920, August 26 The Twentieth Amendment to the Constitution, which establishes woman suffrage, is ratified.	
1921, March 4–1923, August 2 Warren G. Harding, twenty-ninth president.	**1921** Goldwyn releases Rogers from his contract after nearly twenty short films.

The World: 1879–1935	*Will Rogers: 1879–1935*
1921, November 12–1922, February 6 Washington Conference. President Harding calls for a conference with Great Britain, France, Italy, and Japan to discuss naval limitation.	
1922, August 28, 5:15 P.M. The first radio commercial is aired.	**1922** In a brief experiment with production, Rogers turns out *The Ropin' Fool* and *Fruits of Faith*. A third Will Rogers production, *One Day in 365,* is never released. The experiment is a financial disaster, primarily because of distribution problems, but also because the Rogers magic needed sound.
1922–1930 Refunding of debts owed the United States by Allied powers. A controversial issue affecting international relations.	**1922** Rogers speaks to the International Bankers' Association, New York. This was one of many after-dinner talks during a period of financial embarrassment for Rogers. (See list elsewhere in this volume.)
	1923, January 21 A newspaper in Toledo, Ohio *(Toledo Times)* calls Will Rogers the most popular speaker in the country.
1923, August 2 Calvin Coolidge becomes the thirtieth president upon the death of Warren G. Harding.	**1923, April** Rogers writes an open letter to President Warren G. Harding which strains relations between him and the White House. Comments and skits in the *Follies* also upset the president.
1924, February 3 Woodrow Wilson dies.	**1924** Rogers publishes *The Illiterate Digest,* a collection of weekly articles.
1924, February–March Teapot Dome oil scandal. Albert Fall, secretary of the Department of the Interior, is investigated by a Senate Committee for leasing the Teapot Dome Oil Reserve to Harry F. Sinclair (April 7, 1922) and the Elk Hills Reserve to E. L. Doheny (December 11, 1922). He is found guilty of embezzlement, and resigns.	**1924, June 10** The Republican Convention opens. Rogers writes five articles about the Republican Convention; he then rushes to Atlantic City for the *Follies* opening of June 18.

The World: 1879–1935

1924, June 24
The Democratic National Convention begins in Madison Square Garden. The party members are divided into two groups: the followers of Al Smith and those who support John W. Davis. Davis wins the nomination.

1924, June 10
Calvin Coolidge is the only person to be nominated for the presidency at the Republican Convention.

1924
The McNary-Haugen Bill proposes that the Federal Farm Board purchase the annual surplus commodities. It is vetoed by President Coolidge, first in 1927 and again in 1928.

1925
Trial of John Scopes for teaching Darwinian theory. A journalistic *cause célèbre* is used to discredit religion and rural America.

1925, June
Tension between Mexico and the United States is aggravated by Secretary Kellogg's charge that Mexico failed to protect American lives and property rights. The Mexican Petroleum Law and the Alien Land Law had been enacted in December 1925.

1925, October 28–December 17
Court martial of William ("Billy") Mitchell, the army colonel who revealed America's lack of preparedness for the air war to come.

1926
First airmail service between New York and Boston is established.

1926, April
The Book-of-the-Month Club creates a revolution in book selling and publishing.

Will Rogers: 1879–1935

1924
Rogers nominates Calvin Coolidge at the Democratic Convention. Rogers writes telegrams to congratulate major figures (John W. Davis and Al Smith). He includes them with imaginary replies in his column.

1925, May
Death of Maud Lane, sister of Will Rogers; he returns home to Claremore.

1925–1927
Rogers writes a daily article "Worst Story I've Heard Today," but drops the exercise—it was not authentic Rogers material.

1925–1928
Rogers travels all over the United States on lecture tours organized by Charles Wagner, giving Rogers an opportunity to visit hundreds of American towns and cities.

1926, Spring
Rogers is asked by George Horace Lorimer to write articles on the European scene for the *Saturday Evening Post. Letters of a Self-Made Diplomat to His President* is the delightful result.

The World: 1879-1935

1926, November 21
Annie Oakley dies.

1927
BBC chartered. British Cinematography Act provides for a quota system.

U.S. Radio Act creates Federal Radio Commission (later FCC).

Roxy Theatre opens in New York. CBS is formed.

1927, June 20–August 4
Naval Disarmament Conference, Geneva.

1927, September
Dwight W. Morrow is appointed ambassador to Mexico. Asks Will Rogers to help reduce tensions between the two neighbor nations.

1927, October 6
First talking motion picture in which the sound track was actually on the film *(The Jazz Singer).*

1927
The Academy of Motion Picture Arts and Sciences is established.

1927, May 20–21
Charles A. Lindbergh makes the first solo nonstop flight from New York to Paris in *The Spirit of St. Louis.* Rogers celebrates the hero and his accomplishments.

Will Rogers: 1879-1935

1926
During Rogers' European tour, he plays in the *Cochran Revue,* London. He also makes motion pictures, including *Tip-Toes* and a series of twelve short films entitled *Strolling Through Europe with Will Rogers* (see film list).

1926
Rogers begins his daily column "Will Rogers Says." The column will run until his death in 1935. It is his favorite journalistic exercise and reaches 40 million readers.

1927
Rogers speaks at benefit performances for victims of Mississippi River flood; he suffers serious illness and surgery; he is designated Congressman-at-large for the United States of America by the National Press Club, Washington, D.C.

Rogers publishes *There's Not a Bathing Suit in Russia,* a brief look at the Soviet experiment.

Rogers is the first passenger to fly from coast to coast with mail pilots. His love for aviation is evident in his articles.

1927
Rogers makes his last silent film, *A Texas Steer.* The era of sound will prove to be a distinct advantage for Rogers, whose humor depends so much on word play.

1927
In a nationwide hookup, Rogers mimics the voice of President Coolidge and finds himself in some hot water when the president is not amused.

The World: 1879–1935

1928
First motion picture cartoon released by Walt Disney Productions (Mickey Mouse in *Plane Crazy*).

1928, June 12
Republican Convention begins in Kansas City. Herbert Hoover is nominated after much opposition.

1928, June 26
Democratic Convention begins in Houston, Texas. The Democrats nominate Alfred E. Smith for president.

1928, June 27
A journalist for the *Arkansas Democrat* reports: "As was expected, the best 'stuff' about the convention at Kansas City came from Will Rogers. Will saved the day for all of us with his humor."

1928, June 28
First successful airplane flight from San Francisco to Honolulu.

1928
RKO Radio Pictures Corporation is formed by GE/Westinghouse/RCA. They combine to exploit RCA's sound patents in film.

1928, November 6
Herbert Hoover is elected president, 444 electoral votes to 87.

1928, May 15
Flood Control Act appropriates $325 million for relief work in the Mississippi Valley over a ten-year period.

1929, March 4–1933, March 3
Herbert Hoover, thirty-first president.

1929, October
Stock Market Crash, the end of the economic boom of the Coolidge-Hoover era and the beginning of the Depression.

Will Rogers: 1879–1935

1928–1929
Rogers substitutes for his friend Fred Stone in the musical comedy *Three Cheers,* starring Dorothy Stone.

1928
Significant events in 1928: Rogers visits the Pan-American Conference, Havana, and talks of his mock candidacy for president on the Anti-Bunk party ticket.

In February, he launches another lecture tour of the United States. *Life* praises him and carries a full portrait of him on the cover of the May 31, 1928, issue. *Life* keeps the "anti-bunk" campaign rolling, and Rogers writes many articles for *Life* as part of the fun.

1928
Rogers reports on the Democratic Convention for the *New York Times.*

1928
Democratic Convention: Rogers in fun represents the "Anti-Bunk" party.

1928
Rogers gives a performance to raise money for the children's department of the Salvation Army, and on June 17, another one for the benefit of a Kansas City policeman who was killed.

1929
Rogers makes first sound film for Fox Film Corporation, *They Had to See Paris.* Eventually, Rogers makes twenty-one sound films for William Fox.

The World: 1879–1935

1930, November 4
Republicans lose eight seats in the Senate and their majority in the House.

Hoover proposes a policy of decentralized work relief, operated by agencies on a basis of self-help.

1930, January 21–April 22
London Naval Conference leads to a treaty involving the United States, Great Britain, and Japan. Rogers visits the proceedings and comments in his articles.

1930
Drought in Western Plains worsens.

1931, June 20
President Hoover proposes a one-year moratorium on interallied debts and reparations.

1931, June–July
Wiley Post and Harold Gatty fly around the world in eight days, 15 hours, and 51 minutes. Rogers celebrates this achievement for aviation and Oklahoma.

Will Rogers: 1879–1935

1930, April 20
In a radio speech, Rogers praises Herbert Hoover for his food programs and his "wonderful character."

1930
Rogers makes two motion pictures for Fox: *So This Is London* and *Lightnin'*.

1930
January — Rogers flies to the Disarmament Conference in London.

1931
Rogers makes three motion pictures with Fox: *A Connecticut Yankee; Young As You Feel;* and *Ambassador Bill*.

1931
Rogers makes a trip by small plane through Arkansas, Texas, and Oklahoma and raises $225,000 for relief through several performances per day. Americans are moved by his generosity and selflessness.

Rogers is on a national radio broadcast discussing unemployment with President Hoover, Calvin Coolidge, Al Smith, and others.

1931
Rogers visits Nicaragua and other Central American countries and the Caribbean for the benefit of earthquake and fire victims.

1931, November–1932, February
Rogers begins a trip around the world about which he writes for the *Saturday Evening Post*. He tries to restore the public's confidence in Hoover through newspaper articles and radio broadcasts.

The World: 1879–1935

1932, February 2
Reconstruction Finance Corporation (RFC) proposed by President Hoover and established by the Senate and the House to provide financing for banks, life insurance companies, railroads, and farm mortgage associations.

1932, June 2
The Republican Convention begins. President Hoover is nominated for a second term.

1932, June 26
The Democratic Convention begins. Franklin D. Roosevelt and Al Smith are the two nominees, with Roosevelt the ultimate victor.

Governor Murray's votes at the Democratic Presidential Convention go to Will Rogers and then to Franklin Roosevelt.

1932, July 21
Relief and Construction Act expands the scope and functions of the RFC.

1932
Unemployment reaches 13 million; wages 60 percent less than 1929.

1933, February 14
All banks in Michigan close. Business and banking are at a standstill across the nation.

1933
Chicago's World's Fair.

1933
Franklin D. Roosevelt, thirty-second president of the United States.

1933, June 15
The Farm Credit Act is approved.

1933–1935
Other New Deal legislation: The Beer-Wine Revenue Act levies a tax of $5 on every barrel of beer and wine manufactured.

Will Rogers: 1879–1935

1932
Rogers makes two motion pictures with Fox: *Business and Pleasure* and *Down to Earth.*

1932
Florenz ("Flo") Ziegfeld dies bankrupt. Rogers pays for his medical and funeral expenses.

Rogers travels to South America.

Rogers covers the Republican and Democratic conventions.

Rogers speaks for an hour at the Democratic Convention. Some editorial writers try to promote him for president. He is very popular with the delegates and the crowd.

1932
Rogers makes one motion picture with Fox: *Too Busy to Work.* Rogers becomes the highest paid male film star in the United States.

1933
Rogers makes three motion pictures with Fox: *State Fair, Dr. Bull,* and *Mr. Skitch.*

Rogers signs a contract with Gulf Oil Company for fourteen radio talks: $72,000. He will appear on "The Good Gulf Show."

The World: 1879–1935	*Will Rogers: 1879–1935*

1933, continued

The Tennessee Valley Authority Act.

The National Industrial Recovery Act.

The Agricultural Adjustment Act.

1935, July 5
Wagner Labor Relations Act.

1935, August 14
Social Security Act.

1934

Rogers makes two motion pictures with Fox: *Handy Andy* and *Judge Priest.*

1935

Rogers makes three motion pictures with Fox: *The County Chairman, Life Begins at 40,* and *Doubting Thomas.*

Rogers makes a motion picture with 20th Century-Fox: *Steamboat 'Round the Bend* (Rogers' last film), released with *In Old Kentucky* after his death.

1935

Rogers dies in a plane crash with Wiley Post, famous pilot, near Point Barrow, Alaska. The nation mourns its great loss.

1938, November 4

On what would have been Rogers' 58th birthday, the Will Rogers Memorial in Claremore, Oklahoma, is dedicated.

1941

Publication of *Will Rogers: His Wife's Story,* by Betty Rogers.

1944

Betty Rogers dies. Bodies of Will and Betty Rogers are interred in crypt at Claremore Memorial along with remains of Fred Stone Rogers.

WILL ROGERS' SILENT AND SOUND FILMS: A FILMOGRAPHY

This filmography has been assembled from a number of sources. Robert Love provided me with a comprehensive information guide to the films in 1972. In 1979, Anthony Slide generously shared a copy of his reference work, *The Films of Will Rogers* (1979). A total of thirty archives across the world kindly replied to requests for information about some of the more esoteric items such as *Tip-Toes* (1927). Extremely terse entries usually indicate a paucity of print and celluloid data: research simply turned up very little about some of the minor silent motion pictures. Throughout the preparation of this information, I was assisted by Tom Slater, whom I thank for his scrupulous attention to detail.

1. Laughing Bill Hyde

A Goldwyn Pictures Corporation production. Director: Hobart Henley. Based on a story by Rex Beach in *Laughing Bill Hyde and Other Stories* (New York: Harpers, 1917). Photography: Arthur Cadwell. Released: September 30, 1918. 5 reels. With Will Rogers (Laughing Bill Hyde), Anna Lehr (Ponotah), John Sain Polis (Black Jack Burg), Clarence Oliver (Dr. Evan Thomas), Mabel Ballin (Alice), Joseph Herbert (Joseph Wesley Slayforth), Robert Conville (Denny Slevin), and Dan Mason (Danny Dorgan).

Story and Criticism

Laughing Bill Hyde is a good badman who, after leaving prison, moves to Alaska for a new start on life. On the way, he befriends a young doctor, and, upon landing, they both encounter a lovely girl who is part Russian and part Eskimo. Laughing Bill discovers that a mine which rightfully belongs to the girl has been exploited for some time and for great profits without her knowledge. Tapping his criminal past, Laughing Bill steals the gold and spoils the intentions of the villains. In the end, the young doctor is given enough money to marry his fiancé, and Bill has enough funds to marry the native girl.

Mrs. Rex Beach, wife of the story's author, suggested that Will Rogers should play the lead role in this melodrama. Since Ziegfeld's *Follies* were closed down for the summer, Rogers agreed to attempt the new medium at Goldwyn's Fort Lee Studio in New Jersey. The *New York Times* reviewer was highly pleased by the debut, but Goldwyn's records show little profit from the first Rogers venture into film.

2. Almost a Husband

A Goldwyn Pictures Corporation production. Director: Clarence Badger. Based on the story "Old Ebenezer" by Opie Read. Photography: Norbert Brodin. New York premiere: Strand Theatre, October 12, 1919. 5 reels. With Will Rogers (Sam Lyman), Peggy Wood (Eva McElwyn), Herbert Standing (Bander McElwyn), Cullen Landis (Jerry Wilson), Clara Horton (Jane Sheldon), Ed Brady (Zeb Sawyer), Sidney DeGray (John Caruthers), and Gus Saville (Jasper Stagg).

Story and Criticism

In this regional tale, Sam Lyman (Will Rogers) is a school teacher from New England who finds employment in a small village along the Mississippi. A leading banker's daughter, Eva McElwyn (Peggy Wood), is insistently wooed by an obnoxious suitor who is tricked into believing that the girl and Lyman have been wed. Much of the plot entails the various ploys attempted by the disappointed suitor to have the marriage annulled. In the end, a real ceremony confirms the wedlock of the two lead characters—whose performances were commended by the *New York Times* reviewer (October 13, 1919, p. 16, col. 3).

Availability

The Museum of Modern Art has a few scenes from this film.

3. Jubilo

A Goldwyn Pictures Corporation production. Director: Clarence Badger. Screenplay: Robert F. Hill. Based on the *Saturday Evening Post* serial by Ben Ames Williams. Photography: Marcel Le Picard. Released: December 7, 1919. 5 reels, 53 minutes. With Will Rogers (Jubilo), Josie Sedgwick (Rose Hardy), Charles French (Jim Hardy), Willard Louis (Punt), and James Mason (Bert Rooker).

Story and Criticism

As my "Regional Literature and Will Rogers" (1974) attempts to demonstrate, there was a close ideological affinity between the regional stories of the *Saturday Evening Post* and the screen persona of Will Rogers. In the early silent period, Rogers portrayed a series of characters who were slight variations of the "Jubilo" role: whether dressed as tramps, cowboys, or farmers, they are all lazy, rural clowns with hearts of gold. Rogers somewhere noted that he had a special feel for such types: "I like to play tramps. There is something about an old tramp that kinder hits me, especially a kind of good natured one that don't take things too seriously."

Drifting along a country road, Jubilo becomes a witness to a train robbery, and he notices a horse with a unique mark on the hindquarters. Later, he sees the horse again at the Hardy family's ranch. Jubilo stays with the Hardy family, falls in love with the daughter, and unmasks the rival suitor as the criminal. While melodrama keeps the story moving, the real entertainment of the film—exploited for visual comedy by Rogers—comes from watching poor Jubilo adjust to the pains of work and the unaccustomed burden of daily responsibilities around the farm.

Rogers became deeply involved in the production of this film. (See Croy, *Our Will Rogers,* 1953.)

Availability

Both the Museum of Modern Art and the Will Rogers Memorial have prints.

4. Water, Water, Everywhere

A Goldwyn Pictures Corporation production. Director: Clarence Badger. Screenplay: Robert F. Hill. Based on the *Saturday Evening Post* story "A Hard Proposition" by William R. Lighton. Photography: Marcel Le Picard. Released: February 1920. 5 reels. With Will Rogers (Billy Fortune), Irene Rich (Hope Beecher), Roland Lee (Lyman Jennings Jordan), Wade Boteler (Ben Morgan), Marguerite Livingston (Martha Beecher), Lillian Langdon (Fay Bittinger), Lydia Yeamans Titus (Mrs. Red McGee), Milton Brown (Sam Beecher), Victor Potel (Steve Brainard), William Courtwright (Daddy Sammett), and Sydney DeGray (Red McGee).

Story and Criticism

As a cowboy named Billy Fortune, Will Rogers is found in the middle of a small town that is turning to Prohibition. To make the change from fire water to soda water more attractive, the town imports some lovely girls — only to discover that the men folk are now tempted to spend more time away from home than they did during the era of demon rum. The discussion of prohibition gives Rogers ample opportunity to throw darts at both "wets" and "drys." A romantic triangle involving Fortune, the local doctor, and the ingenue, Hope Beecher (played by Irene Rich), keeps the story moving when social satire and other plot complications are not in view.

Even the publicity writer for this film had to admit that the film itself was of little interest other than for Rogers' performance: "It is the little touches and fine shadings that make Rogers' performance so noteworthy. The flicker of an eyelid, a twitching of the lips, the droop of the head, a shy glance aside provokes a gale of laughter or a lump in the throat" (*Motion Picture News,* February 14, 1920, p. 1751).

Availability

The Museum of Modern Art has one scene from this film.

5. The Strange Boarder

A Goldwyn Pictures Corporation production. Director: Clarence Badger. Based on a story by Will Payne. Photography: Marcel Le Picard. Released: May 1920. 5 reels. With Will Rogers (Sam Gardner), Jimmy Rogers (Billy Gardner), Irene Rich (Jane Engraham), James Mason (Kittie Hinch), Doris

Pawn (Florry Hinch), Lionel Belmore (Jake Bloom), Jack Richardson (Westmark), Sydney Deane (Dawson), and Louis J. Durhan (Sergeant Worrill).

Story and Criticism

Will Rogers plays an Arizona rancher who comes to the city for the first time and is swindled out of $10,000 by a group of bunko artists. Although Sam Gardner tries to stay out of trouble, he is arrested by the police in a raid on a saloon where gambling is taking place. He goes to jail where he befriends a young, embittered man named Kittie Hinch, a gambler who vows to get even with a local politician who has stolen his girl. When Hinch is released from jail, he shoots his antagonist, but the Arizona rancher is arrested. In the end, the real killer is identified, and the Rogers character, his son, and a kind-hearted city girl make their home in the metropolis.

The publicity writer for Goldwyn warned exhibitors that *The Strange Boarder* was a picture "in which the star gets a great deal out of a story that is not of the best. . . . As usual, you should concentrate your exploitation on Rogers" (*Motion Picture News,* January 7, 1920, p. 3907).

6. Bumping Into Broadway

Pathé Exchange, Inc. March 18, 1920. Author: Hal E. Roach.

Story and Criticism

Probably the story of a country bumpkin who travels to the big city.

7. The Illiterate Digest

1920 — Weekly. Released by Pathé, Inc.

Story and Criticism

One twelve-minute release of this weekly series is available in the Motion Picture Division of the U.S. Archives in Washington, D.C. Will Rogers is dressed in the cowboy outfit he wore for vaudeville performances, including chaps and what would now be called an "L.L. Bean shirt." Behind him is a curtain that displays trees, and parked along a dirt road is a Model T Ford. In the existing episode, Rogers twirls his rope, shares a winning grin with the screen audience, and then, through verbal "titles," comments on contemporary issues. There is nothing visual about the presentation. However, it is the closest existing record we have of a Will Rogers stage presentation — and that might have been the appeal in 1920 for viewers outside the New York City area.

Portions of the episode described above are part of *Will Rogers' 1920s* (1976).

Availability

The Museum of Modern Art has a brief excerpt from this series. The Motion Picture Division, U.S. Archives, has a longer excerpt.

8. Jes' Call Me Jim

A Goldwyn Pictures Corporation production. Director: Clarence Badger. Screenplay: Edward T. Lowe. Adaptation: Thompson Buchanan. Based on the novel *Seven Oaks* by J. G. Holland. Photography: Marcel Le Picard. Released: June 5, 1920. 5 reels. With Will Rogers (Jim Fenton), Irene Rich (Miss Butterworth), Lionel Belmore (Belcher), Raymond Hatton (Paul Benedict), Jimmy Rogers (Harry Benedict), Bert Sprotte (Buffum), Nick Cogley (Mike Conlin), and Sydney DeGray (Sam Yates).

Story and Criticism

The central character of this melodrama is an inventor named Jim Fenton (Will Rogers) whose invention has been stolen by the villain. To prevent detection of his lucrative crime, the villain keeps Fenton in a cell and prevents him from recovering from a nervous condition which the public believes is a hopeless case of insanity. With the help of Miss Butterworth (Irene Rich), the oppressed inventor finds his way out of captivity and into the arms of his beautiful redeemer. The *New York Times* reviewer felt that the movie was redeemed only by "Rogers' personality and his definite, if artless, impersonation of Jim Fenton" (May 24, 1920, p. 20, col. 3).

Availability

Both the Museum of Modern Art and the Will Rogers Memorial have prints.

9. Cupid, the Cowpuncher

A Goldwyn Pictures Corporation production. Director: Clarence Badger. Screenplay: Edfrid A. Bingham. Based on the novel *Alec Lloyd, Cowpuncher* by Eleanor Gates. Photography: Marcel Le Picard. New York premiere: Capitol Theatre, July 25, 1920. 5 reels. With Will Rogers (Alec Lloyd), Helene Chadwick (Macie Sewell), Andrew Robson (Zack Sewell), Lloyd Whitlock (Dr. Leroy Simpson), Guinn Williams (Hailroil Johnson), Tex Parker (Monkey Mike), Roy Laidlaw (Dr. Billy Trowbridge), Katherine Wallace (Rose), Nelson McDowell (Sheriff Bergin), and Cordelia Callahan (Mrs. Bergin).

Story and Criticism

As a ranch foreman named Alec Lloyd, Will Rogers acts the role of matchmaker for everybody but himself. When he falls in love, he discovers that things can be less tractable for those actually playing the marriage game. The *New York Times* critic singles out Rogers for "pantomimic abilities . . . [which] . . . serve to convey thoughts and feelings; they are expressive" (July 26, 1920, p. 9, col. 5).

10. Honest Hutch

A Goldwyn Pictures Corporation production. Director: Clarence Badger. Based on the story "Old Hutch Lives It Up" by Garret Smith. Photography: Marcel Le Picard. Released: September 1920. 5 reels. With Will Rogers (Honest Hutch), Mary Alden (Mrs. Hutchins), Priscilla Bonner (Ellen), Tully Marshall (Thomas Gunnison), Nick Cogley (Hiram Joy), Eddie, Jeanette, and Yves Trebaol (The Hutchins Children), and Byron Munson (Thomas Gunnison, Jr.).

Story and Criticism

The town loafer (Honest Hutch/Will Rogers) accidentally discovers a buried treasure worth $50,000. Rather than squander the money in a manner that will call attention to himself, he vows to spend the new wealth a little at a time. Unfortunately, he cannot hide the arrogance and punctiliousness which overlay his character now that he considers himself to be among the better people in town. The *New York Times* reviewer enjoyed Rogers in this recreation of his "Jubilo" role (September 26, 1920, Section VI, p. 2, col. 1).

11. Guile of Women

A Goldwyn Pictures Corporation production. Director: Clarence Badger. Screenplay: Edfrid A. Bingham. Based on an original story by Peter Clark MacFarlane. Photography: Marcel Le Picard. Assistant Director: James Flood. Los Angeles premiere: California Theatre, December 26, 1920. 5 reels. With Will Rogers (Tal), Mary Warren (Hulda), Bert Sprotte (Skole), Lionel Belmore (Armstrong), Charles A. Smiley (Captain Larsem), Nick Cogley (Captain Stahl), Doris Pawn (Annie), and Jane Starr (Maid).

Story and Criticism

A Swede named Tal (Will Rogers), due to his awkwardness and inexperience, has a number of misadventures until he discovers the right woman, someone who will appreciate his innocence. The *New York Times* reviewer was disturbed that the "unusually wordy story gives Rogers only occasional opportunities to reveal his peculiar expressiveness and personality" (February 28, 1921, p. 16, col. 2).

12. Boys Will Be Boys

A Goldwyn Pictures Corporation production. Director: Clarence Badger. Screenplay: Edfrid A. Bingham. Based on a *Saturday Evening Post* serial by Irvin S. Cobb and a comedy by Charles O'Brien Kennedy. Photography: Marcel Le Picard. Los Angeles premiere: California Theatre, February 27, 1921. 5 reels. With Will Rogers (Poop O'Day), Irene Rich (Lucy), C. E. Mason (Tom Minor), Sydney Ainsworth (Sublette), Edward Kimball (Judge Priest), H. Milton Ross (Bagby), C. E. Thurston (Sheriff Breck), May Hopkins (Kitty), Cordelia Callahan (Mrs. Hunter), Nick Cogley (Aunt Mandy), and Burton Halbert (Farmer Bell).

Story and Criticism

This would be the first — but certainly not the last — Will Rogers film based on a story by Irvin S. Cobb, a figure in regional literature who had much in common with Will Rogers. The local ne'er-do-well discovers a great sum of cash and goes on a spending spree. The *New York Times* reviewer enjoyed brief moments of Rogers' acting but found the movie tedious, "padded out with so much labored melodrama, comedy and sentimentality that, for scene after scene, it is buried entirely" (May 6, 1921, p. 20, col. 2). Later Will Rogers films would make better use of "Judge Priest" tales by Cobb.

13. An Unwilling Hero

A Goldwyn Pictures Corporation production. Director: Clarence Badger. Screenplay: Arthur F. Statter. Based on the story "Whistling Dick's Christmas Stocking" by O. Henry. Photography: Marcel Le Picard. Los Angeles premiere: California Theatre, May 8, 1921. 5 reels. With Will Rogers (Dick), Molly Malone (Nadine), John Bowers (Hunter), Darrel Foss (Richmond), Jack Curtis (Boston Harry), George Kunkel, Dick Johnson, Larry Fisher and Leo Willis (Hoboes), Nick Cogley (Negro Servant), and Edward Kimball (Lovejoy).

Story and Criticism

A professional tramp, "Whistling Dick," gets off a freight car in New Orleans where he discovers that a new law against vagabonds makes him unwelcome. He leaves town quickly and becomes involved — against his will — in a robbery of a large plantation house. The honest tramp warns the family and is treated like a hero. The family offers him a job, but, realizing that employment is not his cup of tea, the "unwilling hero" departs in the night to continue his rambling ways.

Obviously, this was a Jubilo persona film for Rogers. The appeal of lazy rural characters in American literature and film needs to be explored further.

14. Doubling for Romeo

A Goldwyn Pictures Corporation production. Director: Clarence Badger. Screenplay: Bernard McConville. Based on an original story by Elmer Rice, which in turn was based on William Shakespeare's "Romeo and Juliet." Titles: Will Rogers. Photography: Marcel Le Picard. Art Director: Cedric Gibbons. New York premiere: Capitol Theatre, October 23, 1921. 6 reels. With Will Rogers (Sam/Romeo), Sylvia Breamer (Lulu/Juliet), Raymond Hatton (Steve Woods/Paris), Sydney Ainsworth (Pendleton/Mercutio), Al Hart (Bis Alec/Tybalt), John Cossar (Foster/Capulet), C. E. Thurston (Duffy Saunders/Benvolio), Cordelia Callahan (Maggie/Maid), Roland Rushton (Minister/Friar), Jimmy Rogers (Jimmie Jones), and William Orlamond (Movie Director).

Story and Criticism

In this satire of movie conventions, "Sleepy" Sam Cody (Will Rogers) is told by his girlfriend that he must conform to Hollywood standards of romance. In search of guidance, the country bumpkin travels to the Goldwyn Studios where a juvenile star, Jimmie Jones (Jimmy Rogers), helps him to find employment. *Will Rogers' 1920s* employs a hilarious scene from this picture in which Sam attempts to portray an authentic Hollywood lover. Unfortunately, the simple cowboy is so shy that the "vamp" with whom the scene is played embarrasses him. While attempting a kiss, he knocks over some furniture, disrupting the scene. In other acting assignments, the country boy has constant difficulty fitting into Hollywood's mold of heroism and romance.

Without question, this is the best of Rogers' satires and parodies during the silent years. The *New York Times* reviewer asked rhetorically: ". . . breathes there a man, or a woman, with soul so slushy that he cannot relish its fun?" (October 24, 1921, p. 13, col. 1). The film is still worth watching.

Availability

Both the Museum of Modern Art and the Will Rogers Memorial have prints.

15. A Poor Relation

A Goldwyn Pictures Corporation production. Director: Clarence Badger. Screenplay: Bernard McConville. Based on the comedy drama by Edward E. Kidder. Photography: Marcel Le Picard. Released: December 1921. 5

reels/4,609 feet. With Will Rogers (Noah Vale), Sylvia Breamer (Miss Fay), Wallace MacDonald (Johnny Smith), Sydney Ainsworth (Sterrett), George B. Williams (Mr. Fay), Molly Malone (Scallops), Robert De Vilbess (Rip), Jeanette Trebaol (Patch), and Walter Perry (O'Halley).

Story and Criticism

This melodrama has a plot whose intricacy may not be worth the candle. Noah Vale (Will Rogers) is an unsuccessful inventor interested in perfecting a new device that will win him a fortune. As a pastime, he writes clever epigrams which he saves in the attic of his home. After many twists and turns of plot complications, Noah is "discovered" as a writer and gives up his futile attempts to be an inventor.

16. One Glorious Day

A Famous Players-Lasky production, released by Paramount. Producer: Jesse L. Lasky. Director: James Cruze. Screenplay: Walter Woods. Based on an original story by Walter Woods and A. B. Baringer. Photography: Karl Brown. Released: February 5, 1922. 5 reels. With Will Rogers (Ezra Botts), Lila Lee (Molly McIntyre), Alan Hale (Ben Wadley), John Fox (Ek), George Nichols (Pat Curran), Emily Rait (Mrs. McIntyre), and Clarence Burton (Bert Snead).

Story and Criticism

In this fantasy, a spirit impatient over the long wait for an earthly body to inhabit decides to occupy the soul of Professor Ezra Botts (Will Rogers). Everyone who knows Botts is shocked by the resulting transformation, which resembles the radical transformation chronicled in the delightful 1980 remake, *Heaven Can Wait.*

One Glorious Day proved of interest to its contemporaries for two reasons: first, the issue of spiritualism—in which Professor Botts is dabbling when Ek invades his body—was receiving much attention in literary circles; second, the film borrowed production ideas from a revolutionary new German film called *The Cabinet of Dr. Caligari.* The *New York Times* reviewer was extremely impressed by the technical abilities demonstrated in set design and filming techniques; on the other hand, the comic dimension could not have had an effect if the issue of spiritualism had not been in the air. That Will Rogers' writings in this period comically treated spiritualism and spiritualists is further evidence of the timeliness of this film's social satire.

The *New York Times,* in its wrapup for 1922, listed *One Glorious Day* as one of the top thirty photoplays of the year, saying that in it "The American screen has achieved something distinctive" ("Screen Pictures of 1922," July 2, 1922, Section IV, p. 3, col. 1).

17. The Roping Fool

A Will Rogers production, released by Pathé. Director: Clarence Badger. Screenplay: Will Rogers. Photography: Marcel Le Picard. Released: October 29, 1922. 2 reels. With Will Rogers ("Ropes" Reilly), Irene Rich (the girl), John Ince (the stranger), and Guinn Williams (the foreman).

Story and Criticism

The Roping Fool (1922) was one of the three films which Will Rogers' own film company made. Rogers' brief venture into production failed to yield a profit—at least in part because of distribution problems during an era of "block booking." Of all the Will Rogers silent films shown to college audiences, this one receives the greatest attention. Since it is about roping, it has considerable eye appeal. Rogers painted his ropes white and made extensive use of slow motion to accentuate the rope tricks. Many are as beautiful to watch as they must have been difficult to perform. In addition, there is enough slapstick humor to keep the story moving from one set of tricks to another so that *The Roping Fool* never really descends to the level of a demonstration film. Still, demonstration was at the heart of the matter as Will Rogers, Jr. explains in *Will Rogers' 1920s:*

> He wanted roping to be remembered as an American art, and I think that's why he made *Roping Fool*. In fact, he said: "I made this picture so I could set back in my rocking chair and say 'Now, there, you young ropers, that what I could do when I was your age.'"

In 1924, Will Rogers was forty-five years old, and, according to Will Rogers, Jr., realized that the fine edge he had on some of the more difficult tricks would be lost. The film was indeed a way of fixing in time an art form practiced in his cowboy and vaudeville days.

Availability

Both the Museum of Modern Art and the Will Rogers Memorial have prints and outtakes from this film.

18. Fruits of Faith

A Will Rogers production, released by Pathé. Director: Clarence Badger. Screenplay: Mildred and William Pigott. Photography: Marcel Le Picard. Released: December 24, 1922. 2 reels. With Will Rogers (Larry), Irene Rich (His Wife), and Jimmy Rogers (Baby).

Story and Criticism

Will Rogers plays a Jubilo-type rural hobo in this movie, a slothful individual who will try anything—even prayer—to avoid work. Somehow, he becomes involved in traversing a desert with a mule and a baby (Jimmy Rogers), an adventure that gives Rogers many opportunities for humor and pathos. The *New York Times* reviewer was impressed by "the echoes of smiles, laughter, and applause called forth by the quiet little film" (January 15, 1923, p. 18, col. 3).

19. One Day in 365 (1922)

A Will Rogers production never released.

Story and Criticism

The Will Rogers Memorial has a number of photographs related to the production of this movie, one of three films Rogers attempted through his own company.

The plot is a chronological one, following the domestic routine of the Will Rogers family. The day begins with Dad reading the newspapers at the breakfast table, followed by a series of activities that include a variety show on a miniature stage and horseback activities, and concludes with everybody in bed.

The Rogers children were still a bit too young to make the film very dramatic. In any case, the production was never released. Any student of Will Rogers would cherish an opportunity to see such an "inside story" about the Rogers family.

Availability

Both the Museum of Modern Art and the Will Rogers Memorial have unedited footage from this film.

20. The Headless Horseman

A Sleepy Hollow Corporation production, released by W. W. Hodkinson. Producer: Carl Stearns Clancy. Director: Edward Venturini. Screenplay: Carl Stearns Clancy. Based on the story "The Legend of Sleepy Hollow" by Washington Irving. Photography: Ned Van Buren. New York premiere: Capitol Theatre, December 24, 1922. 50 minutes. With Will Rogers (Ichabod Crane), Lois Meredith (Katrina Van Tassel), Ben Hendricks, Jr. ("Brom" Bones), Mary Foy (Dame Martling), and Charles Graham (Hans Van Ripper).

Story and Criticism

Ichabod Crane (Will Rogers), in this earliest of rural dramas, is a Jubilo character in nineteenth-century New York clothing. Although the movie adheres to Washington Irving's tale, the most that the *New York Times* reviewer could offer in support of the film was that it was "a sincere photoplay which, if not exciting, is at least pleasing to those interested in seeing

'The Legend' illustrated" (December 25, 1922, p. 21, col. 1). The photography in this film is beautiful, but the drama is ineffective.

Availability

Both the Museum of Modern Art and the Will Rogers Memorial have prints of this film. In addition, Blackhawk Films sells a twenty-seven minute abridgment on VHS or Beta-formats.

21. Hollywood

A Famous Players-Lasky production, released by Paramount. Producer: Jesse L. Lasky. Director: James Cruze. Screenplay: Tom Geraghty. Based on an original story by Frank Condon. Photography: Karl Brown. Released: August 19, 1923. 8 reels/8,100 feet. With Hope Drown (Angela Whitaker), Luke Cosgrave (Joel Whitaker), George K. Arthur (Lem Lefferts), Ruby Lafayette (Grandmother Whitaker), Harris Gordon (Dr. Luke Morrison), Will Rogers, Mary Astor, Betty Compson, Ricardo Cortez, Viola Dana, Cecil B. DeMille, Lila Lee, May McAvoy, Pola Negri, Jack Pickford, Anita Stewart, Gloria Swanson, Lois Wilson, etc. (Themselves).

Story and Criticism

Will Rogers played only an incidental part in this showcase for Paramount.

22. Jes' Passin' Through

A Hal E. Roach production, released by Pathé. Director: Charles Parrott. Released: October 14, 1923. 2 reels. With Will Rogers.

Story and Criticism:

This is a "Jubilo" character film in which the protagonist does everything possible to get himself jailed in time for the annual Thanksgiving dinner for the prisoners. The drifter gets himself in a number of scrapes in his struggle to survive. *Moving Picture World* predicted that "Will Rogers' legion of admirers will surely like this one and it should go well with any type of audience" (October 13, 1923, p. 598).

Availability

Both the Museum of Modern Art and the Will Rogers Memorial have prints.

23. Uncensored Movies

A Hal E. Roach production, released by Pathé. Director: Roy Clements. Released: December 9, 1923. 2 reels. With Will Rogers.

Story and Criticism

This comedy consists of a series of unrelated parodies of current films. In each case, Will Rogers plays the leading man and carries to the extreme the characteristics of the film parodied. Spoofed are Tom Mix, Douglas Fairbanks, Sr., Ben Turpin, and Rudolph Valentino. Over forty years later, Mel Brooks would produce on a broader scale similar parodies such as *Young Frankenstein, Blazing Saddles,* and *High Anxiety.*

Availability

Both the Museum of Modern Art and the Will Rogers Memorial have prints. Blackhawk Films sells 16 mm prints.

24. Two Wagons—Both Covered

A Hal E. Roach production, released by Pathé. Director: Rob Wagner. Titles: Will Rogers. Released: January 6, 1924. 2 reels, 22 minutes. With Will Rogers.

Story and Criticism

The Covered Wagon (1923) was one of the first silent films to exploit on-location possibilities for the Western. The James Cruze classic also exploited the presold audience which had enjoyed Emerson Hough's best-seller, an audience consisting of middle-class Americans who would have subscribed to the *Saturday Evening Post.*

As a son of pioneers, Will Rogers was less prone to idealize the Westering generations. *Two Wagons—Both Covered* (1924) recreates scenes from *The Covered Wagon* but always shows the humorous side: Rogers constantly mocked the gestures and demeanor of Ernest Torrence, star of the earlier film; a river is crossed by attaching plastic water wings to cattle and horses; new arrivals to California are attacked by "Escrow Indians" who want the settlers to sign mortgages for housing developments. This delightful film parody starred a man who knew that magazines and popular novels glorified the West beyond recognition.

Availability

The Will Rogers Memorial has a print.

25. The Cowboy Sheik

A Hal E. Roach production, released by Pathé. Director: Jay A. Howe. Released: February 2, 1924. 2 reels, 22 minutes. With Will Rogers.

Story and Criticism

This comedy is an extended spoof of the Rudolph Valentino films which were so popular at the time. Rogers makes a conscious effort to exploit his homeliness in this "romance."

Availability

Both the Museum of Modern Art and the Will Rogers Memorial have prints. Blackhawk Films sells 16 mm prints.

26. The Cake Eater

A Hal E. Roach production, released by Pathé. Titles: Will Rogers. Released: March 2, 1924. 2 reels, 22 minutes. With Will Rogers.

Story and Criticism

In this bunkhouse comedy, the lead character, while ignored by the young woman who has caught his eye, is pursued by a passionate — but unattractive — sister of the man who owns the ranch.

Availability

The Will Rogers Memorial has a print. Blackhawk Films sells 16 mm prints.

27. Big Moments From Little Pictures

A Hal E. Roach production, released by Pathé. Released: March 30, 1924. 2 reels. With Will Rogers.

Story and Criticism

This film is a parody of reigning screen stars, including Rudolph Valentino (a mock scene from *Blood and Sand*), Douglas Fairbanks (a humorous rendering of a scene from *Robin Hood*), and Fred Sterling (a very hurried scene with some Keystone Cops). Will Rogers introduces each segment with a few rope tricks and *Follies*-style patter.

Availability

The Will Rogers Memorial has a print. Blackhawk Films sells 16 mm prints.

28. Highbrow Stuff

A Hal E. Roach production, released by Pathé. Released: April 27, 1924. 2 reels. With Will Rogers.

Story and Criticism

This film attempts to portray the tension between elite culture (which scorns films) and the culture of ordinary Americans. Sophisticates are shown attending little theatre productions instead of going to the movies. While they pretend to like what they see, in reality they are bored by the performances. An especially popular Russian playwright, the darling of the highbrows, is given an opportunity to try his hand at film scripting and is unable to master the new medium. He does very well, however, when a dangerous situation requires him to mount a runaway horse.

As in some of Rogers' later films, he could not resist the opportunity to mock those too sophisticated for popular delights.

29. Going to Congress

A Hal E. Roach production, released by Pathé. Released: May 25, 1924. 2 reels, 22 minutes. With Will Rogers (Alfalfa Doolittle).

Story and Criticism

This delightful film shows how far a candidate must go in the way of promises to reach high office. Alfalfa Doolittle (Will Rogers), an innocuous, lazy storyteller, is selected by the local machine to run for Congress. When he promises to bring rain to the dry fields of voters, Alfalfa is catapulted into office. The story ends as Alfalfa — uncomfortably dressed in a top hat and tails — mounts the stairs of the Capitol, ready to pass legislation that will make his demand for precipitation law.

Availability

The Will Rogers Memorial has a print. Blackhawk Films sells 16 mm prints.

30. Don't Park There

A Hal E. Roach production, released by Pathé. Released: June 22, 1924. 2 reels, 19 minutes. With Will Rogers and Marie Mosquini.

Story and Criticism

Like other comedians of his day, Will Rogers told jokes about the automobile and its impact on American life. Henry Ford often served as the subject for a Will Rogers daily or weekly article. In this film, Rogers brought the phenomenon of the automobile to the screen.

Jubilo is sent to town in a wagon to obtain some patent medicine, but he gets himself involved with a Model T Ford. As a rustic innocent, he knows nothing of the perilous art of driving and less about the new rules and regulations imposed on Americans by this example of machine culture. The film builds to a slapstick climax in which Jubilo loses control of the car and drives through the front window of the drugstore, spontaneously initiating a "drive-in" service. (This hilarious film is used extensively in *Will Rogers' 1920s* [Churchill Films, 1976].)

Availability

The Will Rogers Memorial has a print. Blackhawk Films sells 16 mm prints.

31. Jubilo, Jr.

A Hal E. Roach production, released by Pathé. Director: Robert F. McGowan. Story: Hal E. Roach. Titles: H. M. Walker. Released: June 29, 1924. 2 reels, 28 minutes. With Will Rogers (Jubilo), Mickey Daniels (Jubilo, Jr.), Noah Young (Jubilo's Father), Lyle Tayo (Jubilo's Mother), Mary Kornman, Joe Cobb, Jackie Condon, Andy Samuels, Allen "Farina" Hoskins, Allen Cavan, Richard Daniels, Leo Willis, Joy Winthrop, Otto Himm, and Charley Chase.

Story and Criticism

This film features Will Rogers as he appeared in *Jubilo* (1919), with a flashback to the original "Our Gang" troupe. The movie involves the children and their pranks with Rogers as merely an opening and closing reference point. Naturally, Jubilo, Jr. takes after his namesake.

Availability

The Will Rogers Memorial has a print.

32. Our Congressman

A Hal E. Roach production, released by Pathé. Titles: Will Rogers. Released: July 20, 1924. 2 reels. With Will Rogers (Alfalfa Doolittle).

Story and Criticism

This movie involves more ructions in Washington by the star of *Going to Congress* (1924), the Honorable—if inept—Alfalfa Doolittle.

Availability

The Will Rogers Memorial has a print. Blackhawk Films sells 16 mm prints.

33. A Truthful Liar

A Hal E. Roach production, released by Pathé. Released: August 1924. 2 reels. With Will Rogers (Alfalfa Doolittle).

Story and Criticism

In this "innocent abroad" silent film, Alfalfa Doolittle, a lazy rural story-teller, describes his experience as an ambassador to foreign lands. Later remade as *Ambassador Bill* (1931), the picture gives Rogers a host of opportunities to spoof the stilted manners of high society. A section of this film is used in *Will Rogers' 1920s* where Ambassador Doolittle decides to be introduced to the king, Oklahoma-style.

Availability

The Will Rogers Memorial has a print. Blackhawk Films sells 16 mm prints.

34. *Gee Whiz Genevieve*

A Hal E. Roach production, released by Pathé. Director: Jay A. Howe. Released: September 28, 1924. 2 reels. With Will Rogers, Marie Mosquini, Ena Gregory, Laura Roessing, Mary Foster, Don Maines, and Earl Mohan.

Story and Criticism

This was the last of the Will Rogers–Hal Roach series of two-reel comedies.

35. *Hiking Through Holland with Will Rogers*

A Carl Stearns Clancy production, released by Pathé. Travelesque series. Screenplay: Will Rogers. Released: February 1927. 1 reel. With Will Rogers.

Story and Criticism

In 1926, Will Rogers conducted a detailed inspection of Europe and Russia, reporting his findings through a series of articles in the *Saturday Evening Post*. (This trip and the resulting books are examined in Chapter 2.) A film crew followed Rogers to a number of the stops on the junket, recording location shots which included Rogers before the buildings of Parliament, Rogers looking on amazed at kegs of Irish whiskey, Rogers perplexed by wooden shoes, Rogers spoofing the curiosity associated with the Old Curiosity Shop, and so on.

Unlike the writings produced during the trip, the silent films did not strive to do more than pit an innocent abroad against the quaint differences of European architecture, clothing, and other primarily visual characteristics. In sum, these were glorified home movies which movie-goers could enjoy of their friend, Will Rogers. While not terribly humorous or informative, these travelogues may have meant more to contemporaries who were also following the *Saturday Evening Post* reports. (This description applies to the following items below: 36–41; 43–45; 47–48.)

As usual, the *Tulsa Daily World* took great interest in the venture into documentary: "Rogers' pictures detail his experience with royalty, with dictators, with peasants, with airplanes, railroad trains, strange languages, strange foods, all photographed and described with that mingled sense and nonsense, kindly exaggeration and caustic wit which are so characteristically American in the shrewd, unpretentious Oklahoman" (December 19, 1926, Society Section, p. 9, col. 1).

Availability

Both the Museum of Modern Art and the Will Rogers Memorial have prints.

36. With Will Rogers in Paris

A Carl Stearns Clancy production, released by Pathé. Travelesque series. Screenplay: Will Rogers. Released: February 1927. 1 reel. With Will Rogers.

Story and Criticism

(See entry 35.)

37. With Will Rogers in Dublin

A Carl Stearns Clancy production, released by Pathé. Travelesque series. Screenplay: Will Rogers. Released: February 1927. 1 reel. With Will Rogers.

Story and Criticism

(See entry 35.)

Availability

The Will Rogers Memorial has a print.

38. Roaming the Emerald Isle with Will Rogers

A Carl Stearns Clancy production, released by Pathé. Travelesque series. Screenplay: Will Rogers. Released: May 1927. 1 reel. With Will Rogers.

Story and Criticism

(See entry 35.)

39. Through Switzerland and Bavaria with Will Rogers

A Carl Stearns Clancy production, released by Pathé. Travelesque series. Screenplay: Will Rogers. Released: May 1927. 1 reel. With Will Rogers.

Story and Criticism

(See entry 35.)

Availability

Both the Museum of Modern Art and the Will Rogers Memorial have prints.

40. With Will Rogers in London

A Carl Stearns Clancy production, released by Pathé. Travelesque series. Screenplay: Will Rogers. Released: May 1927. 1 reel. With Will Rogers.

Story and Criticism

(See entry 35.)

Availability

Both the Museum of Modern Art and the Will Rogers Memorial have prints.

41. Hunting For Germans in Berlin with Will Rogers

A Carl Stearns Clancy production, released by Pathé. Travelesque series. Screenplay: Will Rogers. Released: May 1927. 1 reel. With Will Rogers.

Story and Criticism

(See entry 35.)

42. Tiptoes

A British National production, released by Paramount. Producer: J. D. Williams. Director and Screenplay: Herbert Wilcox. Based on the play by Guy Bolton and Fred Thompson. Photography: Roy Oberbaugh. British release: June 1927. 6 reels. With Will Rogers (Hen Kaye), Dorothy Gish (Tiptoes), Nelson Keys (Al Kaye), John Manners (Lord William Montgomery), Miles Mander (Rollo Stevens), Annie Esmond (Aunt), Ivy Ellison (Sister), and Dennis Hoey (Hotelier).

Story and Criticism

Tiptoes is an episodic film with a very loose plot drawn from the musical by the same name. Dorothy Gish plays Tiptoes, a member of an American comedy act. To help the team find engagements, she poses as an American heiress, only to be unmasked as a fraud. The film ends happily, however, with jobs for all and marriage between Tiptoes and an English lord.

At the opening of the film, Will Rogers (as Hen Kaye) has an opportunity to perform but has little chance to shine during the remainder of the film because of the prominence of the love interest. *Kinematograph Weekly* found the film to be at best fair (May 24, 1928, p. 52). The reviewer wanted more Will Rogers and less melodrama.

43. Prowling Around France with Will Rogers

A Carl Stearns Clancy production, released by Pathé. Travelesque series.

Screenplay: Will Rogers. Released: September 18, 1927. 1 reel. With Will Rogers.

Story and Criticism

(See entry 35.)

44. *Winging 'Round Europe with Will Rogers*

A Carl Stearns Clancy production, released by Pathé. Travelesque series. Screenplay: Will Rogers. Released: November 20, 1927. 1 reel. With Will Rogers.

Story and Criticism

(See entry 35.)

45. *Exploring England with Will Rogers*

A Carl Stearns Clancy production, released by Pathé. Travelesque series. Screenplay: Will Rogers. Released: December 18, 1927. 1 reel. With Will Rogers.

Story and Criticism

(See entry 35.)

46. *A Texas Steer*

A Sam E. Rork production, released by First National. Producer: Sam E. Rork. Director: Richard Wallace. Screenplay: Bernard McConville. Titles: Will Rogers and Garrett Graham. Adaptation: Paul Schofield. Based on the musical comedy by Charles Hale Hoyt. Photography: Jack MacKenzie. Film Editor: Frank Lawrence. Comedy Construction: Jack Wagner. Production Manager: Ben Singer. Assistant Director: James F. O'Shea. Released: December 4, 1927. 8 reels. With Will Rogers (Maverick Brander), Louise Fazenda (Mrs. Ma Brander), Sam Hardy (Brassy Gall), Ann Rork (Bossy Brander), Douglas Fairbanks, Jr. (Fairleigh Bright), Lilyan Tashman (Dixie Style), George Marion, Sr. (Fishback), Bud Jamieson (Othello), Arthur Hoyt (Knott Innitt), Mack Swain (Bragg), William Orlamond (Blow), and Lucien Littlefield (Tell).

Story and Criticism

Will Rogers devoted a daily telegram to this movie, a production that filmed some scenes in the Coolidge White House. Like the novice official in *Our Congressman* (1924) and *Going to Congress* (1924), Maverick Brander (Will Rogers) is a bumpkin suddenly thrust into the Washington scene. The energetic representative of Red Dog, Texas, manages to navigate through the dangers of Washington society and succeeds in persuading the House to fund a pet project, the Eagle Rock Dam Bill.

Will Rogers acted as his own critic for *A Texas Steer,* reminding young viewers that they might be too sophisticated to understand the country humor of the movie: "most of you young folks haven't seen it because it went out of style about the time hip flasks and cabarets and the rolled stocking fads got the country in an argument with the grandmothers" (Weekly Article for January 1, 1928). (For additional comments by Rogers, see Chapter 2.)

47. Reeling Down the Rhine with Will Rogers

A Carl Stearns Clancy production, released by Pathé. Travelesque series. Screenplay: Will Rogers. Released: January 15, 1928. 1 reel. With Will Rogers, Jimmy Rogers, and Mrs. Will Rogers.

Story and Criticism

(See entry 35.)

48. Over the Bounding Blue with Will Rogers

A Carl Stearns Clancy production, released by Pathé. Travelesque series. Screenplay: Will Rogers. Released: February 12, 1928. 1 reel. With Will Rogers.

Story and Criticism

(See entry 35.)

Availability

Both the Museum of Modern Art and the Will Rogers Memorial have prints.

49. They Had to See Paris

A Fox Movietone production. Director: Frank Borzage. Screenplay: Sonya Levien. Dialogue: Owen Davis, Sr. Based on the story by Homer Croy. Photography: Chester Lyons and Al Brick. Stage Director: Bernard Steele. Art Director: Harry Oliver. Costumes: Sophie Wachner. Chief Soundman: George Costello. Song: "I Could Do It for You," by Sidney Mitchell, Archie Gottler, and Con Conrad. Film Editor: Margaret B. Clancy. Assistant Director: Lew Borzage. World premiere: Fox Cathay Circle Theatre, Los Angeles, September 18, 1929. 95 minutes. With Will Rogers (Pike Peters), Irene Rich (Mrs. Peters), Marguerite Churchill (Opal

Peters), Owen Davis, Jr. (Ross Peters), Fifi D'orsay (Claudine), Ivan Lebedeff (Marquis de Brissac), Marcelle Corday (Marluise de Brissac), Theodore Lodi (Grand Duke Makiall), Rex Bell (Clark McCurdy), Christiane Yves (Fleuris), Edgar Kennedy (Ed Eggers), Bob Kerr (Tupper), Marcia Manon (Miss Mason), Andre Cheron (Valet), Gregory Gay (Prince Ordinsky), and Mr. Persian Pussy (Claudine's Kitty).

Story and Criticism

Will Rogers was extremely fortunate that silent films became "talkies," for his humor depended so much upon accent, intonation, and phrasing to convey his rustic point of view. He was even more fortunate in the choice of his first sound film, *They Had to See Paris,* for this picture allowed him to portray an archetypal "innocent abroad."

Pike Peters (Will Rogers) and his wife (Irene Rich) leave the American heartland to see a little of the *beau monde.* While in Europe, Pike's daughter (Marguerite Churchill) meets and marries an aristocrat while Pike develops a "good ole boy" relationship with a Grand Duke Makiall: they call each other "Pike" and "Mike." (This twosome would be revived for the Depression era movie *Down to Earth* [1932], which the studio planned as a sequel.) Reviewers found the film refreshing, and—although production standards were still not fully adapted to the new sound technology—it can be asserted that the film is still a delight to watch.

As premiere time approached, Will Rogers hopped on a plane and flew to Tulsa, ostensibly to visit the home folks. Once the film was screened and applauded, Betty Rogers wired: "The picture has opened and you can come home now." It was a successful step into a new movie era. (For anecdotes about this movie, see Homer Croy, *Our Will Rogers,* 1953.)

Availability

Both the Museum of Modern Art and the Will Rogers Memorial have prints.

50. Happy Days

A Fox Grandeur production. Director: Benjamin Stoloff. Staged by Walter Catlett. Story and Dialogue: Sidney Langfield and Edwin Burke. Photography: Lucien Andriot and John Schmitz. Grandeur Cameraman: J. O. Taylor. Lyrics and Music: Joseph McCarthy, James F. Hanley, L. Wolfe Gilbert, and Abel Baer, Conrad, Mitchell and Gottler, James Brockman, Harry Stoddard, and Marcy Klauber. Art Director: Jack Schultze. Costumes: Sophie Wachner. Dances staged by Earl Lindsay. Soundman: Samuel Waite. Film Editor: Clyde Carruth. Assistant Directors: Ad Schaumer, Michael Farley, and Lew Breslow. New York premiere: Roxy Theatre, February 14, 1930. 86 minutes. With Charles E. Evans (Col. Billy

Batcher), Marjorie White (Margie), Richard Keene (Dick), Stuart Erwin
(Jig), Martha Lee Sparks (Nancy Lee), Clifford Dempsey (Sheriff Benton),
James J. Corbett and George MacFarlane (Interlocutors), George Olsen
and His Music, and a Minstrel Ensemble consisting of Janet Gaynor,
Charles Farrell, Victor McLaglen, El Brendel, Edmund Lowe, William Col-
lier, Sr., Tom Patricola, Dixie Lee, George Jessel, "Whispering" Jack
Smith, Sharon Lynn, Lew Brice, Gilbert Emery, The Slate Brothers, Rex
Bell, Will Rogers, Walter Catlett, Marjorie White, Frank Richardson, J.
Harold Murray, Charles E. Evans, Richard Keene, Warner Baxter, Ann
Pennington, David Rollins, Frank Albertson, Paul Page, J. Farrell Mac-
Donald, Nick Stuart, and Lumsden Hare.

Story and Criticism

Rogers supplies a cameo appearance in this Fox extravaganza which attempted to exploit an experimental screen size and a new sound system. The
weak plot involved a minstrel show down on the Mississippi. Each of the
listed performers — among them Rogers — has an opportunity to show what
Fox Grandeur could do. The film is of no value to the student of Will
Rogers.

Availability

The Museum of Modern Art has a print.

51. So This Is London

A Fox Movietone production. Director: John Blystone. Screenplay:
Sonya Levien. Adaptation and Dialogue: Owen Davis, Sr. Adapted from
George M. Cohan's stageplay by Arthur Goodrich. Photography: Charles
G. Clarke. Chief Sound Technician: Frank McKenzie. Settings: Jack
Schultze. Costumes: Sophie Wachner. Film Editor: Jack Dennis. Assistant
Director: Jasper Blystone. Los Angeles premiere: Fox Cathay Circle
Theatre, June 19, 1930. 89 minutes. With Will Rogers (Hiram Draper),
Irene Rich (Mrs. Hiram Draper), Frank Albertson (Junior Draper),
Maureen O'Sullivan (Elinnor Draper), Lumsden Hare (Lord Percy Worth-
ing), Mary Forbes (Lady Worthing), Bramwell Fletcher (Alfred
Honeycutt), Dorthy Christie (Lady Amy Ducksworth), Martha Lee Sparks
(Martha), and Ellen Woodston (A Nurse).

Story and Criticism

In this sequel to *They Had to See Paris* (1929), Rogers again plays an
American businessman who reluctantly ventures abroad. Rogers exploits
the passport application scene to comment on his Indian blood and the vast
differences between frontier life and the bureaucratic society which requires
official papers to prove one's birth. Once in England, Hiram Draper (Will

Rogers) and Mrs. Draper (Irene Rich—who was Mrs. Peters in *They Had to See Paris*) initially establish a hostile relationship with a family of British royalty. Relations eventually mellow, but no opportunity is lost to score hits against aristocratic customs. At the close, Hiram and Lord Worthing join in the tune which both lands have in common: Will Rogers as Hiram Draper bellows "My Country 'Tis of Thee;" Lumsden Hare as Lord Worthing sings the British lyrics for "God Save the King." In some respects, the movie replayed the "Pike" and "Mike" relationship of *They Had to See Paris,* but the contrast between the two films was sufficient to please the *New York Times* reviewer who found the audience to be "in a high state of glee during the screening of this clever comedy" (Mordaunt Hall, May 24, 1930, p. 21, col. 2).

Availability

Both the Museum of Modern Art and the Will Rogers Memorial have prints.

52. Lightnin'

A Fox Movietone production. Director: Henry King. Screenplay: S. N. Behrman and Sonya Levien. Based on the play by Frank Bacon and Winchell Smith, as produced on the stage by John Golden. Photography: Chester Lyons. Art Director: Harry Oliver. Film Editor: Louis Loeffler. Music and Lyrics: Joseph McCarthy and James F. Hanley. Recording Engineer: George Costello. Costumes: Sophie Wachner. Assistant Director: Frank Bettman. New York premiere: Roxy Theatre, November 28, 1930. 94 minutes. With Will Rogers ("Lightnin' " Bill Jones), Louise Dresser (Mrs. Jones), Joel McCrea (John Marvin), Helen Cohan (Milly), Ruth Warren (Margaret Davis), Joyce Compton (Diana), Rex Bell (Ronald), Frank Campeau (Sheriff), Luke Cosgrave (Zeb), Thomas Jefferson (Walter Lannon), Goodee Montgomery (Mrs. Brooks), Phil Tead (Monte Winslow), Walter Percival (Everett Hammond), Charlotte Walker (Mrs. Thatcher), Blanche Le Clair (Mrs. Leonard), Bruce Warren (Mr. Leonard), Antica Nast (Mrs. Lord), Moon Carroll (Mrs. Blue), Bess Flowers (Mrs. Weeks), Gwendolyn Faye (Mrs. Starr), Eva Dennison (Mrs. George), Betty Alden (Mrs. Graham), Lucille Young (Mrs. Young), Betty Sinclair (Mrs. Bigg), Roxanne Curtis (Divorcee), Sharon Lynn (Mrs. Lower), Joseph M. Kerrigan (Judge Townsend), and Jason Robards (Thomas).

Story and Criticism

In this rural tale, Bill Jones owns and operates a hotel which straddles the line dividing California from Nevada, a strange characteristic that attracts even stranger customers—wives in search of divorce and criminals fleeing from the police of both states. Much of the story centers on the proprietor whose inability to work and unwillingness to hurry have earned him the nickname "Lightnin'." Thus, we have a Jubilo-style characterization within a sound film setting.

This was only the third sound film for Will Rogers, but he was quickly gathering a following "which was attested to by the crowds that filed into the big house for the first performance and by the fact that in spite of the wintry blasts a line of patrons was waiting outside." In addition to the head count, Mordaunt Hall was also impressed that "Mr. Rogers does not miss a single chance to make a line tell" (*New York Times,* November 29, 1930, p. 21, col. 4). Clearly, Rogers' work in the sound film was a complete success.

Availability

Both the Museum of Modern Art and the Will Rogers Memorial have prints.

53. *A Connecticut Yankee*

A Fox production. Director: David Butler. Screenplay: William Counselman. Based on the fantasy by Mark Twain. Photography: Ernest Palmer. Film Editor: Irene Mora. Sound: Joseph Aiken. New York premiere: Roxy Theatre, April 10, 1931. 94 minutes. With Will Rogers (Hank/Sir Boss), William Farnum (King Arthur), Myrna Loy (Morgan Le Fay), Maureen O'Sullivan (Alisande), Frank Albertson (Clarence), Mitchell Harris (Merlin), and Brandon Hurst (Sagramor).

Story and Criticism

With adjustments to allow the use of newer technological gadgets such as automobiles, helicopters, machine guns, and radios, this adaptation of Mark Twain was so entertaining to audiences that it also enjoyed a 1936 re-release. Hank Morgan (Will Rogers) adjusts every scene selected to suit Will Rogers themes: the knights slobbering at the round dinner table are addressed as "Fellow Rotarians"; the sun is "forced" to eclipse as a result of a chant involving such potent terms as "prosperity," "farm relief," "freedom for Ireland," and "light wines and beer"; the problem of distribution of manufactured goods is solved by the "potent magic of advertising," a common topic for Will Rogers' writings. In the art of jousting, the lance is replaced by the lasso. This was a big studio production with lavish sets, costumes, and gadgets.

The serious themes of Twain's novel — some of which were also important to Rogers the journalist — are excluded from the film.

Availability

Both the Museum of Modern Art and the Will Rogers Memorial have prints.

54. *Young As You Feel*

A Fox production. Director: Frank Borzage. Screenplay: Edwin Burke. Based on the play *Father and The Boys* by George Ade. Photography: Chester Lyons. Film Editor: Margaret Clancy. Art Director: Jack Schultze. Music and Lyrics: James F. Hanley. Assistant Director: Lew Borzage. New York premiere: Roxy Theatre, August 7, 1931. 78 minutes. With Will Rogers (Lemuel Morehouse), Fifi D'orsay (Fleurette), Lucien Littlefield (Marley), Donald Dillaway (Billy Morehouse), Terrance Ray (Tom Morehouse), Lucille Brown (Dorothy Gregson), Rosalie Roy (Rose Gregson), C. Henry Gordon (Lamson), John T. Murray (Colonel Stanhope), Brandon Hurst (Robbins), Marcia Harris (Mrs. Dentor), Otto Hoffman (Secretary), Joan Standing (Lemuel's Secretary), and Gregory Gaye (Pierre).

Story and Criticism

As Lemuel Morehouse of the Morehouse Meat Packing Company, Will Rogers cuts loose from the daily grind of business that is ruining his health. Turning corporate worries over to his two young sons, Lemuel becomes somewhat of a sybarite: he dresses in the most expensive clothes, throws big parties, and comes close to acquiring a mistress (Fifi D'orsay). Throughout these highjinks, Morehouse keeps his feet on the ground, avoiding the pitfalls of taste which usually await the leisure-class culture vulture. The film develops a fun-loving and virile image for Rogers, the kind of image conveyed by his mature journalism: he knows the world and can enjoy the benefits of wealth without losing the common touch.

Availability

Both the Museum of Modern Art and the Will Rogers Memorial have prints.

55. *Ambassador Bill*

A Fox production. Director: Sam Taylor. Screenplay: Guy Bolton. Suggested by the book *Ambassador from the United States* by Vincent Sheean. Photography: John Mescall. Film Editor: Harold Schuster. Art Director: Duncan Cramer. New York premiere: Roxy Theatre, November 13, 1931. 68 minutes. With Will Rogers (Bill Harper), Marguerite Churchill (The Queen), Greta Nissen (Ilka), Tad Alexander (King Paul), Gustav von Seyffertitz (Prince de Polikoff), Ray Milland (Lotaar), Ferdinand Munier (Senator Pillsbury), Arnold Korff (The General), Ernest Wood (Northfield Slater), Edward Maxwell (Monte), Tom Ricketts (Littleton), Theodore Lodi (French Ambassador), Herbert Bunston (British Ambassador), and Ben Turpin (Butcher).

Story and Criticism

This movie was a remake, with additional scenes, of Will Rogers' *A Truthful Liar* (1924), portions of which are used in *Will Rogers' 1920s* (1976). Ben Harper (Will Rogers) is an unpretentious businessman who finds himself appointed ambassador to Sylvania, a nation with an unstable political climate. In his down-home way, the new ambassador wins the heart of the king, sharing with the lad (who is twelve years old) such riches of American culture as baseball and cowboy outfits. Rogers has numerous opportunities to score hits against politicians, protocol, and pomposity. Slapstick humor is introduced when dialogue fails. A reviewer pronounced it a typical "innocent abroad" role for Rogers, "a good sketch with funny lines and ludicrous situations" (Mordaunt Hall, *New York Times,* November 14, 1931, p. 15, col. 3).

Availability

Both the Museum of Modern Art and the Will Rogers Memorial have prints.

56. Business and Pleasure

A Fox production. Associate Producer: A. L. Rockett. Director: David Butler. Screenplay: William Counselman and Gene Towne. Based on the novel *The Plutocrat* by Booth Tarkington. Photography: Ernest Palmer. Sound: J. E. Aiken. New York premiere: Roxy Theatre, February 12, 1932. 76 minutes. With Will Rogers (Earl Tinker), Jetta Goudal (Madame Momora), Joel McCrea (Lawrence Ogle), Dorothy Peterson (Mrs. Tinker), Peggy Ross (Olivia Tinker), Cyril Ring (Arthur Jones), Jed Prouty (Ben Wackstle), Oscar Apfel (P. D. Weatheright), Vernon Dent (Charlie Turner) and Boris Karloff (Sheik).

Story and Criticism

This film put Will Rogers back into another "innocent abroad" role. Earl Tinker (Will Rogers) owns a razor blade company in Oklahoma. He and his family are aboard an ocean liner en route to the African coast to vacation and to discover the formula for Damascan sword steel. A considerable portion of the movie takes place aboard ship where intrigue is supplied by the presence of an industrial spy (Jetta Goudal) who presses herself upon the American businessman.

Mordaunt Hall was enthusiastic about what he saw, especially in the light of audience reactions: "The Roxy was well filled for the first showing of this film and many a chuckle, giggle, and guffaw was evoked by the comedian's special brand of dry wit" (*New York Times,* February 13, 1932, p. 23, col. 4).

Availability

Both the Museum of Modern Art and the Will Rogers Memorial have prints.

57. Down to Earth

A Fox production. Director: David Butler. Screenplay: Edwin Burke. Based on a story by Homer Croy. Photography: Ernest Palmer. New York premiere: Roxy Theatre, September 1, 1932. 79 minutes. With Will Rogers (Pike Peters), Dorothy Jordan (Julia Pearson), Irene Rich (Idy Peters), Matty Kemp (Ross Peters), Mary Carlisle (Jackie Harper), Clarence Wilson (Ed Eggers), Theodore Lodi (Grand Duke Michael), Brandon Hurst (Butler), Louise Mackintosh (Mrs. Phillips), and Harvey Clark (Cameron).

Story and Criticism

Like the later *Mr. Skitch* (1933), this Homer Croy story comes too close to the realities of the Depression for its humor to function properly. Pike Peters (Will Rogers) is a wealthy Oklahoman whose income cannot keep pace with his social-climbing wife's (Dorothy Jordan) appetite for luxurious parties, cars, and clothes. At a particularly extravagant dress ball, Pike announces that he has lost all his money and that "the circus is over." The concluding scenes show Pike fending for himself in the kitchen, at last out of the tyrannous gaze of his butler and—thankfully—"down to earth."

Mordaunt Hall found the movie to be "mildly merry hot-weather entertainment," which hardly seems a compliment (*New York Times,* September 2, 1932, p. 19, col. 2).

Availability

Both the Museum of Modern Art and the Will Rogers Memorial have prints.

58. Too Busy to Work

A Fox production. Director: John Blystone. Screenplay: Barry Conners and Philip Klein. Based on the story "Jubilo" by Ben Ames Williams. Photography: Charles G. Clarke. Sound: Eugene Grossman. New York premiere: Roxy Theatre, December 2, 1932. 76 minutes. With Will Rogers (Jubilo), Marian Nixon (Rose), Dick Powell (Dan), Frederick Burton (Judge Hardy), Constantine Romanoff (Axel), Douglas Cosgrove (Sheriff), Louise Beavers (Mammy), and Jack O'Hara (Under Sheriff).

Story and Criticism

In this remake of *Jubilo* (1919), Rogers is given the opportunity to comment and sing. The film also gets the rural tramp into an automobile for the kind of slapstick humor which Rogers supplied in a Jubilo-role film, *Don't Park There* (1924). Both *Jubilo* and *Too Busy to Work* were based on a rural tale by Ben Ames Williams, a writer for the *Saturday Evening Post* famous for his regional studies.

The lazy characters in rural literature have pleased anxious city folk since the days of Harriet Beecher Stowe's *Oldtown Folks* (1869). Mordaunt Hall's reaction to the comic sloth of Jubilo (Will Rogers) says much about the appeal of the genre. Hall was almost too impressed. Calling Will Rogers "one of Hollywood's most industrious inhabitants," Hall was surprised that "this actor, writer, flier, and polo enthusiast" could actually look slothful (*New York Times,* December 3, 1932, p. 21, col. 4). It was another tribute to the sense of ease which radiated from the Rogers films of the sound era.

Availability

Both the Museum of Modern Art and the Will Rogers Memorial have prints.

59. State Fair

A Fox production. Director: Henry King. Screenplay: Paul Green and Sonya Levien. Based on the novel by Philip Stong. Photography: Hal Mohr. Art Director: Duncan Cramer. Costumes: Rita Kaufman. Film Editor: R. W. Dischoff. Sound: A. L. Von Kirbach. Assistant Director: Ray Flynn. New York premiere: Radio City Music Hall, January 26, 1933. 95 minutes. With Janet Gaynor (Margy Frake), Will Rogers (Abel Frake), Lew Ayres (Pat Gilbert), Sally Eilers (Emily Joyce), Norman Foster (Wayne Frake), Louise Dresser (Melissa Frake), Frank Craven (The Storekeeper), Victor Jory (The Barker), and Frank Melton (Harry Ware).

Story and Criticism

Abel Frake (Will Rogers), his wife (Louise Dresser), and two children drive to a state fair in an automobile packed with pickles, mincemeat, jams, and an enormous hog named Blue Boy. The Frake children almost fall in love with strangers, Abel nearly suffers from a nervous breakdown in his efforts to instill a winning attitude in Blue Boy, and judges at the food competition are almost knocked out by the alcoholic content of Mrs. Frake's mincemeat. Everyone returns to the Frake farm unscathed, although Blue Boy's future looks doubtful. Now that the trophy has been won, Abel Frake reflects that "what is a winner today may be ham tomorrow."

This film was important to Rogers' late career. Many reviewers hailed the rustic casting and asked for more such parts for the Oklahoman.

Availability

Both the Museum of Modern Art and the Will Rogers Memorial have prints. Rented by Films, Incorporated, Archive Collection.

60. Dr. Bull

A Fox production. Director: John Ford. Screenplay: Paul Green. Continuity: Jane Storm. Based on the novel *The Last Adam* by James Gould Cozzens. Photography: George Schneiderman. Music: Samuel Kaylin. New York premiere: Radio City Music Hall, October 5, 1933. 75 minutes. With Will Rogers (Dr. Bull), Vera Allen (Janet Cardmaker), Marian Nixon (May Tripping), Howard Lally (Joe Tripping), Berton Churchill (Herbert Banning), Louise Dresser (Mrs. Banning), Andy Devine (Larry Ward), Rochelle Hudson (Virginia Banning), Ralph Morgan (Dr. Verney), Tempe Pigott (Grandma), Elizabeth Patterson (Aunt Patricia), Nora Cecil (Aunt Emily), Patsy O'Byrne (Susan), Effie Ellsler (Aunt Myra), Veda Buckland (Mary), and Helen Freeman (Helen Upjohn).

Story and Criticism

Dr. Bull is another late Rogers film drawn from a work of regional literature, in this case a novel by James Gould Cozzens entitled *The Last Adam*. The principal character is a small-town general practitioner in Connecticut who may be behind in the literature of his profession but is certainly ahead of everybody else in seeing into the human heart: a young man needing therapy, a town afflicted by typhoid, a choir lacking volume, and a lonely, beautiful widow (Vera Allen) are all treated according to their particular needs.

Dr. Bull is a warm film, far more humane than its literary model. B. R. Crisler of the *New York Times* found it to be "a homey, lifelike tale, set forth in a leisurely fashion . . . [whose] . . . comedy, as far as the stellar player's work is concerned, is gratifyingly natural" (October 6, 1935, p. 21, col. 2). For more analysis of this film, see Peter C. Rollins, "Regional Literature and Will Rogers," 1974.

Availability

Both the Museum of Modern Art and the Will Rogers Memorial have prints. Rented by Films, Incorporated, Archive Collection.

61. Mr. Skitch

A Fox production. Director: James Cruze. Screenplay: Ralph Spence and Sonya Levien. Based on the story "Green Dice" by Anne Cameron. Photography: John Seitz. Sound: W. S. Flick. New York premiere: Roxy Theatre, December 22, 1933. 70 minutes. With Will Rogers (Mr. Skitch), ZaSu Pitts (Mrs. Skitch), Rochelle Hudson (Emily Skitch), Florence Desmond (Flo), Harry Green (Cohen), Charles Starrett (Harvey Denby), and Eugene Pallette (Cliff).

Story and Criticism

The *Tulsa Daily World* for December 24, 1933, carried an advertisement for this film, calling it "A Tin-can Trek Across America That Leaves You in

Stitches" (p. 7). Indeed, the film traces the trip of Mr. Skitch (Will Rogers) and his wife (ZaSu Pitts) from their Middle West home to California. Many adventures are encountered en route which allow for physical and verbal humor.

Unfortunately, the timing for this story could not have been worse. The reason for the trip is the eviction of the Skitch family from their rather palatial home after a bank failure. Such an opening for the film was too close to Depression realities for humor to function properly. *Mr. Skitch* was simply a bad project, not unlike an attempt to remake *The Grapes of Wrath* as a comedy. Mordaunt Hall of the *New York Times,* while appreciating Rogers' work, found the film "never particularly dramatic" (December 23, 1933, p. 19, col. 1).

Availability

Both the Museum of Modern Art and the Will Rogers Memorial have prints.

62. David Harum

A Fox production. Producer: Winfield Sheehan. Director: James Cruze. Screenplay: Walter Woods. Based on the novel by Edward Noyes Westcott. Photography: Hal Mohr. Musical Director: Louis DeFrancisco. Film Editor: Jack Maury. Recording Engineer: W. S. Flick. New York premiere: Radio City Music Hall, March 1, 1934. 82 minutes. With Will Rogers (David Harum), Louise Dresser (Polly), Evelyn Venable (Ann), Kent Taylor (John), Stepin Fetchit (Sylvester), Noah Beery (Woolsey), Roger Imhof (Edwards), Frank Melton (Edwin), Charles Middleton (Deacon), Sarah Padden (Widow), Lillian Stuart (Sairy), Irene Bentley (Mary), Charles Coleman (Flowers), Jane Darwell (Mrs. Woolsey), and Frank Rice (Robinson).

Story and Criticism

Based on the *fin de siècle* novel by Edward Noyes Westcott, *David Harum* is the Will Rogers sound film which relates best to Depression issues, although most of the commentary is indirect.

The depression of 1893 sends the young man of the film back to the countryside where work still exists. In the "Homeville" setting, John Lennox (Kent Taylor) learns how to appreciate the real things in life and captures the heart of a local beauty (Evelyn Venable). Playing an avuncular role as local deity and matchmaker, Will Rogers assures that character and idealism triumph over impersonal economic conditions. (See Chapter 2 for details about this film.)

Availability

Both the Museum of Modern Art and the Will Rogers Memorial have prints. Rented by Films, Incorporated, Archive Collection.

63. Handy Andy

A Fox production. Director: David Butler. Screenplay: William Counselman and Henry Johnson. Adaptation: Kubec Glasmon. Based on the play *Merry Andrew* by Lewis Beach. Photography: A. Arthur Miller. Music: Richard Whiting. Lyrics: William Counselman. Recording Engineer: F. C. Chapman. New York premiere: Roxy Theatre, August 3, 1934. 81 minutes. With Will Rogers (Andrew Yates), Peggy Wood (Ernestine Yates), Conchita Montenegro (Fleurette), Mary Carlisle (Janice Yates), Roger Imhof ("Doc" Vurneister), Robert Taylor (Lloyd Burmeister), Paul Harvey (Charles Norcross), Grace Goodall (Mattie Norcross), Gregory Gaye (Pierre Martel), Frank Melton (Howard Norcross), Jessie Pringle (Jennis), Adrian Rosley (Armand Duval), Helen Flint (Mrs. Beauregard), Richard Tucker (Mr. Beauregard), Al Logan (Williams), and Charles Teske (Dancer doubling for Will Rogers).

Story and Criticism

As Andrew Yates, Will Rogers plays a retired businessman who has little sympathy for the social and cultural "improvements" which his wife attempts to impose on him. Mordaunt Hall of the *New York Times* was only moderately amused by the production (August 4, 1934, p. 14, col. 5), noting in his review that the Rogers role was a recooked combination of the innocent abroad from *They Had to See Paris* (1929) spiced by a dash of the rural sage of *Dr. Bull* (1933).

Availability

Both the Museum of Modern Art and the Will Rogers Memorial have prints.

64. Judge Priest

A Fox production. Producer: Sol Wurtzel. Director: John Ford. Screenplay: Dudley Nichols and Lamar Trotti. Based on the stories by Irvin S. Cobb. Photography: George Schneiderman. Music and lyrics: Cyril J. Mockridge. Art Director: William Darling. New York premiere: Radio City Music Hall, October 11, 1934. 70 minutes. With Will Rogers (Judge Priest), Tom Brown (Jerome Priest), Anita Louise (Ellie May Gillespie), Brenda Fowler (Caroline Priest), Stepin Fetchit (Jeff), Frank Melton (Flem Talley), Rochelle Hudson (Virginia Maydew), Matt McHugh (Gaby Rives), Roger Imhof (Gaynor), Charley Grapewin (Sergeant Jimmy Bagby), Berton Churchill (Senator Maydew), Henry B. Walthall (Reverend Ashby Brand), Hattie McDaniel (Aunt Dilsey), Hyman Meyer (Felsberg), Louis Mason (Sheriff Birdsong), David Landau (Bob Gillis), Paul McAllister (Doc Lake), Grace Goodall (Mrs. Meydew), Ernest Shield (Milan), Vester Pegg (Herringer), Francis Ford (Juror 12), Paul McVey (Trimble), Winter Hall (Judge Fairleigh), and Duke Lee (Deputy).

Story and Criticism

This John Ford film is steeped in nostalgia for the lost world of the South. Civil War veterans, contented blacks, and harmless villains inhabit Irvin S. Cobb's/John Ford's fictional world. Judge Priest (Will Rogers) in alliance with Jeff Poindexter (Stepin Fetchit) work to assure that conflicts are resolved and lovers united. Andre Sennwald of the *New York Times* realized that the story was pure hokum, but he found the film to be a sentimental delight — perhaps even a relief for the Oklahoman: "let it remind you that Will Rogers, although he bears the burdens of the nation on his shoulders, continues to be a remarkably heart-warming personality" (October 12, 1934, p. 33, col. 1).

Availability

Both the Museum of Modern Art and the Will Rogers Memorial have prints. Rented by Films, Incorporated, Archive Collection.

65. The County Chairman

A Fox production. Producer: Edward V. Butcher. Director: John Blystone. Screenplay: Sam Hellman and Gladys Lehman. Based on a story by George Ade. Photography: Hal Mohr. New York premiere: Roxy Theatre, January 19, 1935. 85 minutes. With Will Rogers (Jim Hackler), Evelyn Venable (Lucy Rigby), Kent Taylor (Ben Jarvey), Louise Dresser (Mrs. Mary Rigby), Frank Melton (Henry Cleaver), Robert McWade (Tom Cruden), Charles Middleton (Riley Cleaver), Stepin Fetchit (Sassafras), Alfred James (Ezra Gibbon), Mickey Rooney (Freckles), Berton Churchill (Elias Rigby), Russell Simpson (Vance Jimmison), William V. Mong (Uncle Eck), Jan Duggan (Abigail Tewksbury), Gay Seabrook (Lorna Cruden), and Erville Alderson (Wilson Prewitt).

Story and Criticism

George Ade supplied the plot for this rural comedy, providing Rogers with a vehicle that was at once rustic and political. As Jim Hackler, Rogers manages the political campaign of a young candidate in Tomahawk County, Wyoming. The handsome officeseeker (Kent Taylor) has a nonpolitical problem: he is in love with Lucy Rigby (Evelyn Venable), the rival candidate's daughter. *The County Chairman* is unique among Will Rogers' sound films for its political commentary, although most of the aphorisms are generalizations on things political rather than specific barbs pointed at contemporary issues.

Frank S. Nugent felt that "Mr. Rogers shines in a role that perfectly suits his personality, talents and his voice" (*New York Times,* January 19, 1935, p. 8, col. 1). Indeed, the blend of ruralism, Western imagery, and politics was perfectly suited for the Oklahoman.

Availability

Both the Museum of Modern Art and the Will Rogers Memorial have prints.

66. Life Begins at 40

A Fox production. Producer: Sol M. Wurtzel. Director: George Marshall. Screenplay: Lamar Trotti. Additional Dialogue: Robert Quillen. Suggested by the book by Walter B. Pitkin. Photography: Harry Jackson. Sound: Bernard Fredericks. Art Direction: Duncan Cramer. Assistant Art Director: Albert Hogsett. Gowns by Lillian. Musical Director: Samuel Kaylin. New York premiere: Radio City Music Hall, April 4, 1935. 75 minutes. With Will Rogers (Kennesaw H. Clark), Rochelle Hudson (Adele Anderson), Richard Cromwell (Lee Austin), George Barbier (Colonel Joseph Abercrombie), Jane Darwell (Ida Harris), Slim Summerville (T. Watterson Meriwhether), Sterling Holloway (Chris), Thomas Beck (Joe Abercrombie), Roger Imhof ("Pappy" Smithers), Charles Sellon (Tom Cotton), John Bradford (Wally Stevens), Ruth Gillette (Mrs. Cotton), Claire Du Brey (Mrs. T. Watterson Meriwhether), and Jed Prouty (Beagle).

Story and Criticism

In this rural tale, Kennesaw Clark (Will Rogers) is an independent journalist who controls just about everyone in the "Homeville" setting. He befriends a young man falsely accused of a crime, managing the situation so that his niece (Rochelle Hudson) finds romance with the upright lad. When a local banker (George Barbier) forecloses on Kennesaw's newspaper, the resourceful editor goes back to premechanized printing and hand delivery. Like so many of the late Will Rogers films, *Life Begins at 40* communicates its homey message through character and atmosphere rather than through plot. Although Fox bought the rights to Walter Pitkin's bestseller of the same title, there is no resemblance between book and film. Andre Sennwald of the *New York Times* found Rogers "a thorough delight regardless of what he is doing, and his country editor takes its place in his gallery of warm and sagacious homespun portraits" (April 5, 1935, p. 21, col. 3).

Availability

Both the Museum of Modern Art and the Will Rogers Memorial have prints.

67. Doubting Thomas

A Fox production. Producer: B. G. DeSylva. Director: David Butler. Screenplay: William Counselman. Adapted by Bartlett Cormack. Based on the play *The Torch Bearers* by George Kelly. New York premiere: Rivoli Theatre, July 11, 1935. 78 minutes. With Will Rogers (Thomas Brown),

Billie Burke (Paula Brown), Alison Skipworth (Mrs. Pampinelli), Sterling Holloway (Spindler), Andrew Tombes (Hossefrosse), Gail Patrick (Florence McCrickett), Frances Grant (Peggy Burns), Frank Albertson (Jimmy Brown), John Qualen (Von Blitzen), Johnny Arthur (Ralph Twiller), Helen Flint (Nelly Fell), Fred Wallace (Teddy), T. Roy Barnes (La Maze), Ruth Warren (Jenny), George Cooper (Stage Hand), Helen Freeman (Mrs. Sheppard), and William Benedict (Caddie).

Story and Criticism

This film sought to satirize mid-Americans who had become over-absorbed in the community theatre movement. Paula Brown (Billie Burke) continually embarrasses her husband (Will Rogers) in her total involvement with an upcoming play. While the film played on a traditional Rogers theme —that normal folk should not aspire to be other than what they are—the *New York Times* critic found the film stale and humorless: "Mr. Rogers is too good a humorist and too valuable as a homespun philosopher to be hidden under this type of story" (July 11, 1935, p. 24, col. 2). Students of Will Rogers in his late period should keep in mind, however, that the New York City response to Rogers' films was often out of tune with that of the rest of the country.

Availability

Both the Museum of Modern Art and the Will Rogers Memorial have prints. Rented by Films, Incorporated, Archive Collection.

68. Steamboat 'Round the Bend

A 20th Century-Fox production. Supervisor: Sol Wurtzel. Producer: W. R. Sheehan. Director: John Ford. Screenplay: Dudley Nichols and Lamar Trotti. Based on the novel by Ben Lucien Burman. Photography: George Schneiderman. Art Director: William Darling. Set Decorator: Albert Hogsett. Music Director: Samuel Kaylin. Film Editor: Alfred DeGaetano. Assistant Director: Edward O'Fearna. New York premiere: Radio City Music Hall, September 19, 1935. 90 minutes. With Will Rogers (Dr. John Pearly), Anne Shirley (Fleety Belle), Irvin S. Cobb (Captain Eli), Eugene Pallette (Sheriff Rufe Jeffers), John McGuire (Duke), Berton Churchill (New Moses), Francis Ford (Efe), Roger Imhof (Pappy), Raymond Hatton (Matt Abel), Hobart Bosworth (Chaplain), Stepin Fetchit (George Lincoln Washington), William Benedict (Breck), Lois Verner (Addie May), and Charles Middleton (Fleety Belle's father).

Story and Criticism

Steamboat . . . was the first Will Rogers film to be released post-humously. (Details about the story and its meaning are supplied in Chapter 2 of this book.) Based on a rural tale by *Saturday Evening Post* author Ben

Lucien Burman, the film takes place along the Mississippi at the turn of the century. Like *In Old Kentucky,* conflicts are resolved by a race — this one between a steamboat captained by Doctor John Pearly (Will Rogers) and a somewhat larger paddle wheeler under the direction of Captain Eli (Irvin S. Cobb). The *New York Times* reviewer Andre Sennwald found little delight in the John Ford film, but nevertheless concluded that the film "finds America's favorite philosopher at his home-spun best" (September 20, 1935, p. 17, col. 2).

Availability

Both the Museum of Modern Art and the Will Rogers Memorial have prints. Rented by Films, Incorporated, Archive Collection.

69. In Old Kentucky

A 20th Century-Fox production. Producer: Edward Butcher. Director: George Marshall. Screenplay: Sam Hellman and Gladys Lehman. Additional Dialogue: Henry Johnson. Based on the play by Charles T. Dazey. Photography: L. W. O'Connell. New York premiere: Roxy Theatre, November 29, 1935. 85 minutes. With Will Rogers (Steve Tapley), Dorothy Wilson (Nancy Martingale), Russell Hardie (Lee Andrews), Charles Sellon (Ezra Martingale), Louise Henry (Arlene Shattuck), Esther Dale (Dolly Breckenridge), Alan Dinehart (Slick Doherty), Charles Richman (Pole Shattuck), Etienne Girardot (Pluvius J. Aspinwall), John Ince (Sheriff), and Bill Robinson (Wash Johnson).

Story and Criticism

People attended this film knowing there would be no sequel: Will Rogers had died the previous summer. (Details about the story and its meaning are supplied in Chapter 2.) A family feud keeps lovers apart in the Middle South. Chance, and the intervention of avuncular Steve Tapley (Will Rogers), mend the quarrel and bring the lovers together in "a first-rate comedy and a handsome epitaph to twentieth century America's first humorist" (*New York Times,* November 29, 1935, p. 24, col. 1).

Availability

The Will Rogers Memorial has a print.

WILL ROGERS' RADIO PROGRAMS FOR "THE GOOD GULF SHOW"

In the early months of 1933, Will Rogers signed a lucrative contract with the Gulf Oil Company. For over $50,000, Rogers agreed to appear on an unspecified number of "Good Gulf Shows" accompanied by an orchestra, other acts, and friends from time to time. By the beginning of June 1935, fifty-three "Good Gulf Shows" had been lightened by the Rogers touch. Fireside Chats by the president often followed immediately after a Rogers presentation, a juxtaposition that probably helped both radio personalities.

The "Good Gulf Shows" with Will Rogers are listed and summarized below. Those bearing an asterisk are on tape at the Will Rogers Memorial and have been reprinted in full in *Radio Broadcasts of Will Rogers* (1983) which are part of *The Writings of Will Rogers*. Verbatim transcripts of all twelve programs produced for E. R. Squibb, the drug company, are also in *Radio Broadcasts of Will Rogers*. Each of the Squibb programs profiles a major contemporary figure, including Charles Lindbergh, Herbert Hoover, Charles Curtis, Alfred Smith, the Prince of Wales, Dwight Morrow, Henry Ford, and others.

* 1. April 30, 1933	28. September 16, 1934
2. May 7, 1933	29. September 30, 1934
3. May 14, 1933	30. October 7, 1934
4. May 21, 1933	31. October 14, 1934
5. May 28, 1933	32. October 21, 1934
6. June 4, 1933	33. October 28, 1934
7. June 11, 1933	34. November 4, 1934
* 8. August 13, 1933	35. November 11, 1934
9. October 29, 1933	36. December 23, 1934
10. November 5, 1933	37. December 30, 1934
11. November 12, 1933	38. January 6, 1935
12. November 19, 1933	39. January 13, 1935
13. November 26, 1933	40. January 20, 1935
14. January 7, 1934	41. January 27, 1935
15. January 14, 1934	42. February 3, 1935
16. January 21, 1934	*43. March 31, 1935
17. January 28, 1934	*44. April 7, 1935
18. February 4, 1934	*45. April 14, 1935
19. February 11, 1934	*46. April 21, 1935
20. February 18, 1934	*47. April 28, 1935
21. February 25, 1934	*48. May 5, 1935
22. March 4, 1934	*49. May 12, 1935
23. June 10, 1934	*50. May 19, 1935
*24. June 17, 1934	*51. May 26, 1935
*25. June 24, 1934	*52. June 2, 1935
26. July 1, 1934	*53. June 9, 1935
*27. July 8, 1934	

*1. April 30, 1933

In this first of the Gulf programs, Will Rogers begins by discussing the recent work of Franklin D. Roosevelt, a logical subject on President's Day.

The Oklahoman offers the president a flattering series of sobriquets: "We elected him because he was a Democrat, and now we honor him because he is a magician. He's the Houdini of Hyde Park." In fact, the entire nation has gone wild about the new national leader: "Talk about sweeping the country. Roosevelt swept the country like a new toothpaste. . . . Why they rushed up and voted for him just like buying tickets for some new Hollywood sex drama, you know." Popular enthusiasm has encouraged an unusual cooperation between the White House and Congress during the opening days of the New Deal.

Rogers closes the program with an address to Roosevelt: "Mr. Roosevelt, we've turned everything over to you. We've given you more power than we have ever given any man. . . . We tried to run the country individually and collectively and along the Democratic line, but boy we've gummed it so. Take it and run it if you want to — deflate or inflate or complicate. Do anything so long as you get us a dollar or two every now and again. God bless you."

Future programs will examine the economic, legislative, and presidential dimensions of bringing America out of the Great Depression.

2. May 7, 1933

Will Rogers opens his second program with an "alarming" statement. He promises to bring an alarm clock to the show each week so that he will finish in time for the closing commercial, a difficult task for the extemporaneous — and garrulous — speaker. When the clock's alarm sounds, he promises to stop: "I don't care whether I am in the middle of reciting Gunga Din or the Declaration of Independence, I am going to stop right when that rings." The clock will become a regular prop, sort of a comic "maguffin."

Rogers notes that a presidential address will follow his show, pairing the Oklahoman with the "Houdini of Hyde Park" for a full evening of radio entertainment: "We are both on here. I am selling Gulf Oil and he is selling the United States. Both of them are good propositions; don't sell either of them short." Rogers goes on to discuss the "bank holiday," inflation, the national budget, the gold standard, economic relations with Europe, and the president's enormous responsibilities in a time of trouble. Rogers closes with a plea for Americans to support the president as he makes major changes in a flawed economy. "I know we all trust him."

3. May 14, 1933

Will Rogers announces that tonight's program comes from Hollywood and that he now has two alarm clocks to warn him when to stop talking. Rogers has just arrived in town after a cross-country flight which has given him some perspective on national issues. First, he is wary of press reports. The papers claim that a tornado hit Oklahoma: "It wasn't a cyclone; I was the big wind that hit the town." Recently, newspapers have demanded a change of name for the Hoover dam. Rogers proposes the simplest of transformations: "Lord, if they feel that way about it, I don't see why they don't just transfer [transpose] the two names." A short stop at the Chicago World's Fair elicits some comments on the state of the world: "They call it the Century of Progress. . . . It is misnamed. . . . I think they ought to call it 'What the Last Hundred Years Has Done to Us,' "

Rogers takes the opportunity to reflect on the flaws of modern life. At the turn of the century, if people were out of work, they just rested outside the country store; they did not become alarming "unemployment" statistics for everybody to worry about. In addition, America was on the gold standard. There was no golf, no chamber of commerce pep talks. The country was peaceful in the golden era before 1900.

Rogers expresses a hope that Roosevelt will use his popularity to right the ship of state: "He is the only dictator by popular demand." Future Sundays may feature them both again: "He will be on here again some of these times when he has something he wants to tell you. I'll be on here again whether I have anything to tell you or not."

4. May 21, 1933

This program is broadcast from the Mayflower Hotel in Washington, D.C., where Will Rogers addresses legislators and their wives in a mock joint session of Congress. Rogers opens with a humorous survey of the chamber. He warns Vice President Garner not to go to sleep and not to interfere: "You will have nothing to do with the running of this meeting. I am running this outfit here." He chides Senator Hiram Johnson and Robert LaFollette for straddling the political fence: "Make up your mind which side you are going to sit on, if you're going to be with the Democrats or the Republicans around here. Hurry about it!" Once order is established, he unveils the basis for his political humor: "I just watch the government and report the facts."

In an unusual move for an address to legislators, Rogers spends most of the time talking about President Roosevelt who is described as a new Moses: "What did Mr. Roosevelt do? He went up on Capitol Hill with a fistful of ideas and hit you Senators over the head, and, you know, forth came twenty of the greatest laws of this time. He not only saw Moses, but raised him ten." Roosevelt's ability to push legislation through Congress, his honesty, his many plans, are touted in a talk which portrays the president with religious imagery: "He swallowed our depression. He has inhaled fear and exhaled confidence."

5. *May 28, 1933*

Tonight, Rogers speaks from Chicago, home of America's other favorite radio program, "Amos 'n' Andy." In an extended dialogue, Rogers employs his version of the "Amos 'n' Andy" voices, injecting numerous malaprops familiar to loyal "Amos 'n' Andy" listeners. Rogers goes on to comment on the World's Fair and the city's success in improving both its economy and image.

The remainder of the program gives an inside view of the White House where Rogers has recently spent the night. Despite his enormous responsibilities, the president is in high spirits: "He has a grin on his face . . . he has got some kind of divine feeling. He knows that things is going to be all right." One morning Rogers asked Mrs. Roosevelt where the president was, and she merely said: "Wherever you hear the laugh." While the president is aware of the suffering which plagues the land, he has not lost his zest for life. Listeners should follow the president's good example.

6. *June 4, 1933*

Rogers tells the audience that he is excited to be back in Hollywood where there is never a dull moment: "Hollywood, heart of iniquity, you might say, and the old Nick himself is in these valleys and sin is just oozing out of them mountains. Compared to Hollywood, Sodom and Gomorrah were a couple of babes in the woods." With so much rain hitting the West coast, Rogers proposes a new federal program to make and give away raincoats to the citizens of California—a proposal which he believes is no less wasteful than current public works efforts.

Rogers has a good time making fun of the C(ivilian) C(onservation) C(orps) reforestation program which ships young city people out to the countryside. As a country person himself, he worries about the results: "With city men and women planting the trees, you know, they are liable to get the wrong end in the ground and in our forest of the future, the roots will be in the air and the limbs in the ground." He predicts that this Democrat program to plant trees will yield lumber when Republicans are in office. Like other fads, political fashions change.

To prevent further class antagonisms, Rogers proposes to do something for the image of the rich. His R(ogers) R(econstruction) R(eturn) T(o) R(espectability) A(ssociation) will build public relations bridges between classes: "When I can stop people throwing rocks at the banker, that will be a little progress. When they finally get to speaking to him, that shows my association is working fine. When they cheer him, that's when I get my bonus." Rogers hopes that many of America's wealthy will follow the example of John D. Rockefeller, devoting their wealth to charitable efforts in a time of need.

7. June 11, 1933

Much of this final program of the first year of the "Good Gulf Show" is devoted to a discussion of the experiment in radio. Rogers admits that he was worried at first about how to handle an invisible audience. Inviting people to the studio solved that problem. At the beginning, he was also concerned that his humor might be too political for a Sunday night audience, but letters have proved that listeners are as intelligent as readers. In general, the whole audience issue — whether he was taking hold or not — bothered him even after three or four programs. (At least three times during his monologue, Rogers indirectly appeals for fan mail.) The Senate has sent a telegram asking Rogers to continue the show: "We have enjoyed your recent talks on the air and want your assurance that you will soon return with your humorous and wholesome comments on national affairs." Rogers thanks his Congressional fans, especially since much of his humor is at their expense.

Rogers' last topic is the London Disarmament Conference which he predicts will be a failure. Too much time is being devoted to formal ceremonies and not enough attention to the matter of peace. As an observer of men and nations, Will Rogers put little stock in the effectiveness of conferences and treaties.

*8. August 13, 1933

This program opens with a tribute to Will Rogers from the Senate read by Colonel Edwin A. Halsey. Seventy-four Senators have signed a message which describes Will Rogers as "the poet laureate of wisecracks:" "No one in America is held in greater affection nor higher esteem and no one person's daily comment is more enjoyed than that of Mr. Rogers."

The program itself is a bit disappointing, consisting of dialogue between Rogers and his friend Fred Stone. The patter skips across such topics as Hollywood, state politics, movie stars, Congress, religion, radio commercials, and comedians. The undistinguished conversation is punctuated by undistinguished duets. It must have been obvious to everyone that Will Rogers was coming back to the air slightly unprepared for his new series of shows. Subsequent performances would be more substantial.

9. October 29, 1933

Will Rogers opens this program with an attempt to explain what President Roosevelt is doing about the gold standard. Rogers claims that the president's own radio address left much to be desired; even the brain trusters had trouble understanding it, "so I better kind of clear up on where the President left off." What follows is a combination of serious information, word play, and homely metaphors designed to translate the abstractions of economic theory into ordinary language. The presentation on gold ends with comic relief, a spoof of the jargon which confuses the public: "What we are trying to do is elevate the commodity prices, plus the cost of production, and increase the purchasing power within the means of the purchaser or plus the cost of production and thereby enhance the buying power plus liquidation and receiving fees. Distribution will naturally seek its level when — capital versus labor minus recognition of Russia — and if Mr. Ford cuts his wages down to N.R.A. level. The whole thing, you know, was laid out by Mr. Einstein." Rogers assures his audience that it is not alone in its confusion about questions of gold and silver.

Brief comments on Hollywood and Democrats close the show.

10. November 5, 1933

U.S. relations with Russia are of concern to Americans, so Rogers opens his program with comments based on his trips to the Soviet Union. During the 1920s, the United States refused to recognize Russia, a policy which Rogers calls arrogant. It was part of the mentality of the boom era, the "Absolutely Financially Nutty" days. Since the early 1920s, the United States has learned that no one plans to repay the debts made during and after the war: "If we didn't recognize nations that owed us, and hadn't paid us, we'd be Robinson Crusoe on a desert island." Economic motives will bring us back to Russia; Rogers assures his audience that President Roosevelt will soon press for recognition: "We'd recognize the devil with a false face on if he'd contract for some pitch forks. And the shape we're in right now, we'd be glad to receive a good will tour from Alla-Babba and his Forty Thieves if they'd take back enough toothpaste and radio tubes with them." Rogers sees the resulting communications among nations as a benefit to all.

Rogers is concerned about how Americans are coping with the stress of the Depression. Paradoxically, the rich seem to be suffering more than the poor. Rogers admires the determination and strength with which really poor Americans are confronting their lot. For the good of all, he hopes that the middle class will regain its confidence and its willingness to move into the marketplace.

11. November 12, 1933

As promised last week, Rogers talks about gold. He discusses it, however, as a sports announcer would describe a football game played between the United States and the rest of the world, using the jargon and breathless pace of sports announcing. A highlight has Hitler trying to block France, only to be tackled by a Jewish spectator: "Hitler is out. Wait 'till I check and see who it is. It's a spectator named Rosenberg. He is a little East Side tailor, but oh what a sock he give that guy Hitler." Rogers alludes to the university professors Roosevelt hired. They are sent back to their classrooms: "They had lots of ideas all right, but they had little experience." The United States wins the game, thanks to "the ingenuity of Coach Roosevelt knowing who to send in at the proper time."

This program is like many Gulf shows which sustain a single metaphor throughout, in this case a metaphor and diction peculiar to radio. Unfortunately, no tape of the program exists.

12. November 19, 1933

Rogers presents a skit in which he plays both President Franklin Roosevelt and Russian diplomat Maksim Litvinoff to show what really went on during ten days of negotiations in Washington. Roosevelt wants Russia to recognize America so that America will gain back some of the self-respect it has lost because of the Depression. Litvinoff asks how America got "in this terrible shapeski?" (an example of Rogers' attempt at a Russian accent). Roosevelt blames it on the Republicans.

Before Russia will recognize America, Litvinoff demands that America "give the Russians the same liberties and religious freedom they enjoy at home." Litvinoff asks if the United States has a five-year plan. Roosevelt answers that the United States has plenty of plans — "If plans do any good, why our nation's saved right now."

The skit ends when Roosevelt learns that Litvinoff is not really Litvinoff. The man to whom he has been talking is really the German actor Emil Jannings (a plant for Hitler). Exasperated, Roosevelt exclaims, "That darn Hitler's got the whole world cuckoo."

13. November 26, 1933

Will Rogers announces that he will be leaving the show for a while to make the film *David Harum* (James Cruze, dir., 1934). The subject of *David Harum* plus the occasion of his 25th wedding anniversary suggest some reflection on his career. Rogers remembers his wedding trip to the big city of St. Louis where Betty was impressed by the hotel's enormous mirrors. Sports were more rugged, travel was more leisurely, and Will Rogers was still a silent vaudeville roping act with Buck McKee riding a horse on stage.

When words replaced the lasso, Will Rogers became a commentator. He supplies memories and evaluations of Theodore Roosevelt, William Howard Taft, Woodrow Wilson, Warren Harding, Calvin Coolidge, and Franklin Roosevelt whom he calls "the answer to a comedian's prayer." Looking back over the experience of being the nation's court jester, Rogers makes a famous generalization: "I started it in 1905, jokin' and kiddin' all about presidents and prominent men since that time. Met 'em all, yet I never met one of 'em that I didn't like."

In his closing, Rogers asks that his listeners not take his remarks about gold too seriously. The whole issue seems to be driving the country crazy: "It's made the dumb guy as smart as the smart guy. . . . This gold thing's gettin' us nuts, you know."

14. January 7, 1934

For the major portion of this program, Rogers humorously recalls events of 1933, concentrating on the speedy work of President Roosevelt: "The President was sworn in about eleven o'clock in the morning, and he started from the Capitol down to the White House, stopped the parade on the way, and phoned and closed all the banks in America." Huey Long figures in this retrospective as comic relief; the Louisiana Senator is ridiculed for his garrulity.

Rogers tries to make a case for the better use of ex-presidents. Theodore Roosevelt and Calvin Coolidge should have been drafted after they left the White House: "We killed them with an inane system of retiring 'em into total unusefulness, just when they had learned and wished to be of public service." Rogers suggests that former presidents would make better advisers than technocrats.

Singing cowboys are another target for Rogers. He says that the only thing that sings worse than a cowboy is a coyote. If a cowboy sings well, then he is not the real thing.

15. January 14, 1934

Rogers' primary topic is President Roosevelt's opening of Congress on January 3, 1934. He observes that Roosevelt is now getting things done by being nice to legislators. Using the soft-sell approach, he plans to obtain $10 billion from the Hill.

Employment is another topic, as is how the Depression has equalized the country by causing higher taxes. It put everyone on the road to the poorhouse: "Everybody hit bottom together. Some hit it in better shape and are able to go on. But that was just luck, so they naturally got to help all the others to get back." Rogers reminds Americans that taxes are a responsibility everyone must share.

In a period of proliferating agencies, Rogers proposes to save the government money by cutting the letters "N" (for national) and "E" (for economy) out of all government acronyms! Rogers also makes more remarks about singing cowboys and the recent liquor tax.

16. January 21, 1934

Using previous remarks about singing cowboys and "doggies" as an excuse, Rogers launches into a program of reminiscence and song. He describes family life on the Oklahoma frontier, an experience which has made him the world's expert: "My whole start in life was gotten from doggies." Having established his rural perspective, Rogers goes on to such issues as politics and politicians; frontier marshals and cowboys; show business and how songwriters borrow tunes from Negro spirituals. The patter is punctuated by song. In the discussion, Rogers uses the word "nigger" at least four times.

17. January 28, 1934

Rogers opens the show with a continuation of his discussion of music and singing. He says he feels like Hamlet, but with a different dilemma: "I never knew what the 'to be' was for, but mine is to sing or not to sing." He also returns to the Negro issue, claiming that he is a friend of Black Americans: "I wasn't only raised among darkies down in Indian Territory, but I was raised *by* them. And Lord, I was five years old out on the ranch before I ever knew there was a white child."

Hollywood, Fred Stone, and other entertainment topics are mentioned, but talk of the death of Blue Boy, the hog that appeared with Rogers in *State Fair,* takes up a large portion of the program. Rogers speculates that the country animal was either a victim of Brown Derby food or the pace of life beyond the "Divorce Divide:" "He passed out. Hollywood life was too fast for him." Rogers regrets the demise of a fellow actor who would never "hog" a scene.

Rogers spends time on the topic of aviation and airmail. As a frequent traveller who paid for his ticket in postage (by the pound), Rogers claims that "for many years, I think I constituted America's flying passengers."

The program closes with speculation about an upcoming dinner at the White House and Rogers' unhappiness with formal attire and formalities.

18. February 4, 1934

Rogers calls this program his "Condition of the Country Address." He presents a mock State of the Union talk intended to give some comic perspective on pressing issues of the day. Here are some topics covered with laughter: the gold standard, the condition of the dollar, the conservative economic opinions of Congressman Ogden Mills.

Deficit spending is examined in human terms. "I figure a country is just like a big family. . . . They have love and arguments and fights and hates and everything, but the one thing that does unite a family is illness." The notion of government intervention may be new and may have its own evils, but helping the poor is a responsibility that transcends economic habit and dogma. Rogers effectively uses an extended metaphor of sickness and cure for a large part of the program. The program ends with an extended eulogy to "Dr. Roosevelt," a political physician who still has faith in humanity.

19. February 11, 1934

President Roosevelt's "scheme" to lower interest rates inspires Rogers to come up with an even more dramatic plan: "The government and everybody would cancel all of their debts. Then everyone would own his own car and home and have paid all his grocery bills."

The Russian-Japanese War is discussed and Rogers explains a plan by which the United States can avoid getting involved; he goes on to tell how wars in general can be avoided. One way is to ban the shipment of goods to either side in a war. Rogers says if a country wants to buy, it can come and pick up the goods. If a manufacturer wants to sell, "let him get on the boat and deliver it personally." Rogers believes that economic boycotts could prevent wars, but that the only two countries that should participate would be Labrador and Mary Byrd Land "because neither one of them has anything to sell." Nations are simply too greedy to avoid the first steps that will inevitably lead them to war; in addition, geographic conditions in Europe and Asia constantly tempt nations into conflict. The United States has been unwise to strip its Navy and Army during an era of disarmament conferences and should begin preparations for the next war.

20. February 18, 1934

After some mention of the Army's takeover of the United States air mail, and an expression of concern for the flyers, Rogers devotes most of the program to foreign affairs. He is perplexed and irritated by the friction in Europe. Politics is plagued with new parties of hate: in the old days, Rogers remembers that Liberal and Conservative were the two obvious choices, "But now—Lord, a country can go Nazi, and Facististi, and Communistic, and Royalist, and New Deal, and Rugged Individualism!"

Rogers traces many of the nationalist conflicts back to the Versailles treaty and to President Wilson's naive idealism. The facts of the map should have been respected over conflicting claims to territory, claims which will soon be settled by armies and air forces. The creation of Austria and Hungary is discussed in some detail, with surprising awareness by Rogers of the contending parties involved at the peace talks. Using his playful approach, Rogers suggests that peace can be obtained by moving Germany to where

Mexico is located and by letting Canada trade places with Ireland. He suggests that the English not be told where Ireland is relocated; the habit of quarreling is so ingrained that the British will only seek out the Irish to continue the fighting.

The clock alarm interrupts Rogers' geopolitical fantasy.

21. February 25, 1934

The entire program is dedicated to the recent air mail scandal and its implications. Rogers begins by describing in graphic detail a trip made from Los Angeles to New York City aboard a commercial airline. He worries about the crew of that plane for, during a recent run, they were lost somewhere over Utah. Rogers tells the audience that he is keeping close tabs on the news from the Western mountains.

The private corporation responsible for the air mail had recently been accused of misusing funds and the scandal had touched Charles Lindbergh, a consultant to the company. Rogers defends Lindbergh as an innocent bystander: "As usual, the innocent do happen to work for the guilty and, of course, suffer worse." He also advocates more faith in governmental leaders. The public should continue to support aviation and be optimistic about the future of this new form of transportation — and defense.

22. March 4, 1935

Will Rogers arrives two minutes late for the program, blaming his tardiness on the thick fog blanketing the California coastline. Rogers spends considerable time discussing the N(ational) R(ecovery) A(ct) and its implications. While impressed by the ambitious and laudable goals of the program, Rogers is worried about Washington bureaucrats becoming too deeply involved in the details of everyday life. He is unhappy with the contentiousness of opponents to NRA and the useless denouncing of the agency. Rogers, exaggerating, says that a code has been formulated for denouncers: "You was allowed to denounce six hours a day and if you wanted to denounce more than that, why you had to take on help."

Rogers proposes his own plan to deal with the airmail crisis. Instead of the government providing a subsidy, the mail service should charge users for the cost of their service. Rogers predicts that his plan will force clients to be more judicious in their use of air mail, relieving taxpayers of cost and pilots of unnecessary hazards.

Rogers takes the time to apologize a second time to his listeners for "using some word [nigger] that was objectionable to some of them" in an earlier broadcast (January 21, 1934). Rogers assures his listeners that he meant no offense.

23. *June 10, 1934*

Rogers asserts that the major activity of the government in the past few months has been appropriating and borrowing money, "mostly from ourselves." Government spending and taxing the rich come in for much discussion. Rogers thinks that if the rich could pay their taxes in person to the president, they "would just fall all over themselves" to do so.

Rogers is thankful that America has "two of the finest neighbors [Canada and Mexico] that any country in the world ever had." He says there is no good reason for America to go to war with Japan or Russia.

Prizefighter Max Baer, the Dionne quintuplets, and the Chicago Fair are briefly discussed. Rogers also speculates on the fate of gangster John Dillinger who has just escaped from prison.

Rogers mentions that the program is sponsored by "the Gulf Oil and Rogers Gas Company."

*24. *June 17, 1934*

Rogers explains why he was late for last week's show and talks about fellow radio comedians Jimmy Durante, Ed Wynn, and Eddie Cantor. He makes some jokes about Wynn's sponsor, Texaco gas, and observes that radio listeners are becoming adept at "tuning out" commercials.

Max Baer's latest fight and a meeting between Hitler and Mussolini are briefly mentioned, with Rogers likening the two events: "Everybody's wondered what the meeting between Mussolini and Hitler was. It was to see, you know, since Baer won, you know, maybe we're wrong about these Jewish people. Better let them come back or something. If they can fight that good, we'd better let them in again, you know."

Rogers says that "if you're driving down the street and a man is hitchhiking, if he's a Finlander, pick him up" since Finland is the only country to pay back its debt to the United States. He also talks about the futility of trying to collect from England and France, despite the heroic efforts of Secretary of State Cordell Hull.

*25. *June 24, 1934*

Tonight, Rogers focuses on the Republican party, claiming that he is lacking really important topics. He concentrates on their wealth, their intelligence, and the size of their party. He calls the Democrats "a semi-heathen tribe [that] could live on little because they've never had anything else." Even though the Republicans are richer and smarter, according to Rogers, the Democrats are able to "come along and level 'em off every once in a while" as they are doing now. Even if some Republicans are voted into Congress, Rogers feels Roosevelt will have no trouble getting their support.

Rogers briefly talks about the war in Paraguay and Bolivia and mentions a poll about the president in *The Literary Digest.*

Rogers reminds listeners that Gulf Oil is the sponsor and calls it "an old Indian secret they got from my Cherokee ancestors down in Oklahoma."

26. July 1, 1934

Rogers admits at the start of the program that the week has not supplied much exciting news. He decides to pay a tribute to the ailing movie star, Marie Dressler. Rogers describes her career on Broadway and then remembers how she set new standards for women actors in Hollywood, demonstrating that acting skill was as important as good looks. Rogers goes on to claim that he would like to make a motion picture with Dressler: "That would be the proudest moment of my life, my whole amusement career, to say that I'd worked with Marie." Rogers' sentiment reflects well upon him.

Rogers goes on to talk about his own acting in *Ah, Wilderness!,* the Eugene O'Neill play. He stresses how a memorized part was difficult to adjust to after being an extemporaneous performer for so many years. Yet there might be a future for him in "drahma:" "I would have loved to have got a crack at that *Hairy Ape.* There's a thing there, you know. And *Desire Under the Elms.* Boy, wouldn't I have been hot under the elms. Rogers and somebody under the elms." Rogers closes by wishing Eugene O'Neill a speedy recovery from the shock of hearing his lines spoken with an Oklahoma accent.

*27. July 8, 1934

Rogers, broadcasting without an audience, asks the listeners at home whether or not they prefer an audience in the studio. He says he has received much mail complaining that laughter and applause take up too much of a comedian's air time. Listeners are told to write to NBC.

Rogers announces that this will be his last broadcast for a few weeks because he is going on a trip. Goodwill tours "have been so successful that no two nations are speaking to each other," so he is taking a "bad will" tour. He plans to go to Honolulu, Japan, Manchuria, Siberia, Finland, "Garboland" (Sweden), Norway, Denmark, and Germany. Rogers calls it a "secret mission" and says that Congress will investigate him when he gets back to "find out why I went." He speculates about the benefits of bringing the president along as a companion: "He would be great to travel with. We could stop now and then to let him catch a fish. If he went with me all through Russia, he would come back with more ideas than General Hugh Johnson and Rex Tugwell combined."

28. September 16, 1934

This broadcast is from England in the form of a mock telephone call from traveler Will Rogers to America. Rogers makes maximum use of the device; for example, he says early on to the Depression audience: "Is this America? It don't sound like your voice; it sounds sad." The first American he speaks to is a rich man in California who is dejected because the stock market has gone to hell: "H as in Huey. E as in the third letter of Huey. L as in Long. And another L as in Long." Rogers reminds the rich man that the stock market is only a small fragment of what makes America great.

Rogers then asks to speak with an ordinary American. To him he relates observations about the comeback of England and the hardships of being a Communist in Russia where the responsibilities of governing force ideologues to be pragmatic. Rogers cautions all Americans to be happy with their imperfect government: "*We* don't know what form of government it is, but whatever it is, it's ours, and you can bet your life we won't change it, and as bad off as we are, we are better than anybody else I have seen."

29. September 30, 1934

In this program, Will Rogers returns from his "Bad Will Tour" of the world. Rogers attempts to provide a global perspective on the problems of the United States during the Depression. Many listeners may be out of work, but "I've been in countries on this trip where our unemployed would be arrested for being capitalists." Wealthy Americans are worried about the New Deal violations of the Constitution, a problem which also can be put in perspective: "I've been in some countries that wouldn't know what it was." In sum, Americans should be thankful that they have been saved from the worst pangs of a world-wide depression.

Rogers announces a mock plan to deal with fears of the rich. He rejects the Russian solution: "They bumped off all the rich. . . . They ain't any good. We've got to keep the rich 'cause we've got to live off 'em." Instead of more government control, Rogers advocates that the president send all the "rugged individualists" into the market place to prove their mettle. They should not be bound by government controls; on the other hand, they should not be eligible for government loans: "Give them one year's trial and just see how rugged they could get."

30. October 7, 1934

In a show broadcast from Texas, Will Rogers is interviewed over the airwaves by "Hired Hand" Huff of the *Fort Worth Star-Telegram*. Recent topics such as the World Series and pitcher Dizzy Dean are discussed, but the most important and extended dialogue focuses on the similarities between recent talks by Will Rogers and President Roosevelt. Huff presses Rogers on the matter: "Some people are wondering if the president is writing your speeches, or you're writing the president's speeches."

Rogers has a simple explanation. He and President Roosevelt have a similar grasp on political matters because they have both travelled much and understand power. The American rich need to follow the British example and "bet on" America. Henry Ford has set the right example by investing in new factories during bad times; the country will come out of the Depression much faster if other investors follow Ford's example. Rogers takes pride that he and the president are of like mind on this matter.

31. October 14, 1934

Rogers gives the first of his "intellectual and unreliable talks" on Russia. He says explaining Russia is not easy, even though he was there in August, 1934 and he has even read some books on the subject. Stalin and the government are discussed, as are Russian movies, hotels, and the Russian work week. He has no answer to the question, "Is Russia happy?" but he does assert that all countries have the right to their own systems: "I don't know how Russia's run. Nobody knows how it's run. It's not run our way. The government of Russia to me is like a suit of clothes. Now it don't fit 'em very good, but it's the best one they got."

References to Roosevelt, Wall Street, the NRA, and Congress are scattered throughout the talk. Rogers thinks the chances of the United States turning Communist are slim because consumers are better off than elsewhere: "That's one thing about America. We don't give everybody a job, but everybody's certainly got a car."

32. October 21, 1934

In this program, Rogers finally gets to tell about his Russian travels: "Last Sunday night I told you I was going to tell you about Siberia, and the Trans-Siberian railroad in Russia. And to show you I'm not a politician, I'm going to keep my word."

Typically, Rogers is as interested in details of the environment as in political matters. The geographical approach also helps to organize the talk as Rogers moves from Manchuria to Siberia to central Russia. Along the way, digressions touch on Chinese and Russian mores; F.D.R.; comparisons between the U.S. and Russian reforms; college professors and social planning; the relative strengths of Japanese and Chinese cultures. Rogers' concern about future conflicts in the Far East were prescient.

33. October 28, 1934

This evening Rogers continues his survey of Russian conditions. Religion still flourishes among adults even though the Communist regime has constantly propagandized against the church: "If you're a believer in some Supreme Being, no matter what religion, you don't give that up as easy as you change your government." Secular heroes such as Lenin have replaced religious figures for the youth of the nation: "I'd rather have the Lenin statue building contract in Russia than to have the Ford automobile building rights there."

The Rogers family was given a tour of Soviet motion picture operations during the production of *The Three Songs of Lenin* (Dziga Vertov, dir., 1934). The film and other public information activities of the Russians impressed Rogers enormously, but he predicts that many Russian "atheists" will have second thoughts on the last day of their lives. The lack of facilities and public crowding are discussed at length; the pervasive hunger seems to add to a portrait of inefficiency and privation. Lawyers, divorce, marriage, and children are topics which round out the cowboy philosopher's reflections on the Soviet experiment.

34. November 4, 1934

After a few opening comments about elections and their influence on the rhythm of American life, Rogers shifts attention back to his trip across the Soviet Union. Finland is of special interest to Rogers because it has been the only country to pay back loans made after the Great War. Rogers has fun playing with the language, talking about the food and, of course, providing a critique of Finnish politics. He is particularly struck by the use of electric balloting in the Finnish Diet: "They vote by electricity. We vote by air."

Rogers is, as usual, aware of the geopolitical pressures affecting Finland: "They sort of used to be under Russia. . . . I don't mean 'sort of under' Russia, because when you're under Russia, you ain't sort of—you're just under." Finnish athletes such as Paavo Nurmi, the famous Olympic marathon runner, impress Rogers for their unusual talents and achievements. In general, Rogers reflects a very positive view toward the nation which pays its debts. Unfortunately, the Russians, the Finns, and European citizens generally—despite the affable nature of individuals—need to eschew war, "but somebody must sell 'em the idea for they keep on having them." So ends Rogers' world-wide survey of men and nations.

35. November 11, 1934

Because of recent elections, Rogers uses most of the time in this program to critique the American political system with special emphasis on the death—and possible future resurrection—of the Republican party. He pronounces the party temporarily dead: "He passed away . . . he passed away because he wanted to live like a pioneer. He couldn't change with modern civilization." Rogers charts the illness of the patient, beginning with the paralytic stroke which hit the party during the stock market crash. The family and doctors did not realize that drastic measures were needed to deal with the problem: "They had always come out of these cramp colics without having to give up anything, and there was no reason why this one should be any different." When a tombstone was carved, the epitaph read: "Here lies a rugged individual, but he wasn't rugged enough to compete with the Democrats."

Continuing with the death motif, Rogers goes on to consider an afterlife for the Republican party. He predicts that the Democrats will eventually fall from grace, at which time there will be a need for a Republican return, swinging the pendulum back from left to right in a nation which seems to require a two-party system. The clock alarm halts these rambling speculations.

36. December 23, 1934

After a break in the program, Rogers returns to the air shortly before Christmas. Some remarks on politics and sports precede the major topic of discussion, aviation. Russia and Japan seem to be squaring off over Manchuria and Rogers predicts that air power will decide which of the two antagonists will prevail. As he pointed out some seven years earlier in *There's Not a Bathing Suit in Russia* (1927/1973), the Russians had become very air-minded. Parachute clubs all over Russia received government support and provided the nation with continuous paramilitary training of importance in a conflict-ridden world; even Russian women were jumping out of planes.

Commercial aviation in the United States and the exploration for new routes are discussed at length. Rogers narrates his experiences of flight over the desert of Mesopotamia, stressing the contrast between modern transport and the traditional ways of the desert: here, as elsewhere, the contrast of old and new fascinated him. He also reminisces about the beautiful, fertile valleys encountered during this Mediterranean trip. Rogers' ability to paint word pictures as well as his responsiveness to new experiences comes through in this program.

37. December 30, 1934

The subject of aviation continues from the previous program, with a special visit by Eugene Vidals, an administrator with the Federal Aviation

Authority. Vidals opens the program by describing Will Rogers as "aviation's star passenger and one of its greatest boosters." Vidals claims that the progress of civilian aviation in America can be measured in the decline of air sick boxes needed by Will Rogers in his cross-country trips over the years. "Ten years ago he was asking for and using one air sickness receptacle for fifty miles. Five years ago, about one for five hundred miles. Lately—none." Vidals goes on to cite the work of the Roosevelt administration to make the air lanes safe; he predicts that general aviation will some day rival automobility.

Rogers arrives dressed in a motion picture costume, for which he jokingly blames the NRA and its leader Hugh Johnson: "Got us working day and night here, and everything." Rogers thanks Vidals for attending and compliments him on not being a fuzzy-headed brain truster. Rogers goes on to chide his American audience for not supporting domestic aviation. Americans either fly in Europe or favor European aircraft in the United States; when travelling abroad, they readily use the air, but in the United States they timidly board trains. Considerable time is spent describing Mrs. Rogers' use of air transportation, followed by a glowing tribute to Amelia Earhart.

The program closes with comments on Sister Aimee McPherson, Mae West, Shirley Temple, and selected politicians.

38. January 6, 1935

This program has no particular focus, shifting from topic to topic and ending in a strange attempt to derive humor from the trial of Bruno Hauptmann, the accused (and later convicted) kidnapper of the Lindbergh baby. The Republicans are lambasted for being too negative: "Their plan has just. been denouncing. They meet and denounce, and never suggest anything—just denounce." The president is kidded for giving away money: "It's going to take years and years. And the Republicans groaned." Huey Long is mentioned in a humorous context.

Over half of the program focuses on a recent football game between Stanford and Alabama. Rogers, as an Oklahoman with Confederate roots, gloats over the superior skill and tactics of the Alabama team. A number of Civil War references are thrown in to accentuate the regional rivalry reflected by the game.

39. January 13, 1935

The most poignant moments of this program involve a letter sent by a listener reproving Rogers for joking about the Lindbergh case. Rogers is shocked that anyone would think he was trying to embarrass the family:

"Why, nothing would hurt me worse than to think that I had in any way tried to joke about the case." Rogers follows with a series of anecdotes indicating that he is a close friend of the Lindbergh family; in fact, he and Betty Rogers were among the last people to see the kidnapped child. His eloquent defense is received by applause from the studio audience. What Rogers meant in the earlier presentation (January 6, 1935) was that the attorney was handling the case in a *manner* which Rogers resented. Not the Lindberghs, but courtroom histrionics were on his mind during the previous show.

Substantive portions of the program touch on such topics as the Supreme Court and New Deal legislation; the economy and economic jargon; the meaning of modern womanhood. With regard to women, Rogers seems to revere both the traditional and the liberated models: while he admires the accomplishments of Amelia Earhart ("She goes about her job and does it great."), he is in awe of the mother of the Dionne quintuplets ("The greatest woman in the world is the one that has babies. And the more babies you have, the greater woman you are.").

40. January 20, 1935

In addition to addressing contemporary matters, Will Rogers talks about his radio style. In the early days of the program he studied for each broadcast: "I'd sit down and even went so far as to write out a little something — figure out how many minutes it would run, and had this thing all down like these old fellows read 'em off and everything." Gradually, his vaudeville style seemed more appropriate to the medium; he decided to work with a live audience and to have the lights in the studio up so that he could follow audience responses. If the audience laughed, then he could assume that listeners were laughing. (It should be noted that Rogers often repeated over the air what he had already used in daily and weekly articles; the programs were thus not completely spontaneous.)

Aviation is again a topic. Rogers describes some cross-country jaunts with Jimmy Doolittle and Wiley Post. Rogers highlights the discomfort of wearing the pressurized suit which Post requires on high altitude flights: "You've got to stay in there, and that's about as long as anyone breathed one mess of oxygen. You can't stick your head out at thirty-five thousand feet, and mix with that other air, you know." Mobility is an implicit theme. Rogers mentions recent jaunts — often by air — to Notre Dame, New York, Alabama, and Washington. He seems to be setting an example for others in the area of flight.

President Roosevelt's quarrel with the Supreme Court is discussed at length. Rogers confides that the president is unhappy with the recalcitrance of the "nine old men" on the court.

41. January 27, 1935

Rogers devotes this program to the discussion of the World Court and the prospects for international peace. One of the problems for the United States is its habit of asserting "moral leadership." We are only kidding ourselves: "It's almost like telling an old man that he's got sex appeal." We become entangled in other countries' affairs when we can't really handle our own: "Now Nicaragua, Santo Domingo, all these—we fixed everybody's business down there, but our own." The United States has also been misled by a faith in conferences. A close observer of the Versailles debacle, Rogers sums up the problem: "We never lost a war and we never won a conference in our lives."

As a result of his travels, Rogers concludes that wars have been avoided because everybody is too poor: "Nobody's got any money. They can't fight till they borrow somethin', and there ain't nobody to borrow it from." The main point with respect to the World Court issue is that conditions—economic and financial—have more to do with the world peace than the conferences and judicial bodies. Linking court problems to recent American history, Rogers observes that World Court decisions might be declared null and void by the United States Supreme Court, thus making a farce out of the elaborate and expensive effort! Oklahoma's world traveller concludes that nations should focus on their own problems; he pleads for the toleration of differences among nations.

42. February 3, 1935

This Gulf program comes from Carnegie Hall. Rogers says that both he and the orchestra are a bit overwhelmed by the fancy surroundings. Early in the program, Amelia Earhart visits with Rogers on the subject of her recent flight to Hawaii. Rogers lavishes considerable praise on the quiet young woman.

The defeat of the World Court bill in Congress is praised by Rogers. He shrugs off the complaint that his comments on a previous program—just before the bill was considered by Congress—had any effect upon the outcome: "If anyone could accuse me of influencing anybody, it would have to be a half-witted Senator. . . . If I'd known what they was going to do, I wouldn't have been blatherin' around last Sunday night." Discussion of the World Court leads to the gold standard issue before the Supreme Court and to matters at the Lindbergh trial. In all cases, Rogers is unhappy with the uses which lawyers and publicity seekers find for such bodies. Rogers would rather admire the direct and honest achievements of a Lindbergh or an Earhart.

* 43. March 31, 1935

After a seven-week vacation from the program, Will Rogers returns with a number of crises to discuss. He accuses Germany of taking advantage of his absence: "Hitler broke out on me. I thought I had him covered. He broke out on me and tore up the Versailles treaty." Rogers then recycles a number of remarks written years earlier about the silliness of Woodrow Wilson's peace plan. England and France anticipate a war with Germany; Rogers comments on their swift realignment with Russia against a common enemy. He imagines Anthony Eden (then a junior diplomat) telling the Russians that the British would like to share a war with them. As an isolationist, Rogers warns his American audience to expect—and to resist—similar invitations from the British.

Rogers links Italy's invasion of Ethiopia to private assurances made by allies during the Versailles conference. Evidently Mussolini was given free rein in Africa: "If you ever want anything in Africa, our heads will be turned. So he remembered that. That guy never forgets anything. So he's off down in there." According to Rogers, the blame for the invasion should be distributed broadly.

Shifting to the nation's capital, Rogers explains his attitude as a Washington reporter: "The Senate is my particular hobby. And I go down and see them, and go in—drop in the old joke factory there and see what the boys . . . see what the boys is doin'." He is pleased with a recent bill introduced to bar war profits, although he offers an improvement: "I think it would be still a better idea and would keep us out of a lot of wars if they put in the bill there that not only couldn't we make any [profits] out of our own war, but we couldn't make any out of anybody's war." Rogers is definitely not impressed by former President Hoover's criticism of the New Deal in a recent, highly publicized speech: "I kind of gathered from just reading between the lines that he really wasn't in a hundred per cent with all that was going on in Washington." Rogers says that the most often asked question concerns government spending; people want to know how long it can go on. His response is more aimed at entertainment than insights: "I says—well, it will go on just as long as the Republicans has got any money. That's all I know about it."

* 44. April 7, 1935

In this program, Rogers tries to explore the basis for criticism of Roosevelt's spending policies; in addition, he takes a look at specific cases of taxes new and old. He urges the public to support current fiscal experiments by both state and federal governments.

The Roosevelt plan has come under considerable fire from the press, but much of the criticism stems from the fact that Republicans own the newspapers. Rogers tries to simplify the rationale behind deficit spending: in times of financial stress, someone must stimulate purchasing by the public to get the economy working again. Rogers focuses on his own dilemma as a film star. People need jobs or relief payments so that they can afford to attend their local theatres; when they show up for a Will Rogers film, then Hollywood and its actors can survive, hopefully using their purchasing power to generate additional jobs in the economy. For all their complaints, even bankers profit: "When the man comes to pay his loan with government money, they don't say—no, I can't take it." Rogers' point is that, while deficit spending is attacked as a partisan measure, it actually helps everybody in the economy, even the propertied classes.

Rogers ridicules the reluctance to pay taxes. For example, the movie industry is loudly opposing new California taxes: "Mr. Sam Goldwyn this morning said we're going to England." Rogers reminds the film industry that it is dependent upon the good will of the American public; furthermore, it is only right that Hollywood do its share of the work to get the nation back into the black. Since the Pilgrims, Rogers explains, Americans have complained about taxes: "Of course, we know our government is costing us more than it's worth, but do you know any cheaper government? If you do, we'll just sell you a ticket there anytime." Rogers mentions a few specific contrasts around the world: "There's no income tax in Russia, but there's no income. . . . You don't have to pay a poll tax to vote in Italy, you know, but nobody votes."

* 45. April 14, 1935

A philosophical strand connects the otherwise desultory topics of this program. Rogers is reflecting in various ways on the rise and fall of American civilization. A debate between Provincetown and Plymouth, Massachusetts, about where on Cape Cod the Pilgrims first landed, invites some comments on the nature of early settlement. As a Cherokee, Rogers claims to have a special perspective on the Pilgrims, a viewpoint which takes into account the greed and rapacity of the conquest of New England in the seventeenth century: "You never in your life seen a picture of one of those old Pilgrims praying that he didn't have a gun right by the side of him. That was to see that he got what he was praying for." Discussion of the Dust Bowl conditions leads to a consideration of pioneers. They, too, have been glorified beyond justification; in fact, the problems in the West can be linked to a misuse of the land by early settlers: "I think if we stopped and looked history in the face, the Pioneer wasn't a thing in the world but a guy that wanted something for nothing. He was a guy that wanted to live off of everything that Nature had done . . . He thought it was nature he was living off, but it was really future generations." Finally, Rogers turns to the current political turmoil, offering a Panglossian defense of conditions in his own region of the country. If civilizations must rise before they fall, then he is proud of coming from that part of the country which has been selected to fall first. In fact, this short term disaster can be interpreted to be a profound blessing. As a contrast, Rogers predicts that Washington will be the last city to fall "on account of its being the least civilized, it will be the last place to be covered up."

* 46. April 21, 1935

Dealing as it does with various plans to save the nation, this program is probably one of the most thoughtful and clever of the Gulf series. Not only is the Rogers wit at full tilt, the Oklahoman had actually prepared for the program by reading books by the major figures mentioned.

Dr. Francis Townsend, author of the Townsend Plan is described by Rogers as "a conscientious, well meaning, humanitarian old gentleman." Rogers worries that publicity surrounding the plan may have fostered unrealistic expectations among the old. While critical of details of the plan, Rogers admits that Dr. Townsend got Congress to act—an accomplishment in itself. Rogers briefly alludes to competing plans to share government revenues with citizens.

Government plans seem to yield unexpected results: "Somebody had a plan to teach hogs birth control, and now it is a habit with them. You can find a deer quicker than you can a hog. Somebody had a plan to plow under every third acre of wheat, and the wind came along and blew out the other two acres." The silliness of Father Charles Coughlin is linked to previous utopian schemes: "Jesus said: 'Love thy neighbor as thyself,' but I bet there ain't two people in your block that's speaking to each other." Rogers' exasperation with the multitude of plans does not prevent him from offering his own.

The Rogers Plan is to end all plans: "There ain't but one place that a plan will really work and that's on paper. The minute you get it off paper and get it out in the air it blows away." The slogans and propaganda which have accompanied recent proposals remind Rogers of the Great War hysteria which prevented Americans from dealing with problems sensibly. Too often, parties advocating plans—whether Democratic or Republican—use ideas as political weapons. Bordering on a philosophical statement, Rogers offers another perspective: "Go through life haphazardly, even more than we are now. There is nothing in the world as common as an idea and there is nothing in the world as hard to carry out as an idea." In the future, Rogers advocates that anyone hearing plans over the radio immediately turn their dial: "The plan will go right back into the nutshell where it belongs."

* 47. April 28, 1935

This Sunday program comes immediately before an address to the nation by President Roosevelt. Rogers takes advantage of the forum to continue his talk about plans and to speculate about what the president might be getting ready to say. Despite his attempt to put an end to plans, Rogers announces that there have been some new proposals put forward. For example, Henry Morgenthau, Jr., secretary of the Treasury, has proposed a major increase in inheritance taxes. Rogers has lots of fun playing with the way in which the plan morbidly anticipates revenue over the next years. Rogers wonders if the president will announce some new plan of his own.

In ordinary language, Rogers attempts to explain the trauma of the Depression and to justify the need for government spending. He likens the financial crash to a train accident at a crossing. Americans were hit once and now hesitate to invest and spend as a result of the trauma. As a result, the government must enter the marketplace, hopefully encouraging dazed citizens to become involved again in productive work: "We are so scared now that we drive up to the track and we won't do anything. We are just standing there. . . . We won't trust our own eyesight. If a train goes by and it looks like everything is OK and we might be able to cross, we won't do it. We are so scared we think it might turn around and come back and hit us again."

Rogers says the role of the president is to get America moving again, a task which demands both new legislation and a resurgence of public confidence. Neither the legislative goals nor the psychological change will be easy to effect without humor, flexibility, and willingness to avoid dogmatic plans.

* 48. May 5, 1935

In this program, a metaphor of gambling is sustained throughout in an effort to describe a tendency running through American history. While the historical survey is in jest, Rogers does attempt to show an irresponsible characteristic in American life: Americans love to spend and live in the future. The stock market crash was only one example of the results of such carelessness: "Our whole depression was brought on by gambling, not alone in the stock market, but in expanding and borrowing, and going in debt all just to make some money quick." Through humor, Rogers attempts to exorcise this flaw. The Puritans, the Quakers of early Philadelphia, Harvard and Yale Universities in the eighteenth century, the Revolutionary War, the War of 1812, and the Kentucky Derby are some of the instances of the gambling itch surveyed by the plains historian.

Rogers devises a mock lottery, a plan with an unwieldy acronym: R(ogers) L(ottery) U(ntil) I C(an) T(hink) O(f) a B(etter) P(lan). The proceeds of the lottery will be used for relief of the unemployed during the Depression. The benefit of the Rogers plan—as compared with taxation—is that even the rich will hold tickets for the drawing. As a result, they will participate enthusiastically: "You can always get money out of a rich guy if you show him where there is a chance he is liable to bring something home with him." Rogers proposes that the lottery somehow be connected with presidential elections, at last giving the events "dignity and prestige."

The entire show is an exercise in extended metaphor designed to spoof the contending income tax proposals before the country.

* 49. May 12, 1935

This broadcast takes place on Mother's Day, a holiday which Rogers feels is an inadequate gesture. In a fashion mocking the many plans for every aspect of American life, Rogers comes up with his own plan. Like his other panaceas, this plan has a very awkward acronym: R(emember) M(others) I(n) A S(ubstantial) W(ay) D(ay). The event would run throughout the year. January would carry "Mother's Forgotten Christmas Presents Day." On "Mother's Transportation Day," the lady of the house would receive a present with wheels: "The modern mother she don't want lilacs or a corsage of pansies, or something, but give her a car, Chevy, Ford. Those that couldn't afford it, give her a bicycle." Rogers has a lot of fun with his holiday plan.

The concluding half of the program focuses on Congress and a serious, deep-seated resentment pervading American society. Members of the Senate have lost their sense of humor and, thereby, their sense of perspective. They need to remember the gift of laughter to relieve them of the pressures of their work and to give them a realistic grasp of the nation's problems. The rich need to relax; they are frozen into positions of unconstructive antagonism toward the president and his programs. The middle and lower classes also need to counteract a festering class animosity. Rogers, in a serious vein, predicts that the country will not come out of the Depression unless everybody backs off unconstructive positions: "We have got a conflict now where everything, any class, one class is arrayed against another one, and that's the way we are going through, and none of us will admit that maybe we was in the wrong." Rogers pleads for more national unity to pull the country through hard times.

* 50. May 19, 1935

Since this broadcast originates from Sacramento, California, Rogers has a perfect opportunity to poke fun at state legislators and government interference in general. Rogers was in the area making one of his last films, *Steamboat 'Round the Bend* (John Ford, dir., 1935).

A recent bill raising taxes for motion picture personnel is spoofed as a typical legislative error. The solons think that actors will be an excellent source of revenue, but Rogers warns that they are going to be surprised: "It won't hook us so bad because we don't have to pay on what we are advertised to get. We only have to pay on what we get." Other bills dealing with marriage laws, the right of Indians to buy liquor, the salaries of legislators, all receive withering commentary by the erstwhile mayor of Beverly Hills.

Irvin S. Cobb, co-star of *Steamboat 'Round the Bend,* joins Rogers in a hilarious dialogue about Hollywood. Cobb (Kentucky) and Rogers (Oklahoma) talk about the "liberated" life of the movie capitol and the difficulties of adjusting to mores in a city of free love and yes men. In their exchange, as in *Steamboat,* both men celebrate the virtues of an America before Hollywood, radio, and taxes.

* 51. May 26, 1935

The theme of legislative plans carries over from previous programs: this evening, the focus is the contending schemes for paying a bonus to veterans of World War I. As usual, Rogers has his own plan although he avoids an acronymic approach: "After all, a bill is nothing but a plan and a plan is nothing but a bill, and both of them is nothing but a pipedream anyhow, a pipedream on paper."

While apparently talking about relief measures such as the bonus, he relates the discussion to war. His plan is simply to tax anyone on income derived from war profits: "All these fellows [senators] have been hollering about 'take the profits out of the next war!' Well, my scheme is why not take it out of the last one, too?" Although fanciful in the extreme, Rogers' mock plan does illuminate the problem of greed and the rewards which some in American society have reaped from human suffering. Because he claims not to be experienced in legislative processes, Rogers warns that he will hand over the project to his favorite plan enthusiast, Huey Long.

Like so many of the writings and radio programs of Will Rogers, serious messages are mixed in with pure playfulness.

* 52. June 2, 1935

Most of this broadcast focuses on the famous Supreme Court decision which held that the N(ational) R(ecovery) A(ct) of the New Deal was in violation of the Constitution. The Schechter Brothers, owners of a poultry business in Brooklyn, were accused of shipping spoiled food across state lines and of improper labor practices. In his discussion, Rogers assays the devastating effect of this decision for the New Deal; he questions the usefulness of a Court which prevents a nation from flexibly coping with its challenges.

As an innocent to the complexities of politics, Rogers ponders how a regulation against bad food could be oppressive. He simply cannot understand the logic of the court and its "old motheaten copy of the Constitution." He is concerned that President Roosevelt's ability to lead has been compromised: "He is just another President now, all over a plate of chickens." The impact upon history parallels other great moments but, in this case, history is being played as farce: "We fought England over a mess of tea, which nobody over here ever drinks anyhow, and now the whole social structure of the North American continent is changed by Brooklyn buying a sick chicken."

Throughout the program, Rogers fears for a country whose institutions cannot keep pace with the times.

* 53. *June 9, 1935*

In his final Gulf program, Rogers continues to talk about the NRA decision by the Supreme Court while exploring partisan tensions of the country which the decision reflects. Rogers shows awareness of the labor practices dimension of the decision—specifically the minimum wage and work hours restrictions of the NRA codes. Again, he pleads for flexibility. Granting to Republicans the point that the Constitution of the United States has helped enormously through the years, Rogers reminds them that not everyone has prospered: "There's a lot of folks that haven't got anywhere under them [the current laws] you know, and the prospects ain't any too bright for them to get any further." A worthwhile approach is one which helps everyone, not just those at the top. President Roosevelt may be excessive in his goal to bring prosperity by helping those at the bottom of the social ladder; on the other hand, Republicans seem too eager to let the rich continue unrestrained, a practice which has already proven its limitations. Rogers pleads for a centrist approach: "I have never heard of anybody suggesting that they might start it in the middle, so I hereby make that suggestion, to start recovery halfway between the two. Because it is the middle-class that does everything anyhow." Rogers warns that much of America's current partisan acerbity stems from an unwillingness to honor the contributions of the middle class majority.

A significant portion of this program is taken up with ridicule of party rivalry. Rogers mockingly suggests that each party be placed in geographic isolation: give the Democrats the West, send Republicans to the East. He predicts a complete cessation of hostilities as a result of such segregation: "I personally can't picture a more ideal existence all around. The only trouble would be neither one would be happy because they wouldn't have nobody to lay anything on to." This exaggeration is obviously introduced to satirize squabbling when the nation is in trouble and the national interest—not party interest—should be the top priority.

With summer coming on, Rogers advises the audience not to worry: "Don't get all heated up and argue and get mad over these problems all summer. . . . Everybody is trying to save the country, only they are trying to do it in different ways. It is too big, the country is too big for all of them put together to spoil anyhow." Will Rogers completed his last Gulf radio program on a reassuring note.

OCCASIONAL TALKS BY WILL ROGERS

Will Rogers was a much sought after speaker. Frequently, the *New York Times* carried a summary of the presentations together with quotable quotes. These presentations have been ignored by most students of the Will Rogers legacy. They are summarized briefly here as an incentive to future researchers.

1. "Speech for Ogden Mills"

Group: General public
Topic: Congressional candidacy of Ogden Mills

Rogers told the audience that he had never gone into politics because he wanted to live an honest life; his jokes implied that Representative Mills, who was a wealthy man, had become considerably richer since he had taken office. Still, Rogers claimed that he was able to support Mills because he had not yet actually met the congressman. Mills endured the speech with a very sombre look on his face. (See *New York Times,* June 13, 1920, Sec. 6, p. 2, col. 3.)

2. "Merchants' Drive Nets 1,825 Members"

Group: Merchants Association
Topic: Politics and the world situation

Rogers used this occasion as a forum for ridiculing Prohibition, but the Merchants Association itself naturally did not escape his taunts. According to Rogers, a man's first priority should be his own family, and then he should be left alone to enjoy himself. His first comment to the new members of the Association was, "Some people belong to everything in town but their own families." Later, he tells them, when receiving a list of Association achievements, "It says here you have enrolled 32,000 children to keep the streets clean. It says nothing about what you have done yourselves to keep them clean." His humor lends more dignity to his description of an individual from his home state: "He said, 'I am neither an Elk nor an Eagle nor a Shriner. I am just an ordinary drunkard.' " This comment sums up Rogers' feelings toward both unnatural laws and unnatural associations in general. Rogers also addressed issues such as the recent elections, the Hall murder in New Jersey, and the situation in Turkey. (See *New York Times,* November 18, 1922, p. 18, col. 1.)

3. *"Modern Triumvirate Guests of Friars"*

Group: Friars Club
Topic: Hollywood and baseball

At a dinner devoted to Broadway movies and baseball, Rogers' sharp comments quickly deflated the seriousness with which these fields of entertainment were being discussed. He called movies "a lot of stories with different names to them," and he referred to baseball players as "glorified rounders." Focusing further on the sport, Rogers said, "Baseball is not an industry . . . and, as the Yankees played it, not even a game." His comment reveals both his knowledge of the national pastime and the innocence with which he viewed it, particularly considering this was barely a year after the infamous "Black Sox Scandal." (See *New York Times,* November 20, 1922, p. 21, col. 1.)

4. *"Rogers Pokes Fun at Advertising Men"*

Group: Advertising Club
Topic: Advertising and world events

As a commentator on the changing nature of American life, Rogers was provided with the perfect forum. His comments focused on the transformation of commercialism from an area dominated by quality into one dominated by the creation of appetites among consumers: "What would happen if you fellows ever got down and told the truth? . . . Did it ever appeal to you to get the people you work for to improve the article they're selling with the money they are using to advertise it? Of course, that's a revolutionary idea. It'll never happen." These opening comments gave him a basis to discuss other events of the day: Clemenceau's visit, New Yorkers' eating habits, Turkey's wars, progressives' attempts to amend the Constitution, and Prohibition agents who were going out beyond the three-mile limit to confiscate liquor aboard ships. Appropriately for this event, his comments emphasize that problems are caused by people who want more than what they can reasonably have. (See *New York Times,* December 8, 1922, p. 30, col. 1.)

5. *"Hits Publicly Dry and Privately Wet"*

Group: Molly Pitcher Club
Topic: Prohibition

Rogers added his voice to a number of other speakers who were attacking the hypocrisy of Prohibitionists. The law was passed, he said, when a number of senators, "having nothing else to do at the moment," went around to local Washington bars gathering enough members for a quorum to get the legislation through. Rogers did claim to have selfish reasons for wanting the country "wet." He said he liked to have an audience that had drunk "just enough to see the point of the joke and [was] sober enough to applaud." (See *New York Times,* December 18, 1922, p. 19, col. 6.)

6. *"Will Rogers Tells Ford How to Win"*

Group: Authors' League
Topic: Ford running for president, world events, crime in New York

Rogers used this occasion to poke some gentle fun at prosperity and Prohibition. He started by saying that Henry Ford could win the presidency if he would only tell all of America what it wanted to hear most. "He'd only have to make one speech," said Rogers. "Voters, if I'm elected, I'll change the front of the Model T." Building on the myth of American prosperity, Rogers complained about crime in New York by saying that "it's getting so that a woman can't go out at two o'clock in the morning with $500,000 worth of jewels."

Turning his attention to world events, Rogers found something positive to say. He felt that the international debt situation could be solved if France would buy all the light beer and wine from Germany and then sell it to the United States. This move would also help bring the country back to where it was before Prohibition. As for now, he said, the country was having trouble finding delegates to send to European conferences, and when we did find one, we could not be sure he would come back. (See *New York Times,* January 8, 1923, p. 17, col. 3.)

7. *"Will Rogers Calls Auto Makers 'Gyps' "*

Group: National Automobile Chamber of Commerce
Topic: The auto industry

Automobiles were causing a lot of euphoria in the country, which gave this dinner the perfect atmosphere for Rogers to bring everyone back down to earth, if only for a little while. He began by calling manufacturers "gyps" and said that none of them would honestly be able to swear on a Bible that he had not stolen a patent. "You cannot get one of them to do that, and if you could find him you would have to send outside the industry to get a Bible." He chided the auto advertisements which claimed to have all the best bodies when he knew that Flo Ziegfeld had hired all the best ones, and he said that the most interesting part of the auto show "was the salesman's dress suits." He expressed his admiration for Henry Ford, giving him a vote of confidence for the presidency. "I would like to see him take hold of the country and put it on a paying basis. Give him a percentage of what he can save." (See *New York Times,* January 10, 1923, p. 13, col. 20.)

8. *"Rogers Compares Autos with Wives"*

Group: Automobile Accessories Manufacturers
Topic: The auto industry

This occasion gave Rogers a second consecutive evening to rib the automobile industry, and he claimed that he had discovered he was wrong the previous night in his remarks to the manufacturers. The accessories producers were the real cause of the industry's troubles. "You are the Lenins and Trotskys of the business," he told them. "I find the manufacturers are only tools in your hands. You make the brittle parts, sell 'em to him, and he has to be the goat and try and peddle them to the public." Compared to the "unfortunate millionaires" he had addressed the previous night, Rogers found this group to be the real controllers of the business because they made all the essential "accessories" such as doors that actually shut, 1,400 different styles of knobs, and wheels. "When I think of all the accessories on a Ford car, I weep," said Rogers. "Why, if all those accessories were put on one car Ford himself couldn't identify the original parts." Rogers again took a jibe at Prohibition by stating that the auto industry was second only to bootlegging, and he claimed that the soldiers recently returned from Germany would have been home sooner if anybody in the War Department had known where they were. (See *New York Times,* January 11, 1923, p. 21, col. 5.)

9. *"Salvation Army Bids Broadway Farewell"*

Group: Friends of Rheba Crawford
Topic: Crawford's work

Rogers admitted that some people might be surprised to see him paying tribute to the evangelist Rheba Crawford, but his remarks showed that he was an admirer of a sincerely honest person. "I don't know offhand of anyone who started off with the same wonderful God-given personality and endowed with such good common sense." He compared her with New York churchgoers who "look around for the box office first thing," and popular ministers in whose churches "the seats are in the hands of the speculators." Rogers could naturally not resist using humor in his compliments of Crawford. He claimed that he had seen bootleggers leave some of her meetings "and cut off $5 a case." Rogers' kindness and honesty were such that he was not at all out-of-place in this tribute to a beloved spiritual leader. (See *New York Times,* February 26, 1923, p. 13, col. 3.)

10. "Will Rogers Silenced"

Group: New Building Superintendents Association
Topic: Limited remarks

Rogers' only recorded comment to the superintendents was that Carnegie Hall was a "swell joint and so I guess many of you ain't ever been here before." But he was stopped from making any more comments by a drunk in the balcony who made so much noise that Rogers did not try to compete with him. (The report does not indicate that the man was acting out of antagonism toward Rogers.) (See *New York Times,* April 1, 1928, p. 22, col. 2.)

11. "Will Rogers on Harding"

Group: National Association of Manufacturers
Topic: Harding's speeches

After telling the manufacturers that he had never "appeared before a finer bunch of gyps in the world than you are," Rogers decided to advise President Harding on what issues to address during his upcoming speaking tour. Accurately reflecting the sincere interests of the people, Rogers told him to avoid "junk" like the International Court and the League of Nations and to comment on whether Valentino was going to be making any more pictures, where people could park their cars, and "who is the latest dancing champion and how many hours she danced." "We want to know can Willard whip this Firpo? Those are the things this country is interested in right now." (See *New York Times,* May 16, 1923, p. 5, col. 2.)

12. "Stage Pays Honor to Cardinal Hayes"

Group: Catholic Actors Guild
Topic: Appointment of Hayes as cardinal

Rogers honored the new cardinal in his typically comic manner and was also able to mix in jibes at President Coolidge, Hollywood, and the Catholic Church. Proclaiming himself to have been "the original 'Hayes-for-Cardinal' man," Rogers expressed his admiration in characteristic fashion by saying, "He has got a better job, but he is just the same fellow." Rogers wondered if the Prince of Wales could have told President Coolidge a joke during his recent visit. "We can't even tell him an American joke." He also mentioned that even Hollywood had printed the news of Hayes' appointment to cardinal "in the first story of a spiritual nature they had ever printed." He said that in reading the story he had been surprised to find out "how it took three days to learn how to wear a red hat." But he added that he was always proud to say that he had once been laughed at by a cardinal. (See *New York Times,* October 8, 1924, p. 16, col. 1.)

13. "Rogers Aids Y.W.C.A. Drive"

Group: Workers of YWCA budget campaign
Topic: Fund raising

Rogers' only recorded remark at this function sounded a note of bleak irony. He said that what the country needed was another war to make people give. Other speakers also noted the difficulty of raising funds in the midst of the stock market boom. (See *New York Times,* November 27, 1924, p. 3, col. 2.)

14. "Will Rogers and Tom Mix"

Group: Dinner for Tom Mix
Topic: Early experiences with Mix

Rogers entertained the audience with a story about how, when he first met Mix while both of them were performing in Colonel Zack Mulhall's Wild West Show, the two had once been forced to steal their pay from the owner. (See *New York Times,* April 12, 1925, Sec. 8, p. 5, cols. 6–7.)

15. "Will Rogers Jokes on Schwab's Genius"

Group: Pennsylvania Society
Topic: Schwab's legal troubles

Charles Schwab's autobiography provided the basis for most of Rogers' humor on this occasion. Rogers joked about the large gaps in it and about how Schwab had gone from being a dollar-a-day stake driver to president of Bethlehem Steel. Although Schwab was being brought to court by the government at the time and Rogers was not sure what the charges were, he did not hesitate to give the steelmaker his highest praise: "There isn't a man, woman, or child in this country who doesn't believe Charley Schwab is right. . . . When they make more Charley Schwabs this country will be better." (See *New York Times,* April 22, 1925, p. 24, col. 4.)

16. "Peals of Laughter Greet Will Rogers"

Group: General public at Carnegie Hall
Topic: Current events

In what was practically a one-man show, Rogers covered a broad range of topics, including the Florida real estate boom, the Ku Klux Klan, Prohibition, New York traffic conditions, Congress, and the younger generation. His most memorable remarks included his description of the Florida state emblem as an all-day sucker and his advice to flappers not to "follow fashion any further than you are physically able." The addition of his rope tricks during his monologue made the performance a typical Rogers evening. (See *New York Times,* April 12, 1926, p. 18, col. 1.)

17. *"New [Radio Station] WEAF Offers a Gala Program"*

Group: Listening audience
Topic: Travels and meetings with President Coolidge

The report of this event states only that the title of Mr. Rogers' talk was "Fifteen Minutes With a Diplomat," in which he reviewed his recent trip to Europe, travels through the West, and his visit with President Coolidge at the White House. (See *New York Times,* November 16, 1926, p. 22, col. 2.)

18. *"Ziegfeld Theatre's Cornerstone Laid"*

Group: General public
Topic: Theatre location

Rogers' comments at this event were also only briefly noted. He said that Ziegfeld had chosen the location because of the absence of saloons. Rogers lamented this fact: "Since the saloons have disappeared there have been many more theatres, and this accounts for the fact that the entertainment is not as good as it was." Several other celebrities were also present. (See *New York Times,* December 10, 1926, p. 30, col. 2.)

19. *"Will Rogers Inducted into Office of Mayor"*

Group: General public
Topic: Beverly Hills

This lighthearted event provided Rogers with a chance to do some gentle ribbing of the wealthy community and of himself. "It's an unique town," he said, "we've got two swimming pools to every Bible." Douglas Fairbanks, Sr. was present to demand that private swimming pools, bridle paths, and golf courses be cared for out of public funds. Rogers, who described his touring as "God's gift to those who didn't see Queen Marie," did not promise an honest administration, but he said he would split everything 50-50 and give the town an even break. (See *New York Times,* December 22, 1926, p. 24, col. 6.)

20. *"Will Rogers Fed Up on 'Peaches' and Mush"*

Group: Canners' Association
Topic: Public morality

This speech marked a distinct change in attitude in Rogers' comments. Whereas he had previously been upset with pious moralists, he now focused his remarks on a number of scandals. He attacked the judge in the recent "Peaches" and "Papa" Browning divorce case by saying that "what he lacked in judgment by letting the public in on the case . . . he's making up nicely in publicity." He claimed that "most mothers-in-law nowadays are looking for alimony for their daughters." He also referred to the Charlie Chaplin paternity case by stating that it had not taken place under his administration as mayor of Beverly Hills. Besides these opinions, he also felt that the United States should stay out of China and Nicaragua: "Can you imagine America settling an election in another country when all the Senators elected at the last election are being refused their seats?" (See *New York Times,* January 27, 1927, p. 3, col. 2.)

21. *"Rogers Satirizes Own Foreign Policy"*

Group: General public
Topic: Foreign policy

China and Nicaragua, along with Mexico, were once again the focus of Rogers' remarks on this occasion. Reflecting American attitudes after World War I, he said that "Every time we start out on a humanitarian mission we come back with both legs in a sling." In regard to China, he commented: "These Chinese get mighty few pleasures out of life, so they thought they'd have a civil war. And they can't even have that without us and England hornin' in on it." Rogers' call for America to stay at home included the missionaries in China who, he said, must be all trying to convert each other, and his own audience. He told the women present, "Every one of you ought to be home cookin' lunch instead of bein' here." According to Rogers, Americans should mind their own business and stick to things they know. Foreign interventions and meddling in the affairs of others always lead to trouble. (See *New York Times,* January 29, 1927, p. 2, col. 8.)

22. *"Will Rogers Joins in Lamb's Gambol"*

Group: Lambs' Club
Topic: Beverly Hills, New York Mayor Jimmy Walker, Thomas Lipton

Rogers used this speech to again emphasize his position at the center of traditional American morality by stating that, as mayor of Beverly Hills, his jurisdiction "was the decentest end of Hollywood." He added that his only platform had been that any woman "must give two days' notice" before she left her husband. He joked that New York's mayor had turned down the presidency of the American Baseball League because he never woke up early enough to see the games, and he praised Sir Thomas Lipton (of Lipton Tea) for his work in furthering international goodwill. (See *New York Times,* April 25, 1927, p. 23, col. 1.)

23. *"Obregon Dinner to Rogers"*

Group: Dinner guests of ex-President Obregón of Mexico
Topic: Lindbergh's D.C.-to-Mexico flight

In this speech at a dinner for the former Mexican president Álvaro Obregón, Rogers' only recorded comment was in praise of Charles Lindbergh's prospective flight from Washington, D.C., to Mexico City: "It will stop them from shooting for a while." Rogers also announced his plans to fly over the Valley of Mexico with the chief of the Mexican presidential staff, General José Alvarez, the following day. (See *New York Times,* December 10, 1927, p. 14, col. 4.)

24. *"All America Used as Radio Studio"*

Group: Nationwide radio audience
Topic: President Coolidge, Dodge cars

This program was notable for two reasons. It was the first nationwide broadcast featuring performances in four different locations, and it featured a controversial imitation of President Coolidge by Rogers, who served as host. Speaking from his living room in Beverly Hills, Rogers introduced the Paul Whiteman Orchestra, which performed in New York, Fred and Dorothy Stone, who sang some musical comedy numbers from their dressing room in a Chicago theatre, and Al Jolson, who sang from his hotel room in New Orleans. Rogers perfectly captured Coolidge's noncommittal nature in his imitation of the president: "Well, we're going to bury the Nicaraguan matter, and as far as the farmers are concerned, we're not going to bother about a McNary-Haugen bill. . . . We are simply going to pray for rain and better crops." Rogers' remarks must have taken some of the enjoyment out of the program for "Silent Cal."

The front-page treatment given to the story by the *Times* indicates the extent to which it was considered an engineering marvel. The Dodge Brothers produced the show, and Rogers gave them ample credit in his "advertisement" for their new line of cars, indicating that consumers now owed the company a favor as a result of being provided with this program. "I am not asking you to buy a car, mind you," he said, "I am just telling you about it. After a company extends you the courtesy of giving you a great big splendid program, the least you can do is to give their car a trial." Evidently, the *Times* felt the same way, for it followed the report of the program with an article detailing the new Dodge "Victory Six." (See *New York Times,* January 5, 1928, p. 1, col. 2; p. 24, cols. 1–4.)

25. "Will Rogers Pleads at Flood Hearing"

Group: House Committee on Flood Control
Topic: Aid for Mississippi Valley

Rogers made use of his appearance to satirize congressmen, himself, and tardy governmental relief. Referring to himself as "a Congressman at large," Rogers claimed to be one of the few representatives to have actually heard about the flood. Rogers did not blame Capitol Hill alone for having misplaced priorities, however. Of his fund-raising for the Red Cross, he said: "I have been around the country on my little tour and every night, after I had gotten all I could get for myself, I felt that the flood ought to get what was left." Rogers' real knowledge of conditions plus his personal example in providing charity did much to dramatize the need for government help. (See *New York Times,* January 13, 1928, p. 25, col. 8.)

26. "Democratic Women Honor Mrs. Wilson"

Group: Women Democrats
Topic: The presidential election

In a breakfast speech that seemingly had little significance at the time, Rogers repeated what is perhaps his most memorable statement, that he had never met a man he did not like. Although the statement is memorable chiefly because it characterizes the man so well, on this occasion it also had a political context that most people have forgotten. The speech was given on the morning of the day on which the Democrats were to nominate Al Smith for president and the party was torn on the issue of Prohibition. Some Southern states were even adamantly opposed to Smith. So, Rogers' statement, which is generally thought of as a kindly humanitarian thought, was also a special plea for unity within the Democratic party. Unfortunately, his call went unheeded, as the convention erupted in fighting that night, fighting that eventually involved the police. Whether or not Rogers' remark would have made any difference is certainly doubtful, but its intended effect was diminished in any case by the entrance of Mrs. Woodrow Wilson during his speech. In the report of the event, Rogers' comments received only a single paragraph; his now famous saying was not highlighted. (See *New York Times,* June 28, 1928, p. 2, col. 5.)

27. "Rogers in Brooklyn Pulpit"

Group: General public
Topic: Trying to see other points of view

Rogers told parishioners that they should never disagree with someone until they attempted to understand the other's perspective: "first, walk around behind him and see what he's lookin' at, and then see if he ain't a bit right." Rogers was at the church to assist the pastor, who was engaged in an attendance contest with some California ministers. (See *New York Times,* November 26, 1928, p. 31, col. 5.)

28. *"New York Puzzles Mackey"*

Group: Republican Women of Pennsylvania
Topic: Candidates for the next secretary of state

Rogers used this occasion to endorse Dwight W. Morrow, ambassador to Mexico, as the next secretary of state, adding that he had "no ulterior motives in the matter outside of wanting Morrow's job in Mexico." He also stated that Ambassador Henry Fletcher, in Rome, would be a good choice. (See *New York Times,* December 18, 1928, p. 16, col. 6.)

29. *"Will Rogers' Quips Aid Broadway Temple"*

Group: Bankers' Club
Topic: Broadway Temple Fund

Rogers was a member of the Broadway Temple Committee and one of the earliest contributors to its building fund. His speech at this event was designed to help raise more money. His remarks focused on rumors that the Temple would be located in a "Semitic neighborhood." Rogers explained, "We wanted to keep it in a day's travel of New York. . . . That's why we won't be able to move it to a Protestant neighborhood." He also amused the audience with anecdotes and jests about prominent people. (See *New York Times,* December 29, 1928, p. 22, col. 1.)

30. *"Will Rogers Enlivens Automotive Dinner"*

Group: Society of Automotive Engineers
Topic: National politics

This event featured another one of Rogers' most memorable statements: "People ask me where I get my jokes. I just watch Congress and report the facts." Returning to some of his favorite themes, Rogers talked about Prohibition and organizations in general. When the audience stood to applaud him, he told them, "Sit down—you'll tip your bottles over." He said he did not like societies because the country was being "clubbed to death." Referring to millionaire John Raskob's joining of the Democratic party, he noted that Raskob would be able to pay the party's debt and take it off his income taxes as a "contribution to a legitimate charity." (See *New York Times,* January 11, 1929, p. 13, col. 3.)

31. "Beverly Hills Revisited"

Group: Beverly Hills Chamber of Commerce
Topic: Beverly Hills

Rogers told stories about the settlement and development of Beverly Hills, referring to it as one of the earliest towns in California, "settled about 1914 . . . Beverly Hills was settled by renegade actors from Hollywood." He remembered that "About 1919 was the real estate slump and the restrictions were removed, and that is when I came in." Most of his humor was naturally aimed at the wealth of the community, which he said had become one of the best known towns in the world. But he hoped that it would not get too good, because then it would be just like Pasadena. (See *New York Times,* July 28, 1929, Sec. 8, p. 5, cols. 2–3.)

32. "Alabama Squad Sees Will Rogers at Work"

Group: University of Alabama football team
Topic: Unknown

The University of Alabama football squad, in California to play Washington State in the Rose Bowl, visited Rogers on a movie set and then lunched with him while he acted as master of ceremonies. No specific remarks of his are recorded. (See *New York Times,* December 30, 1930, p. 17, cols. 3–4.)

33. " 'Watch Coolidge in 1932,' Says Rogers"

Group: General public
Topic: Republican handling of the Depression

Accurately described in the *Times* as playing the "role of a Robin Hood to the drought stricken Southwest," Rogers made stops in Fayetteville and Rogers, Arkansas, and in Oklahoma City in his tour of the region to help raise funds. In Fayetteville, he laid much of the blame for the country's troubles directly where he thought it belonged. "I hate even to suspect it, but it looks like the Lord is on the Republicans' side," he said. "Of course, if he is, he's misinformed, but the result is always the same." Not wanting his audience to forget about whom to vote for, Rogers claimed that the Republicans always had three bad years and then one good one during an election year: "Watch Coolidge in 1932," he chided. "Even if Coolidge doesn't choose to run, the Republican slogan will be 'Hoover Pulled Us Through.' " The warmth of his reception was evident in Oklahoma, where the House of Representatives named him "the State's most useful citizen." (See *New York Times,* February 10, 1931, p. 5, col. 5.)

34. "Will Rogers Arrives in Panama to See if Brookhart Was Right"

Group: General public in Panama
Topic: U.S. presence in Latin America

Speaking at a benefit performance for Nicaragua earthquake victims, Rogers told his Panama City audience that "the United States is no good — no work, no money, no beer." Understanding how to relate to his audience better than Senator Smith W. Brookhart, who had been concerned about the prevalence of liquor in the Canal Zone, Rogers opened by speaking in Spanish, declaring that he had come to wallow in sin with the people: "I've sure enjoyed it," he added. Referring again to the senator, Rogers said that the United States' intentions were misunderstood by the Latin Americans who cannot "savvy why we have Marines in Nicaragua to defend a canal we are not even going to build." But in a serious manner, he noted that the marines had been helpful in relieving the suffering and that they should leave while the people still had a good impression. (See *New York Times,* April 13, 1931, p. 21, col. 7.)

35. "Schwab Says Bonus Holds Able Staffs"

Group: American Newspaper Publishers Association
Topic: Defending Schwab, challenge of radio to newspapers

In another talk to defend Charles Schwab against the charge of giving a bonus of over $1 million to his corporation's president, Rogers compared the steelmaker's troubles to his own difficulties with Clara Bow in an imaginary Nevada gambling incident. Speaking of Schwab's noted optimism, Rogers said, "Every rich man wants to be known as a regular guy. That's why Rockefeller and I sometimes exchange new dimes." Rogers also satirized President Hoover, former President Coolidge, and various current news events. Referring to newspaper publishers' complaints about unfair competition from radio, he said, "I don't think you've got anything in the world to fear from radio, but if you have, all you've got to do to destroy radio is to poison Amos 'n' Andy." He then remarked on the threat of television removing all the pictures from the papers and leaving nothing but editorials. (See *New York Times,* April 28, 1931, p. 16, cols. 4-5.)

36. "Heard on Hookup of 150 Stations"

Group: General public
Topic: Relief for Depression victims

Once again, Rogers spoke from his home in Beverly Hills on a gigantic radio hookup. The *Times* only notes that he "interspersed bits of homely philosophy in his extemporaneous appeal to the people to meet the situation [of the unemployed]." His appearance on the same program with President Hoover showed Rogers' ability to put aside political differences in order to achieve a necessary end.

This famous "Bacon and Beans and Limousines" broadcast – or at least Will Rogers' part of it – is reprinted in Chapter 3, pp. 94–96. (See *New York Times,* October 19, 1931, p. 8, col. 4.)

37. "Manchuria in Luck, Will Rogers Holds"

Group: Foreign Community Club in Mukden
Topic: Manchurian conflict

Rogers, who was sending "daily reports" home to Senator William Borah on the Manchurian situation, said that the League of Nations' decision to send a commission to the area reminded him of a sheriff who went to inspect a stable after the horse was stolen. Rogers said that he would be willing to lower his price for investigating the situation since he had been offered the governorship of Northern Manchuria. But, reverting to old themes, he claimed that he had really made the journey "to introduce Prohibition, due to the success of the great experiment in America." In referring to the Depression, Rogers took a very balanced stance. He said that he was glad to see all the journalists there because it proved that they had jobs, but he also said that he was tired of hearing people blame Hoover for the situation. The Aleutian Islands were in the same condition, he said, and as far as he knew, Hoover had never been there. (See *New York Times,* December 15, 1931, p. 25, col. 5.)

38. "Rogers Reviews Air Controversy"

Group: General public
Topic: Airmail controversy

The purpose of this talk was merely to calm people down in relation to a controversy over airmail. Rogers was again trying to serve a unifying function, this time in relation to a dispute between Charles Lindbergh and President Roosevelt. In regard to Lindbergh, he said, "I told the folks he could probably give the President a lot of good information and that they could have been good friends. It was too bad a thing like this came up and I hope it can be straightened out." Rogers also reported that he had advised the fliers to be careful and not take unnecessary chances.

As a friend of aviation, Rogers feared that hasty decisions or ill-chosen words might endanger the nascent industry. (See *New York Times,* February 26, 1934, p. 5, col. 1.)

7

ARCHIVAL MATERIALS: THE WILL ROGERS MEMORIAL AND ELSEWHERE

PRESERVING THE LEGACY: THE WILL ROGERS MEMORIAL

The Will Rogers Memorial in Claremore was built with funds from the state of Oklahoma and private donations after a movement in Congress to supply federal monies was vetoed by President Franklin Roosevelt. Complete records of the financial and public relations dimensions of the Memorial movement are at the Memorial, including a ream of testimonials used in the radio campaign to raise money for the institution. When the Memorial was dedicated on November 4, 1938, a national hookup allowed the nation to hear voices of worthies in Washington, Claremore, and California celebrate the accomplishments of the great man. A complete transcript of the program is available at the Memorial.

Paula Love, a niece of Rogers, was selected as the first curator of the collection, a role she filled with tenacity and devotion. She was ably assisted by Robert Love, her husband, a man dedicated to the memory of Will Rogers. Bob always had a place in his house for stray dogs and visiting scholars.

There were discussions of the Memorial in Congress (1938), along with other forms of tribute. In *Between Sittings* (1951), Jo Davidson described the process by which he completed the statue of Rogers which stands in the rotunda at the Memorial and in the nation's capital. Davidson screened a few of Rogers' late sound films for inspiration and even hired a model to pose in Rogers' actual clothing. In this manner, Davidson felt he had captured the man: "I sensed the grace and ease with which Will Rogers wore his clothes. They expressed the careless freedom of his personality" (p. 300). The resulting work of art skillfully blends the man with the myth: like Rogers himself, it radiates a sense of transcendence and restlessness at the same time.

Basic Data About the Will Rogers Memorial

Staff

Director: Mrs. Reba N. Collins, Ed.D.
Curator: Mr. Greg Malak

Address

The Will Rogers Memorial
P.O. Box 157
Claremore, Oklahoma 74017

Phone

(918) 341-0719

Holdings

In addition to the manuscript materials, a host of other items described on the following pages. Founded in 1938, the Will Rogers Memorial is an open collection.

Screenings

A new theatre and study wing allows the Memorial to schedule screenings of Will Rogers' silent and sound films. Special study and screening rooms will be available for researchers.

Library

Every book which mentions Will Rogers—even books with only an incidental reference—has been collected over the years. Other works related to vaudeville, movies, and radio are also on the shelves of this handsome, paneled library.

Museum

The Memorial has a number of displays of Will Rogers memorabilia including photographs, artifacts, and clothing. Samples of his writing and a quaint diorama tracing his life are on display. Considerable effort has been made to present the multiple facts of Oklahoma's great man. A thorough tour of the beautiful facility takes at least three hours, not including motion picture screening time. Millions of tourists have taken advantage of the opportunity.

Other Activities

During special times of the year, events related to the Will Rogers heritage take place on the grounds of the Memorial or at Will Rogers College, a small commuter school across the street.

Research Opportunities

The Will Rogers Memorial's first responsibility is to preserve the artifacts, papers, and other documents related to the Will Rogers heritage. Research questions and arrangements should be directed to Dr. Collins, the director of the Memorial. Dr. Collins is a Will Rogers scholar in her own right (Ed.D. diss., 1967). Frequently, the advice and encouragement of Will Rogers, Jr. are helpful during a significant research project. He is unequivocably dedicated to the preservation and understanding of his father's heritage and has been a constant help to many with the same interests.

The Rogers Company

Will Rogers, Jr. can be reached at the Rogers Company, 9538 Brighton Way, Room 202, Beverly Hills, California 90210. (213) 272-3602.

Sales

The Memorial contains a book and souvenir shop with items that relate to Oklahoma history and the life of Will Rogers. Books about Will Rogers—many of them recently reprinted—are available. (*The Writings of Will Rogers* are available directly from the Oklahoma State University Press or at the Memorial's shop.)

Daily, Weekly, Miscellaneous Articles, and Books

The Writings of Will Rogers have been edited with painstaking detail; still, the researcher with an interest in the process of Will Rogers' writing may wish to inspect the hundreds of manuscripts available in the Memorial vault. For the usual needs of research, these manuscripts will not prove important, but all of them do show how Will Rogers wrote and then how he revised his ideas.

Recordings

The Memorial has a number of aluminum discs on which the "Good Gulf Show" radio programs by Will Rogers were recorded in the 1930s. All of these have been conveyed to sound tape and are available for study. Typed transcriptions of the recordings are also available for inspection. Miscellaneous earlier recordings from the 1920s are also available, as are transcripts from radio shows never recorded. A volume in *The Writings of Will Rogers* collects most of this material in a carefully edited collection.

Many of the Memorial's aural holdings are available in the marketplace or through its bookstore.

Motion Pictures

Over the years, Robert Love made a great effort to find and preserve the films of Will Rogers. In the late 1960s, with the combined assistance of the Rockefeller Foundation and the Museum of Modern Art, the extant films were put through an expensive process of conversion from nitrate to cellulose acetate stock, thus preserving them in a nonflammable format. Preservation negatives are in the custody of the Museum of Modern Art, which also has prints for scholars to view. Much of the effort in this preservation process was contributed by a devoted Will Rogers fan, Mrs. Eileen Bowser, curator of the Museum of Modern Art (MOMA) Film Department (11 West 53rd Street, New York City, New York 10019).

The Will Rogers Memorial has duplicate materials of those possessed by MOMA. The design of the new wing of the Memorial includes study rooms where scholars can watch the rich cinematic heritage which Rogers contributed. The library has literally thousands of production stills from the seventy films. In addition, many Memorial scrapbooks contain reviews, publicity circulars, and other print documents which illuminate the movies.

The inventory of motion pictures in this volume indicates what films are available and in what format. At the time this book goes to press, the films of Will Rogers are no longer protected by copyright.

The Daily Calendar

For more than twenty years, the Will Rogers Memorial has been filling in a calendar of the life of Will Rogers, a document that runs to some five or six bound volumes and that has blank spaces for every day and hour of his life. It is difficult to exaggerate the importance of this document to any researcher. It is often very important to know where Rogers was on the day he produced a daily, weekly, or special article because the context of his life affected the content of his remarks. The chronological order of the Daily Calendar becomes a mighty sword to cut through such mysteries. Not every day is complete, but some days are crowded with details about hotels visited, trains taken, people met, speeches given. I consider this to be an indispensable source, a map of time which often gives background data essential for an understanding of the man and his ideas.

The Continuing Collection Process

Items related to the Will Rogers heritage are turning up at the Will Rogers Memorial every day. Many of these items are useless; on the other hand, the nature of historical collections is such that valuable and unique materials suddenly materialize out of attics and garages. The collection process at the Memorial continues.

Manuscript Holdings at the Will Rogers Memorial: The Personal Side of Will Rogers

Letters to Family and Friends, 1893-1903

These are original letters from Will Rogers to members of his family during the troubling time of his youth. Also included are letters written home during his wanderings through South America, Africa, and Asia. Anyone interested in the perceptiveness and articulateness of a future social commentator must study these letters *in the original*. (Many were published in the local newspaper, and copies of the newspaper versions appear in a number of biographies.)

Letters to Betty Blake, 1900-1908

Roach (1972) and Mrs. Rogers herself agree that marriage and parenthood would be important settling influences in the life of a restless young man. These personal letters reveal the inner mind of a man attempting to make his way in the world of show business while at the same time looking for emotional stability. Anyone with an interest in the psychodynamics of Will Rogers must study these important intimate documents.

Manuscript Holdings in Filing Cabinet Number Three, Will Rogers Memorial

I. Original Wires in Relation to Tour Series—Elmira, New York, Stop
This was the kickoff of what would become a series of tours taking Rogers to over one hundred towns and cities each season.

Telegrams to: Bates, Tom, New York; Bergman, Leonard, New York; Blackmer, Sidney, New York; Buck, Gene, Boston; Erlanger, A. L., New York; Kastor, Arthur, New York; Ochs, Al, Boston; Toplitsky, Joe, New York.

II. Lecture Routine: 1925-1926
Ten pages of prepared stories, gags, allusions. A clear case—among many—that Rogers did his homework and that, while his stage manner seemed spontaneous, he was an artist who spent time on his act. The lecture is packed with contemporary issues and personalities.
Personalities: Dawes, Charles G.; Mellon, Andrew; Mitchell, William ("Billy"); Wales, Prince of.
Topics: European Squabbles; Florida; Gridiron Dinner; Politicians and Politics; Traffic Problems.

III. Lecture Routine: 1926-1927
Eleven pages of material similar to II format.
Personalities: Coolidge; Mussolini.
Topics: European Tour; Fraternities, College; Halls, Night of; Mussolini; Naples; Night He Slept at White House; Opera; Writing for the Public.

IV. Lecture Routine: 1927-1928
This routine was transcribed by a professional service. The material fills fifty-four pages, and a host of personalities and topics are covered.

V. Original Lecture Notes: 1925-1928
Forty-seven pages of notes which relate to the presentations in II-IV. Most of these notes concern specific cities and worthies: Rogers was known—as Bob Hope is today—for studying up before delivering a lecture so that he could relate to his audience.

VI. Manuscript for the *Farm Journal*
A seven-page article entitled "How to Throw a Lasso" and some related correspondence with editor. May never have been published.

VII. Miscellaneous Notes
Fifty-two pages of materials for performances, articles, and so on. Like other such items, these materials provide a basis for studying the evolution of Rogers' humor from idea to public information.
Personalities: Allen, Henry; Amundsen, Roald; Borah, William; Brewing, Dave; Coolidge, Calvin; Hoover, Herbert; Kaiser; Long, Huey; O'Connor, Tommy; Pope; Queen Mary; Rockefeller, John D. (and Poets); Roosevelt, Theodore; Wilson, Woodrow.
Topics: California; China; Missionaries; War with United States; Clubs; Congress; Cuba; Depression; Horse Trading; Humor in Politics; Inflation; Japanese Affairs; Jerusalem; Klan; Mexico; New Deal; New York; Nicaragua; Pacific Electric; Philippine Independence; Prohibition; Subway; Supreme Court; Taxicabs; Technocracy; Traffic, New York; Vermont Election; Wall Street.

VIII. Unclassified Originals
Twenty-five pages of notes for performances, articles, the 1920s, and 1930s.

Beach, Rex; Bryan; Coolidge, Calvin; Daniels, Bebe; Garrett, E. B.; Glying (Glyn), Miss Elinor; Goldwyn, Samuel; Fitzmorris, Charlie, Chief of Police; Ford, Henry; Hayes, Cardinal; "Huges (Hughes), Rupert"; Hylan, John F., Mayor of New York; Johnson, Hiram; "Knoblock, Mr."; McNaught Syndicate; Max the Barber; "Morris, Governin"; Mussolini; Nazimova, Alla; Porter, Mrs. Gene Stratton; Rinehart, Mary Roberts; Rogers, William; Seudh, (Scott) Leroy; Thompson, Mayor of Chicago; Thompson, Mrs. Hiram; Walton, Jack; Watling, Mr. and Mrs. Mamie Thorne; Wilson, Woodrow.

Topics: Astor Hotel, New York; Barbers; Bootleg; Chicago; China; Christmas; Congress; Crossword Puzzles; Disarm; England; Follies; Hearst Papers; Italy; Japan; Los Angeles; Movies; Muscle Shoals; New York; Notre Dame; Princeton; Prohibition; Richfield Oil; Russia; Russian Oil; Santa Claus; Stanford; West Point, N.Y. (Cadets).

IX. Unclassified Daily Telegrams

Twenty-two original telegrams or carbons, many from the very last days of his life during the Alaskan tour.

Personalities: Bass, Tom, death of; Beach, Rex; Coolidge; Crosson, Joe; Hurley, Pat; Jones, Bobby; Ochs, Adolph, death of; Post, Wiley; Rockefeller, John D.

Topics: Alaska; Election; England; Football Games, Post Season; Juneau, Alaska; Los Angeles; Navajo Indians Conference; Robbery; Unemployment; U.S Treasury Bonds; Voting.

X. Movie Notes

Forty-five pages of typed material dealing with over one hundred motion picture personalities and an equal number of topics for the 1920s. Rogers comments on his own silent films in these notes, beginning with his earliest and working his way through the list. There also seem to be materials for or titles from a series of short films he made in the early 1920s, *The Illiterate Digest.*

Personalities: Arbuckle, Roscoe; Badger, Clarence; Bara, Theda; Beach, Mrs. Rex; Beban, George (Valentino); Bender, Peter; Bow, Clara; Briscoe, A. C.; Briscoe, Beanie; Bryan; Buchanan, Tommy; Bushman, Frances; "Cannedy, Madge"; Carrigan, Warren; Caruso; Chaplin; Clemenceau; Coward, Noel; Cryce, John (Mayor); Daniels, Bebe; Davies, Marion; de Mille, Cecil; Dempsey, Jack; Fairbanks, Douglas; Ford; Fox; Garbo, Greta; Garfield, Henry A.; George (King); Goldwyn, Samuel; Grayson, Cary T. (Admiral); Hardy, Sam; Hawks, J. G.; Hayes, Will; Hearst; Holmes, Burton; Hoover, Herbert; Houdini; Hoyt, Charles; Jackson, Mr. Dale; Joan of Arc; Kaiser; Lasky, Jesse L.; Lehr, Abraham; Lloyd, Frank; Lloyd George; McAdoo, William; McElsin, George; Moore, Tom; Nightingale, Florence; Normand, Mabel; Nye, Bill; O'Neill, Eugene; Pickford, Mary; Pershing, John (General); Roach, Hal; Roark, Sam; Rogers, Will; Roosevelt; Ross, Betsy; Rothatel, Mr. Joseph; Ruth, Babe; Sawyer, Zeb; Shakespeare; Sherwin, Louis; Valentino (funeral of); Victoria (Queen); Wales (Prince of); Wallace, Hugh C.; Webster, Daniel; Wheatly, Ann; Willard, Mark; Ziegfeld, Florenz.

XI. Movie Notes

Almost a Husband (1919); *America;* Atlanta; Audiences; *Ben Hur* (1925); Beverly Hills; Bible; *Big Parade, The* (1925); *Birth of a Nation* (1915); Boer War;

Bolsheviks; Boston; Bucking Pictures; Buicks; Bull Montana; California; Chamber of Commerce; Cincinnati; Cleveland; Claremore; Columbus, Ohio; Corn Plasters; Democrats; England; First National Film Studio; Gillettes; Grauman's Egyptian Theatre; Greenwich Village; Holland; Hollywood; Ireland; Italy; Kansas; London; Long Island; Los Angeles; Methodist Convention; Mexico; New York; Oberchains; Oologah, Oklahoma; Orchestra; Paris; Pictures (Movies); Preachers (1920); Press Agents; Prohibition; Republicans; Rome; *Romeo and Juliet; Roping Fool;* Russia; *Saturday Evening Post;* Slavery; Soldier Bonus; South Africa; Streetcars; Taxes; *Ten Commandments;* Traffic in New York City; Turkey; Washington; *Water, Water, Everywhere* (1919); Willard House.

XII. Original Notes for Victor Records, 1922-1924
Nine pages of text for the short records he made in the early 1920s. Speeches are to Traffic Chiefs (1), Bankers (2), or deal with such topics as Henry Ford and wars (2). Some of the recordings still exist at the Memorial and on the market.
Personalities: Coué, Dr. Émile; Ford, Henry.
Topics: America; Armenians; Asia; Bootlegging; Canada; Democrats; England; Follies; France; Germany; Interest Hounds; Ireland; Japan; Peace Conference; Pedestrians; Prohibition; Republicans; Taxicab Drivers; Traffic Club, Chicago; Turkey; United States; Vice-president; Victor Records; War.

XIII. Unpublished Manuscripts (Perhaps)
Thirty-two pages of material, some of it on stationery for hotels and nightclubs. Much of it typed on his Royal portable. At least seventy-five personalities and an equal number of current topics appear in these materials, 1914-1928.
Personalities: Amos & Andy; Beach, Mr. & Mrs. Rex; Brodie, Steve; Coolidge; Fairbanks, Doug; Harvey, Fred; Hays, Will; Lasky, Jesse; Negri, Pola; Roach, Hal; Rockefeller, John D.; Rogers, Will; Roosevelt; Schwab, Charles M.; Swanson, Gloria; Wilson; Ziegfeld; Zukor, Adolph.
Topics: America; Authors Club; Barnum (Circus); Charleston, the; Cherokee; Democracy; Eighteenth Amendment; Farm Relief; Germans; Grauman's Theatre; Hollywood; Movie Industry; Oklahoma; Politicians; Prohibition; Ranching; Scientists; Tammany; Wall Street.

XIV. Unclassified Radio Speeches
Thirteen pages of material from the 1927-1934 period.
Personalities: Chandler, Harry; Cohen, Major John; Garbo, Greta; Hearst, William R.; Long, Huey; Roosevelt, Franklin D.; Warner, Jack.
Topics: Editor's Banquet; Germany; Hollywood; Publishers.

XV. Miscellaneous *Saturday Evening Post* Articles
Four pages of material, only some of which was used in *Saturady Evening Post* articles.
Topics: Japan; Manchurians.

XVI. The Autobiography
This should not be confused with the anthology edited by Donald Day (1949). Rogers here recorded on six sides of paper, single-spaced, the details he thought

would be important for an eventual autobiography. Internal evidence shows that the book had been urged by George Horace Lorimer, editor of the *Saturday Evening Post* and a regular patron of Rogers. Both Betty Rogers (1941) and Donald Day (1949) drew heavily from these materials.

XVII. Introduction for Charles M. Russell's *Trails Plowed Under*
Two drafts of the Introduction plus some memorabilia from Russell to Rogers.

XVIII. Unpublished (unclassified) Radio Notes
One hundred fifteen pages of notes for radio programs; the earliest is 1927, and the latest is 1935. There are many talks here not recorded in any other manner. On the other hand, such presentations as his talk on unemployment (1931) is in written form. As with the lecture notes, these documents show that Rogers studied for his presentations and that his extemporaneous manner was the product of an artist.
Personalities: Barrymore, John; Coolidge (imitated by Rogers); Franklin, Benjamin; Hayes, Will; Hoover; Kodak; McNamee, Graham; Mayer, Louis B.; Bull, Montana; Mickey Mouse; Rich, Irene; Rockefeller, John D.; Rogers, Jimmy, Mary and Bill; Rolph, Jim; Roosevelt, Franklin D.; Smith, Al; Stone, Fred, Dorothy, Paula, and Carol; Warner, Jack; Whiteman, Paul; Ziegfeld.
Topics: Autos; Banking; Cuba; Democrats; Dodge Bros. Car; France; General Electric; General Motors; W. K. Kellogg, Ranch; Mexico; Milk Fund, 1934; Oklahoma; Olympic Games; Pennsylvania Railroad System; Pioneer Woman Statue, Ponca City; Republicans; Sears Roebuck; Sedan.

XIX. Death Notification Telegram and Post-Death Telegrams
Content is self-evident.

XX. Unclassified Magazine Articles
Twenty-six sheets of material, most of it for *Life Magazine,* although some of the material touches on Henry Ford and was written for *The American Magazine.* Time period: 1928-1930.
Personalities: Clemenceau; Ford, Henry.
Topics: Allied Debt Conference; Anti-Bunk Party; *Life Magazine;* Liquor; Turkey.

XXI. Notes for Magazine Articles
Twenty-three pages of typed notes; fifteen deal with Asian issues, and five focus on Al Smith and his prospects for election.

XXII. "Bucking a Head Wind"
Nineteen pages of material later published in the *Saturday Evening Post* (January 28, 1928).

XXIII. Notes for *Ether and Me* and *A Hole in One*
Seventeen pages of notes for a series originally published in the *Saturday Evening Post* (November 5 and 12, 1927) and later published in book form. Also, the original manuscript.

XXIV. Unclassified Miscellaneous Notes
For a talk to Tulsa Realtors, and perhaps others.
Personalities: Borah, Senator.
Topics: California; Claremore; Democratic Convention; Education; Indians—
Osages; New York; Republican Convention; Rodeo; Tulsa; United States; Weather.

Other Manuscript Holdings, Will Rogers Memorial

I. Original Vaudeville Routine—Notes
Thirty-one pages of notes from a period heretofore undocumented. Some material
as early as 1912, including gags "for missing the nose" of his horse.
Personalities: Caruso; Ford, Henry; Foy, Eddie; Hoover; Kaiser; McAdoo;
Roosevelt, Theodore; Root, Elihu; Wilson (President); Ziegfeld.
Topics: Cabarets; Cowboys; Follies; Unicycles.

II. Original "War Stories"
Thirteen pages of material, some of which appeared in his book on the Peace
Conference in 1919.
Personalities: Bush, Mrs. Guy T.; Chaplin, Charlie; Lloyd George, David; Hard-
ing (President); Joffe (Marshal), Joseph; Schwab, Charles M.; Valentino.
Topics: Austria; Bolsheviks; China; Japan; Germany; Rumania; Turks; War.

III. Follies: Original Notes
Seventy-eight pages of material, 1916-1924.
Personalities: Beach, Rex; Daniels, Bebe; Debs, Eugene; Gibson, Charles; Gold-
wyn, Sam; Grayson, (Admiral) Cary; Hart, Bill; Harvey, Fred; Hayes, Will;
Hughes, Rupert; Jennings, Al; Lloyd George, David (resigned); McAdoo, William;
Maeterlinck, Maurice; Moore, Owen; Mussolini; O'Connor sisters; Pershing, John;
Pickford, Mary; Rinehart, Mary Roberts; Roosevelt, Theodore (Colonel); Sinclair,
Harry; Smith, Al; Stillman, James; Wales (Prince of); Washington (President);
Well, H. G.; Willard, Jess; Wilson, Woodrow (President).
Topics: Anti-beer Bill; Aviation; Beauty Parlors; Belgium; Bryan's Resignation;
Bull Fight in Mexico; Chamber of Commerce; Democratic Nominations;
Disarmament Conference; Follies' Conference; Japan; Jews; League of Nations;
Mississippi Valley; Mulligan Stew Bill; Oklahoma; Old Men in St. Petersburg; New
Poor; Pike's Peak; Prohibition; Radios and Advertising; Railroads; Real Estate;
Rumania; Television and Advertising; *Ten Commandments;* Turks; White Sox;
Wilson's Five-Point Peace Terms to Congress.

IV. Early Articles by Will Rogers for Selznick News
Five pages of material, 1922-1923.
Personalities: Coué, Dr. Émile; Harvey, George B. (Ambassador); Morgan, J. P.
Topics: Football; Prohibition; Return of U.S. Troops; Safety Week; Turkey;
Woman in the Senate.

V. Original Articles, Foreign Countries
Fifteen pages of material, throughout career.

Topics and Places: Americans; China; Cricket; Democrats; Germans; Hong Kong; Ireland; Mexico; Russia; South America.

VI. Original Notes for Books and Lecture Tour
Seven pages of material, throughout career.
Personalities: Dempsey, Jack; Noah.
Topics: Bible; Movies; New York as an Uncivilized Town; Prohibition; Russian Vodka.

VII. Original Notes for Magazine Articles
Seven pages of material, most of which was published in *The American Magazine.*

VIII. Original Scripts for the Stage
Two pages of material.
Topics: Los Angeles; Movies; Ropes; Traffic Problems; Veterans.

IX. Notes to Introduce People or to Speak About Them
Sixteen pages of material.
Personalities: Brougher, Dr.; De Palacio, Lucas; Fitch, Honorable Tom; Robinson, Joseph T.; Shaw, Frank L.

X. Original Miscellaneous Notes
Eight pages of material.
Personalities: Hughes, Patrick (Secretary); McAdoo, William; Wales (Prince of).
Topics: Disarmament; Elections in the United States; Japan; League of Nations; Prohibition; Railroads; U.S.-Mexican Relations.

XI. Original Notes
Forty-six pages of material.
Personalities: Barnum, P. T.; Coolidge; Garbo, Greta; Gompers, Samuel; Lloyd George, David (his *Memoirs*); Mitchell; Ruth, "Babe"; Stone, Dorothy; Villa, Pancho.
Topics: Banking Picking Up; British Golf Players; Cabarettes; Congress; Democrats as Cannibals; Democrats in Need of Etiquette; Fords; *Grand Hotel* (opening); Mexican Development; Republicans; Scientists.

XII. Miscellaneous Original Notes: Not Identified
Thirty-nine pages of material.
Personalities: Coolidge (his speech on Armistice Day); Kaiser; Small, Len (Governor of Illinois).
Topics: Aviation; Democrats and Corruption; Depression; Los Angeles; Peace Conference in Washington; Polo; Presidential Messages; South, the; Wales, Prince of; War.

XIII. Miscellaneous Original Notes (Some DT Notes):
Twenty-three pages of material.
Personalities: Chevalier; Garbo; Hoover; Mellon, Andrew; Roosevelt, Franklin D.; Wales (Prince of); Wesley, John.

Topics: Depression; General Motors, U.S. Steel, and Dupont; Pan American Conference; Roosevelt's letter to Federal Trade Commission; Stock Market Crash; Telephone Girls.

XIV. Miscellaneous Original Notes for Daily Telegrams
Twenty-two pages of material.
Personalities: Brisbane, Albert; Coolidge; Hoover; Lindbergh; McAdoo, William; Shipstead, Henrik, Senator from Minnesota; Smith.
Topics: Democratic Party; Elections; Evolution; Farmers; Ford Car; Greece; Oologah, Oklahoma; Prohibition; Senate, the; Telephone Talks in Canada.

XV. Original Notes for Gulf Radio, Etc.
Thirty-two pages of material.
Personalities: Dillinger, John; Ford, Henry; Johnson, Mr. Hugh; Long, Huey; Longworth, Mrs. Alice; McPherson, Sister Aimee; Roosevelt, Franklin D.
Topics: England; Gold Bill; Japan; Roosevelt and Conference; Russia; Senate, the; Wickersham Report; Women Investors in America.

XVI. Original Notes: Possibly for Speeches
Ten pages of material.
Personalities: Dempsey, Jack; Roosevelt, F. D.
Topics: Conventions; Mothers' Day; Olympics; Sports, Professional.

XVII. Unclassified Original Notes, Re: Politics
Forty pages of material.
Personalities: Bryan, W. J.; Cobb, Irvin; Dawes, Charles G., Hoover; McAdoo, William; Pershing; Smith, Al; Underwood, Oscar; Wilson, President.
Topics: Armenians and Turks; Boston Police Strike; Election of Governor of New York; Farmers; Farmers and Interests; Movies; Railroads; Republican National Committee; Tammany Hall; Turkey.

XVIII. Original Speeches by Will Rogers
One hundred eighty-nine pages of material for a total of 132 speeches. The earliest speech seems to be in the 1914-1916 period; the latest seems to be from 1932, just after Rogers' tour of South America.
Personalities: Beach, Mrs.; Belasco, David; Bow, Clara; Cantor; Chaplin, Charlie; Coolidge; Davis, John; Dunn, Katherine; Fairbanks, Douglas; Follies; Garbo, Greta; Goldwyn, Samuel; Harding, Warren; Harvey, George; Hayes, Will; Houdini; James, Jesse; Kaiser; Kellogg, Mr. W. K.; McAdoo, William; O'Neill, Eugene; Pickford, Mary; Rolph, James R. (Governor); Rothafel, Mr. Joseph; Shubert, Jacob; Smith, Al; Ziegfeld; Zukor, Adolph.
Topics: Accessories; Agriculture; America; American Farm Bureau Federal Convention; Armistice Day; Autos; Bankers; Bootleggers; Beauty Parlors; Child Labor; Colleges and Professors; Comedians; Corset Manufacturers; Cotton; Dawes Plan; Democrats; Disarmament Party; European War; Farmers; Federal Aid to States; Follies; Ford Cars; France; Geneva Peace Conference; Golf; Immigration; League of Nations; Nobel Prize; Polo Clubs; Prize Fights; Real Estate; Russia; Russian Ballet; Stanley Theatre; Taxes; Turkey; U.S. Indians; Wales (Prince of); Washington Arms Conference; Women's Clubs; Wool; World Court.

XIX. Original Speeches by Will Rogers
One hundred thirty-eight pages of material for a total of eighty-two speeches: the earliest is a charity venture of 1914; the latest reaches into the fall of 1933.
Personalities: Buck, Gene; Caruso, Coolidge; Coué, Dr. Émile; Fairbanks, Douglas; Ford; Goldwyn, Sam; Harding (President); Hayes, Will; Hearst, William R.; James, Jesse; Mills, Ogden L.; Mussolini.
Topics: Armenia; Autos; Bicycles; Bull Fighting; Corsets; Democrats; Follies; Fur Merchants; Indians (Osages and Cherokees); Jews; Ku Klux Klan; Mortgages and Loans; Oklahoma; Prohibition Bill; Republicans; Rockefeller Foundation; Womens' Clubs; Ziegfeld's Funeral.

XX. Speeches in Foreign Countries
Eighteen pages of material for a total of fourteen speeches.
Personalities: Coolidge, President; Hurley, Pat; Lloyd George, David; Morrow, Dwight; Villa, Pancho; Wales (Prince of).
Topics: Americans in London; Irish Home Rule; Italian Celebrations; Mexico; Philippines; Prohibition; Russia and Booze; Venice.

XXI. Original Wires from Will Rogers
Nearly 200 wires from Will Rogers to various individuals, 1919 to 1935. Some are trivial; others have become quite famous.
Names of some Addressees: Bryan, Charley; Cherokee Students of Haskell Institute; Davies, John W.; Fairbanks, Warren L.; Goldwyn, Sam; Harrison, Walter; Hughes, Rupert; Longworth, Nick; McAdoo, W. G.; McLean, Ned; Post, Wiley; Rich, Irene; Roach, Hal; Roosevelt, Belle; Roosevelt (Governor); Smith, Al; Thompson, William (Mayor); Tucker, Sophie.

XXII. "Three Cheers," 1928-1929: Original Notes, Script, Program, etc.
A thirty-seven page script, miscellaneous programs, reviews, and stories about Rogers' pinch-hitting for his friend Fred Stone in the play. Also twenty pages of notes for the substitute Oklahoma actor.

XXIII. Introductions to Books
Materials related to *Fashions in Food* (1931), *The Cowboy Philosopher on the Peace Conference* (1919), and *Good Medicine* (1929) for a total of ten pages.

MATERIAL RELATING TO WILL ROGERS IN THE SPECIAL COLLECTIONS AND SCRIPT COLLECTION OF THE MARGARET HERRICK LIBRARY, ACADEMY OF MOTION PICTURE ARTS AND SCIENCES
(8949 Wilshire Boulevard, Beverly Hills, California 90211)

Hollywood Museum Collection
Frank Borzage Scrapbooks
They Had to See Paris (Fox, 1929)
   Scrapbook of stills, mostly scenes from film
Young As You Feel (Fox, 1931)
   Scrapbook of stills, mostly scenes from film

Paramount Collection

Paramount Script Collection
One Glorious Day (Paramount, 1922)
   Script material including scenario, continuities, and synopses
Hollywood (Paramount, 1923)
   Script material including story, scenario, continuities, and synopses

Henry Ginsberg Collection

Irvin S. Cobb letter, ca. 1932
   Letter from Irvin S. Cobb to Henry Ginsberg regarding Cobb playing Judge Priest in short comedies for Hal Roach, ca. 1932
   Note: In this letter, Cobb relays Winfield Sheehan's request that Roach forego production of these comedies due to Fox Film's intention of starring Rogers as Judge Priest in a series of features.

Vertical File Material

Will Rogers contract, 1920
   Contract between Will Rogers and Fox Film Corporation engaging Rogers as a performer and assistant in the production of four motion pictures between June 1, 1929, and September 30, 1930, dated March 22, 1929.

Script Collection (one copy for each)
   So This Is London (Fox, 1930)
   Business and Pleasure (Fox, 1932)
   Down to Earth (Fox, 1932)
   State Fair (Fox, 1933)
   Mr. Skitch (Fox, 1933)
   Judge Priest (Fox, 1934)
   Life Begins at Forty (Fox, 1935)
   Steamboat 'Round the Bend (20th Century-Fox, 1935)
   In Old Kentucky (20th Century-Fox, 1935)

MATERIAL RELATING TO WILL ROGERS AT THE ARCHIVES OF THE PERFORMING ARTS, UNIVERSITY LIBRARY, UNIVERSITY OF SOUTHERN CALIFORNIA, LOS ANGELES, CALIFORNIA 90007

20th Century-Fox Screenplay Collection:
Script material for twenty (20) sound films. Script for every sound film made by Will Rogers.

MGM Screenplay Collection:
Script material for thirteen (13) films produced by Samuel Goldwyn, 1919-1921.

Warner Brothers:
Script material and legal material for the film *A Texas Steer* (1927).

Hal Roach Studio (also at the Will Rogers Memorial):
Weekly salary listings of the Hal Roach Film Company.

From June 9, 1923-May 17, 1924.

The "WM/Will Rogers Co." is listed on each of the weekly payroll summaries. Rogers is listed on all except for the first (June 9) and last (May 17).

Date books from 1923 and 1924 which note which Hal Roach film units were working on each day of the year.

June 11, 1923 (first day Will Rogers Company worked) through May 12, 1924 (Rogers Company terminated).

Three pages from an office ledger which indicates the earnings of Rogers' films.

Monthly earnings statements from Pathé Exchange, Inc., the distributor of Hal Roach films (December 22, 1923-January 17, 1925).

Additional information about each Rogers film which indicates the film's production number, release date, and foreign earnings.

Anthony Slide:

An interview with Hal Roach in which Rogers is briefly mentioned.

Hal Mohr Taped Interviews:

Four tapes with the chief cinematographer for a number of Rogers sound films. Mohr met his wife on the set of *David Harum.*

NATIONAL ARCHIVES: DIVISION OF MOTION PICTURES AND SOUND RECORDINGS
(National Archives and Records Service, Washington, D.C. 20408)

MOTION PICTURE SECTION

The *Universal Newsreel* catalog has an entry for Will Rogers and a few news items related to him.

The Ford Motor Company Collection also has some material related to Rogers, including footage at the Edison birthday celebration in 1929 hosted by Henry Ford at Greenfield Village. In addition, there is some footage from one of the episodes of the topical film series, *The Illiterate Digest* (1924).

SOUND RECORDING SECTION

Six monologues recorded during 1933-1935.

Topics include the Dust Bowl and President's Day. Dates on items are April 30, 1933; April 1, 1935; April 14, 1935; April 21, 1935; and May 12, 1935. A total of thirty minutes.

"My Opinion on Politics" (ca. 1932). Three minutes.

"The Good Gulf Show" (May 8, 1933). Thirty minutes. Memorial has same recording but dates it as the April 30 broadcast.

Biography and Sound Series: Will Rogers, 56 minutes

"Topics of the Day: Crime in New York City and Allied Subjects," February 6, 1923. Three minutes.

"Talk on the Depression," October 18, 1931. Eight minutes.

INDEX

About the Author

PETER C. ROLLINS is Associate Professor of English at Oklahoma State University. He is the editor of *Hollywood as Historian* and author of *Benjamin L. Whorf: Lost Generation Theories of Mind, Language, and Religion.* He was involved in the making of two documentaries: *Will Rogers' 1920s* and *Television's Vietnam.* He has published on Will Rogers and popular culture in the *Journal of Popular film and Television,* the *Journal of Popular Culture, Film and History,* and *American Quarterly.*